C O L O

Front Range Crags

by Peter Hubbel

Chockstone Press

Evergreen, Colorado

Front Range Crags

ISBN 0-934641-61-7

Front and Back Cover: Robyn Erbesfield on **Evil**, Clear Creek Canyon. Photo by Beth Wald.

Acknowledgements

Special thanks to the following people: Alan Mosiman, Gene Ellis, and Steve Holonitch for their help with the Jackson Creek and Castlewood Canyon areas. Also many thanks to Alvino Pon, Harry Kent, Steve Komito and Alan Mosiman for route information on The Piz Badille.

Phil Berggren for his help with Castlewood Canyon, specifically with the ice climbing areas.

Alvino Pon for his help with South St. Vrain Canyon, Pinecliffe, The Piz Badille and Clear Creek.

Richard and Scott Berk for all of their early North Table Mountain information.

Dave Rice for the Gross Reservoir information. Craig Luebben for information and proofing the Big Thompson Canyon and Cache La Poudre areas. Claude (CT) Traufield for the many climbless mileage checks and explorations and for proofreading. Alan Nelson for all of his initial Clear Creek Canyon work. Ken Trout for proofing yet another of my guides. (Happily, too.) Tod Anderson for information on North Table Mountain, Clear Creek Canyon and Castlewood Canyon. Dan Trygstad for help with the Highway 285 area. Mary Katherine Norman for proofreading and for sticking with me through this endeavor. Mark Rolofson for North Table Mountain, South St. Vrain and Buttonrock information. Thanks also to the following people: Steve Hong, A. Brown, A. Stocks, Tom Bohanon, Jeffery Butterfield, Steve Komito, Charles Tabor, George Bracksieck, Deaun Schovajsa, Fred Knapp, and Ryan Nassibene and Ted Evans.

Extra special thanks to Eric and Dana at The Mountain Miser for the original idea for this guide.

To the loving memory of my father, E. Gordon Hubbel, who saw the conception of the idea, but left this world prior to seeing the finished product.

Table of Contents

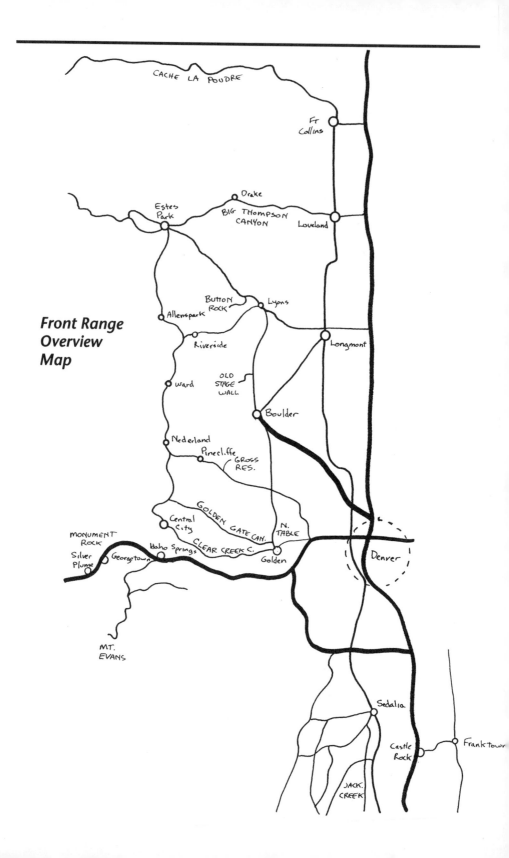

*Front Range
Overview
Map*

Introduction:

The purpose of this guidebook is to introduce climbers to the many smaller climbing areas scattered throughout the Front Range. Almost all are located within an hours' drive or less from any major metro area. Some of the areas covered are as little as 15 minutes away. All provide year round climbing since many of the rocks have good eastern or southern exposure. Many of the areas also have ice climbs, which are noted in the text.

This guide was written with the newcomer in mind and so people familiar with certain areas will find some of the information a little redundant. Written directions, mileages and overview maps should suffice to get climbers to the rock and area with minimal wasted effort.

The rock types and climbing are quite varied ranging from classic granite and basalt to sandstone and Castlewood Conglomerate. The climbing, length and altitudes are as diverse as the individual rock types. Climbs range in height from as little as 30' bolted sport climbs to 700' mixed free and aid routes. Altitudes vary from 6,200 feet above sea level in Castlewood Canyon, to above 13,000 feet on Mt. Evans. Each area has its own weather pattern, environment, and ecology.

Some of the areas covered have previously been included as parts of larger guides or more popular and bigger areas. These guides are referenced in the text. Also included are emergency numbers (911 is the most universal), equipment dealers, resolers, guide services, climbing gyms, recreational opportunities other than climbing and camping information.

Topos and Routes

On the topo drawings, most of the trees were left out, included only where they provided a reference point, such as a belay. As much rock was shown as space permitted. This was done intentionally to let people know areas to put up new routes.

Many of the climbs are listed as "unknown." The author has included these climbs in the hopes that other climbers will provide feedback to "fill in the blanks" for the next edition. Some of the climbs will not reflect the first ascentionists' rock or route names, but only the information that was currently available. The author would appreciate this information so that corrections may be made in future editions.

The author is actively seeking information on any new routes, name changes, corrections, etc. on any of the areas covered

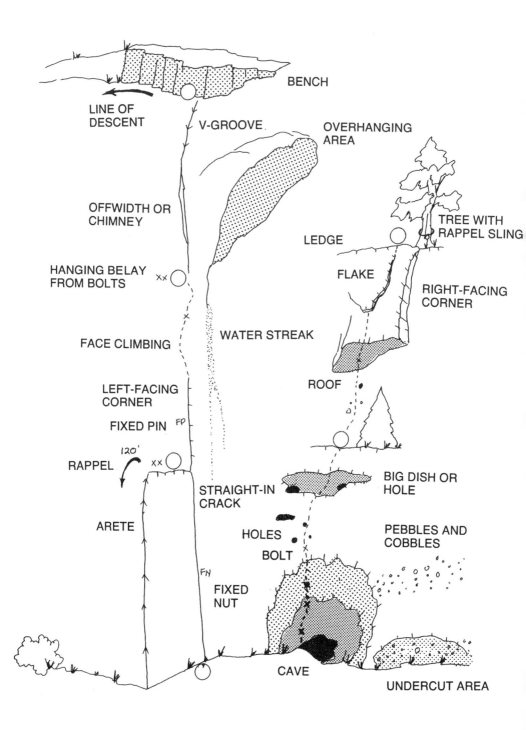

BENCH

LINE OF
DESCENT

V-GROOVE

OVERHANGING
AREA

OFFWIDTH OR
CHIMNEY

TREE WITH
RAPPEL SLING

LEDGE

HANGING BELAY
FROM BOLTS

FLAKE

RIGHT-FACING
CORNER

FACE CLIMBING

WATER STREAK

LEFT-FACING
CORNER

ROOF

FIXED PIN

120'

RAPPEL

BIG DISH OR
HOLE

STRAIGHT-IN
CRACK

HOLES

PEBBLES AND
COBBLES

ARETE

BOLT

FIXED
NUT

CAVE

UNDERCUT AREA

2

in this guidebook. The author is specifically looking for information on the following areas: Lyons Sandstone, South St. Vrain Canyon, Apple Valley Road, The Piz Badille, Crosier Dome, Mt. Evans, Monument Rock, Devil's Head and the south end "Winter Canyon" area of Castlewood Canyon. Please send any information for these areas, in topo format with an overview map, to: Front Range Climbs, Chockstone Press, PO Box 3505, Evergreen, CO 80439.

Protection and Caution

It is assumed that anyone using this book has all of the current toys on their racks. Many of the climbs listed will be found to be inadequately protected without small camming units such as LoweBalls, Cobras, Slugs, TCUs and Perrin wedges.

Many of the rocks involve river crossings. These rocks are best approached when the river is either low or frozen, not during spring runoff. Please think about what you are doing before you cross the rivers.

Some issues need mentioning and are important to us as climbers.

State Park Regulations

The following is from the Colorado State Parks 1993 regulations:

Climbing Hardware:

h. It shall be unlawful to place fixed or permanent rock climbing hardware, unless the climber first obtains a special-activities permit from the park manager. Removal of previously placed fixed or permanent climbing hardware is prohibited.

Violation-Penalty:

Any person who violates any provisions of these regulations shall be subject to the penalties set forth in Title 33, Colorado Revised Statues, as amended.

Many of the climbs included in this guidebook are in State Parks. Please follow all regulations.

Considerations

Due to the growing popularity of our sport, thanks in part to the media, many access and environmental issues are being raised, most notably with the National Park Service. These issues include the introduction of bills that will directly impact how, when, and where we will climb.

Please, GET INVOLVED. When there are options, such as writing your congressman or representative—write them. Support the Access Fund. These folks are your friends and have reopened one area that was closed in this book, North Table Mountain.

Be discreet. Color your bolts, use unobtrusive colors for your rap slings. Please park well off the road so as not to hinder traffic, not just to be polite, but to keep from irritating the locals who live up many of these canyons. As always, please pick up any trash you come across.

Leave the routes as you find them. Don't remove bolt hangers, fixed nuts or pins. This has been an issue in some of these areas and needs to stop. Respect the time, effort and money spent on routes listed as projects.

Two things this guide book is not—it isn't an instructional climbing guide and will not take the place of climbing instruction. It also isn't a first ascent book, though the author is keeping track of this information for historical reasons.

Be safe and have fun climbing!

Alvino Pon on **Upside the Cranium**, Monkey Skull, South St. Vrain. Photo by Ruel Chapman.

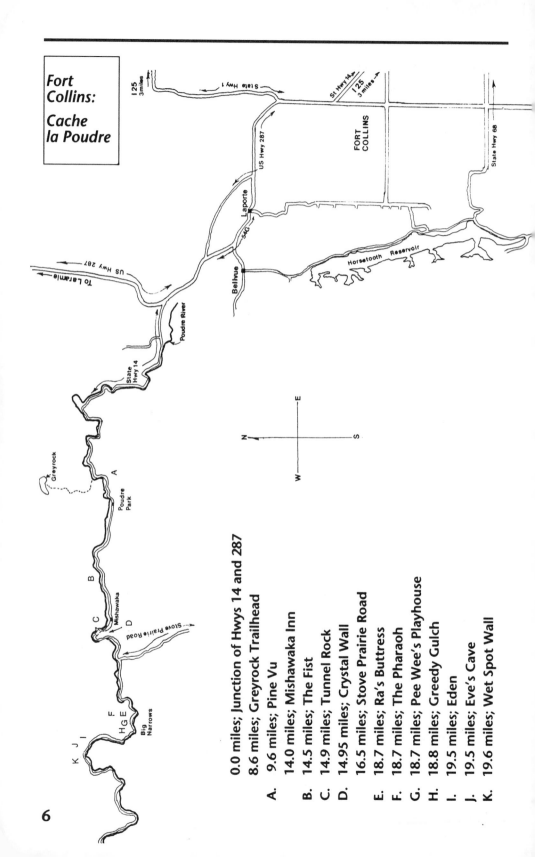

Fort Collins:

Cache la Poudre

0.0 miles; Junction of Hwys 14 and 287

8.6 miles; Greyrock Trailhead

A. 9.6 miles; Pine Vu

B. 14.0 miles; Mishawaka Inn

C. 14.5 miles; The Fist

D. 14.9 miles; Tunnel Rock

E. 14.95 miles; Crystal Wall

F. 16.5 miles; Stove Prairie Road

G. 18.7 miles; Ra's Buttress

H. 18.7 miles; The Pharaoh

I. 18.7 miles; Pee Wee's Playhouse

J. 18.8 miles; Greedy Gulch

K. 19.5 miles; Eden

L. 19.5 miles; Eve's Cave

M. 19.6 miles; Wet Spot Wall

FORT COLLINS

Cache la Poudre

Located just outside of Ft. Collins on Hwy 14, the Cache La Poudre River Canyon is one of the State's premier recreational areas. Some of the attractions include fishing, mountain biking, rafting and kayaking, cross-country skiing, and climbing. The climbing is on some fairly old granite and certain areas are rotten. Some rockfall is to be expected and wearing a helmet is advisable. Many of the climbs are true bolt-protected sport routes, but the majority of them require a selection of gear in addition to quick draws.

Craig Luebben and some of the other Desert Ice Mountain Guides are responsible for the majority of the routes here, primarily the bolted climbs. They also do quite a lot of their guiding in this canyon.

Directions:

From I-25, go north to State Highway 14 exit and west towards Ft. Collins. Go right on Highway 1 to Highway 287. Follow Highway 287 north, heading towards Laramie. When you reach the Highway 14 exit, turn left (west).

Considerations

Due to the close proximity of the road, please use the available parking pull-outs and do not block or hinder other traffic.

Some of these routes are listed as "projects," please respect the time and effort of the people working on these routes.

There have also been instances of hangers being stolen off existing routes. Again, respect the first ascent party's time, effort and money by leaving the hangers in place so that other climbers will enjoy the routes.

Please pick up any trash, whether or not it is yours, and dispose of it properly.

Emergency numbers

911

Estes-Poudre District Ranger
148 Remington St.
Ft. Collins, CO 80524
(303)482-3822

Larimer County Sheriff's Department
911 or (303)498-5100

Arapaho National Forest
(303)498-1100

Roosevelt National Forest
(303)498-1100

Camping and Recreation

Overnight camping is permitted. Please use any of the established camp sites. More information can be requested from:

Colorado State Parks:
Main Office
1313 Sherman St., Room 618
Denver, CO 80203
(303)866-3437

North Region
3842 S. Mason, #8
Ft. Collins, CO 80525
(303)226-6641

For information on the excellent bouldering to be found at Horsetooth Reservoir, please use *A Guide to Front Range Bouldering* by Bob Horan, available at most climbing stores, or from Chockstone Press. For information on Greyrock, please use *A Rockclimber's Guide to Greyrock* by Craig Luebben, available at most mountain shops or by writing directly to Craig at 2100 West Drake, Ft. Collins, Colorado 80524.

> **Note: The Northern Colorado Water District has conducted a survey for a proposed dam that will allow it to dam up to 12.5 miles of the lower canyon. This proposed dam would ruin the river, destroy wildlife habitats, and wipe out the existing recreation pleasures. A group called "Friends of the Poudre" has been fighting this proposal with some success. They can be reached at 250 Poudre River Road, Bellvue, Colorado 80512.**

Cache la Poudre Rocks and Routes:

A. Pine Vu
1. The Iliad (open project)
2. The Odyssey 5.11c/d
3. Don't Damn It! 5.7 R   Pro: Miscellaneous to 2".

B. The Fist
4. Abbey Ale 5.10a

C. Tunnel Rock
5. Easy Day For a Frog 5.12a   Pro: #0 to .5 Friend.
6. Bigger Than Yo Dick 5.11b   Pro: #2 Friend.
7. Guinevere 5.11c or 5.10b

D. Crystal Wall (aka Tunnel Wall)
8. Mood For a Day 5.10a   Pro: To 3".
9. Fantastic Planet 5.11c or 5.10a   Pro: To 3".
10. Thursday Afternoon Hooky 5.10b R   Pro: To 3".
11. Nancy 5.8+   Overhanging offwidth chimney. Pro: To 5".
12. Pumpin' Puff Muffins 5.10b   Obvious offwidth.
    Pro: Two #3.5 Friends, five 4" to 6".

E. Ra's Buttress
13. Warm Beer and Cold Women 5.10a   Pro: To 4".
14. Hungry Wolf 5.11c   Pro: Two 3" pieces at beginning of 2nd pitch.
15. Gypsy Soul 5.12b   Pro: Two 3" pieces at beginning of 2nd pitch.
16. Dirt 5.6   Pro: To 3".
17. NCR (Not Craig's Route) 5.7   Pro: To 3.5".
18. Narrow Minded 5.9-   Pro: To 8", extra 5" to 8".
19. Sorcerer's Apprentice 5.11b
20. Black Magic 5.12a   Pro: To 2.5".
21. Dark Star 5.11a   Pro: To 2.5".

F. The Pharaoh
22. Lettuce Pray 5.9-   Pro: To 4".
23. The Devil Made Me Do It 5.6/5.7   Pro: To 4".

G. Pee Wee's Playhouse
24. Made You Look! 5.11b   Pro: To 2.5".
25. Pee Wee's Big Stem 5.10a   Pro: To 3.5".
26. Pee Wee's Pretty Pumped 5.11d   Pro: To 2.5".
27. The Pee Wee Erect 5.11a   Pro: To 2.5".

H. Greedy Gulch (Two hundred feet west of Pee Wee's Playhouse on the north side of the road.)
28. Someday Never Comes 5.12b   Pro: To #4 Rock.

29. **Crossing Over** 5.12b
30. **Yankee Doodle** 5.8   Not shown.On west facing slab 100 feet upstream from Greedy Gulch. Pro: To #.5 Friend, 3 bolts.

I. Eden

31. **Billy's Face** 5.10b R
32. **Nod** 5.6
33. **East of Eden** 5.9+   Pro: To 3.5".
34. **Fish and Whistle** 5.10c R   Pro: Many small to 1.5".
35. **West of Eden** 5.10b R   Pro: Many small to 2".
36. **Garden of Eden** 5.11a   Missing bolts. Pro: To 3", #2 and #3 LoweBalls.

J. Eve's Cave

37. **Piece of Shit** 5.10d TR
38. **Temptation** 5.11c   Pro: To #0 or #.5 Friend.
39. **Original Sin** 5.10c   Pro: To 3.5".
40. **The Adulteress** 5.11b   Pro: To to 2".
41. **Over The Edge** 5.11c   Pro: To ¾".
42. **Roadkill** 5.9+   Pro: To to 2.5".

K. Wet Spot Wall

43. **Fight Like a Brave** 5.11c   Pro: To 4".
44. **Delicious Demon** 5.11b
45. **Project** 5.11d
46. **Snake Eyes** 5.12b   Pro: To 2".
47. **Snake Trail** 5.11b   Pro: To 3".

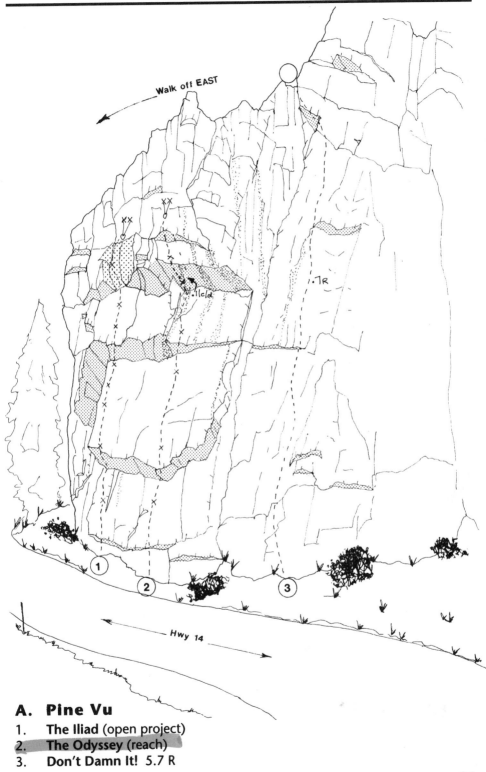

A. Pine Vu

1. **The Iliad** (open project)
2. **The Odyssey** (reach)
3. **Don't Damn It!** 5.7 R

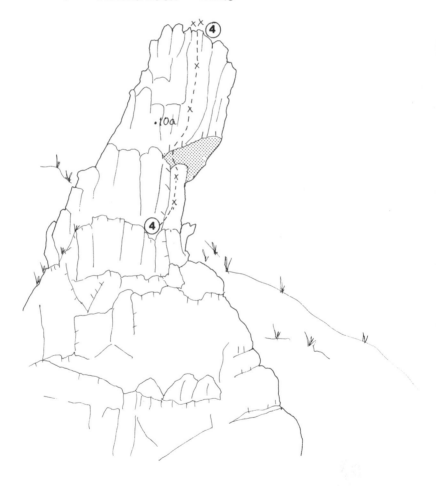

← TUNNEL ROCK   1/2 mile

.10a

B.   The Fist
4.   Abbey Ale 5.10a

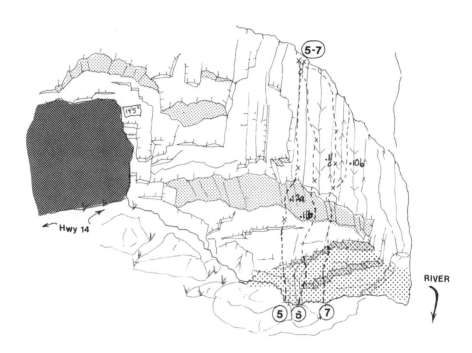

C. Tunnel Rock
5. **Easy Day For a Frog** 5.12a
6. **Bigger Than Yo Dick** 5.11b
7. **Guinevere** 5.11c or 5.10b

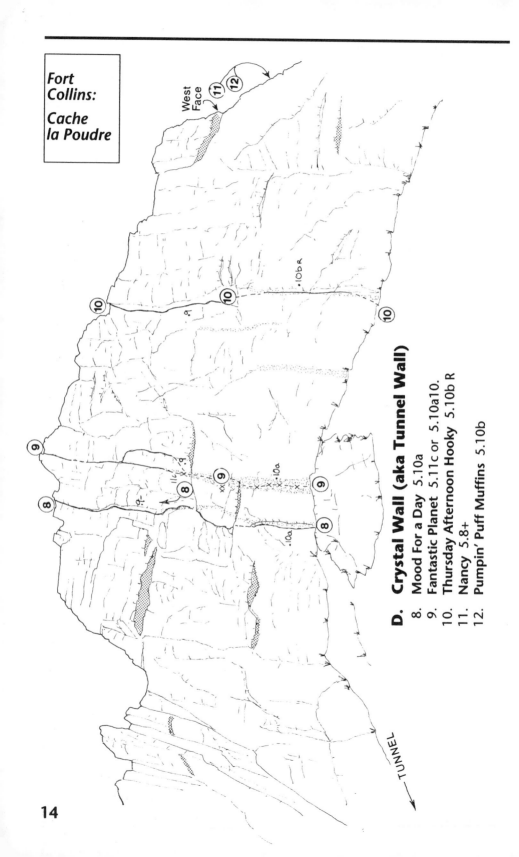

West Face

TUNNEL

D. Crystal Wall (aka Tunnel Wall)

8. Mood For a Day 5.10a
9. Fantastic Planet 5.11c or 5.10a10.
10. Thursday Afternoon Hooky 5.10b R
11. Nancy 5.8+
12. Pumpin' Puff Muffins 5.10b

D. Crystal Wall (aka Tunnel Wall) West Face

10. Thursday Afternoon Hooky 5.10b R
11. Nancy 5.8+
12. Pumpin' Puff Muffins 5.10b

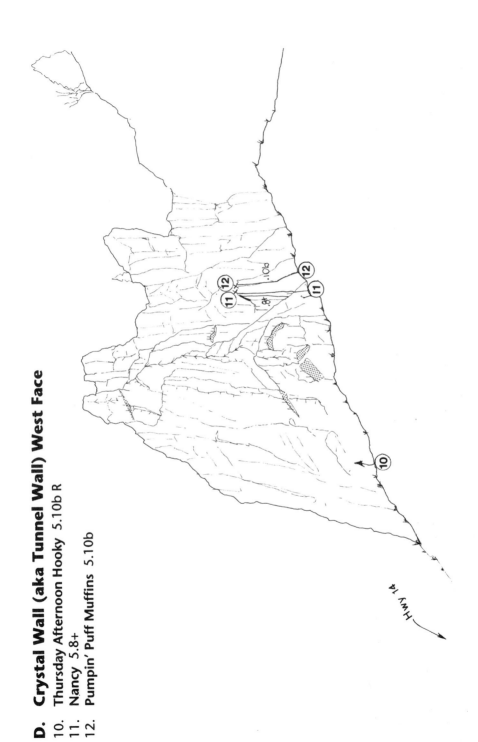

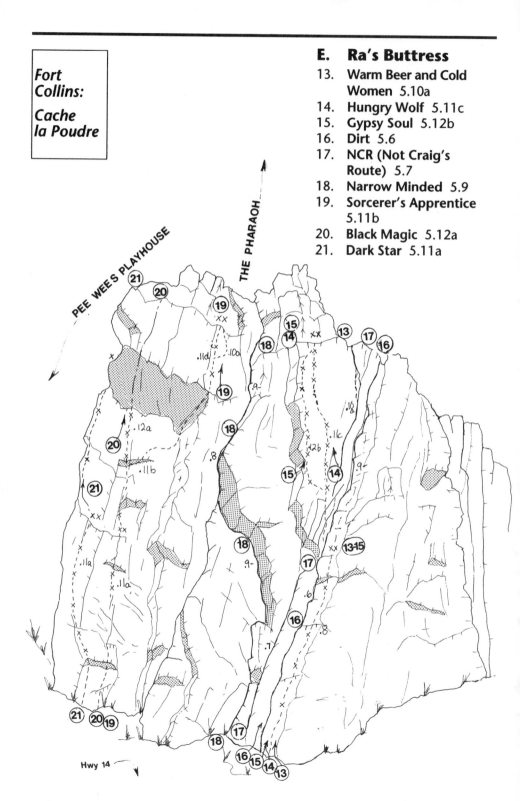

Fort Collins:

Cache la Poudre

E. Ra's Buttress

13. **Warm Beer and Cold Women** 5.10a
14. **Hungry Wolf** 5.11c
15. **Gypsy Soul** 5.12b
16. **Dirt** 5.6
17. **NCR (Not Craig's Route)** 5.7
18. **Narrow Minded** 5.9
19. **Sorcerer's Apprentice** 5.11b
20. **Black Magic** 5.12a
21. **Dark Star** 5.11a

F. The Pharaoh

22. Lettuce Pray 5.9
23. The Devil Made Me Do It 5.6/5.7

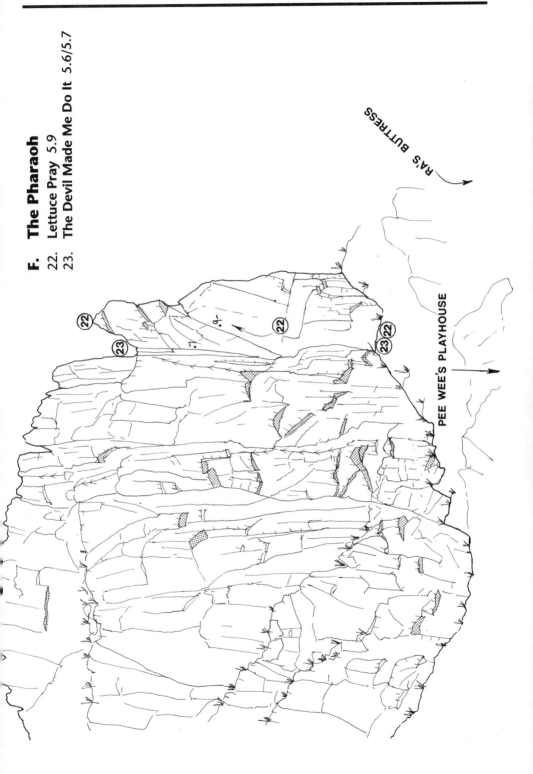

RA'S BUTTRESS

PEE WEE'S PLAYHOUSE

22. Lettuce Pray 5.9
23. The Devil Made Me Do It 5.6/5.7

G. Pee Wee's Playhouse

24. Made You Look! 5.11b
25. Pee Wee's Big Stem 5.10a
26. Pee Wee's Pretty Pumped 5.11d
27. The Pee Wee Erect 5.11a

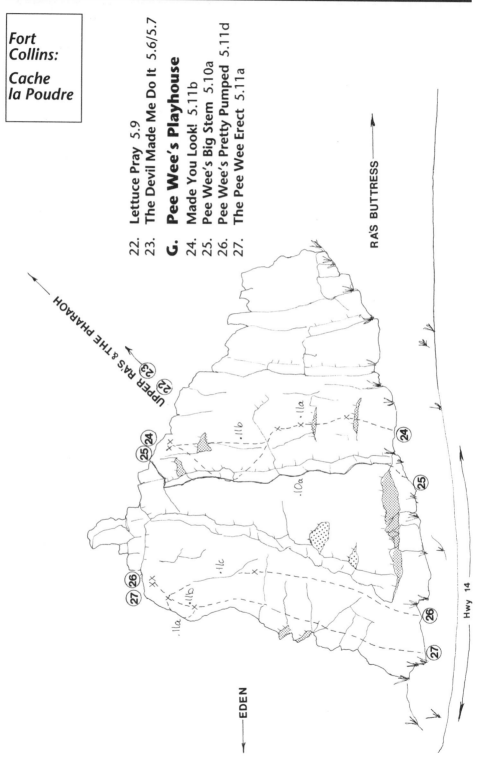

H. Greedy Gulch

28. Someday Never Comes 5.12b
29. Crossing Over 5.12b
30. Yankee Doodle 5.8

PEE WEE'S PLAYHOUSE 300'

Hwy 14

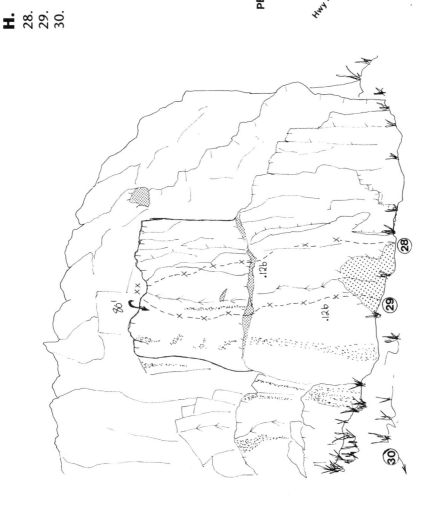

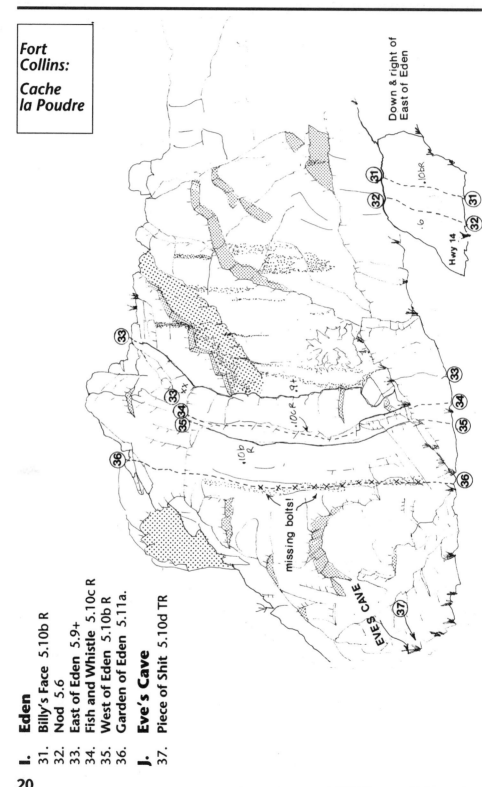

Fort Collins:

Cache la Poudre

I. Eden
31. Billy's Face 5.10b R
32. Nod 5.6
33. East of Eden 5.9+
34. Fish and Whistle 5.10c R
35. West of Eden 5.10b R
36. Garden of Eden 5.11a.

J. Eve's Cave
37. Piece of Shit 5.10d TR

J. Eve's Cave

37. Piece of Shit 5.10d TR
38. Temptation 5.11c.
39. Original Sin 5.10c
40. The Adulteress 5.11b
41. Over The Edge 5.11c
42. Roadkill 5.9+

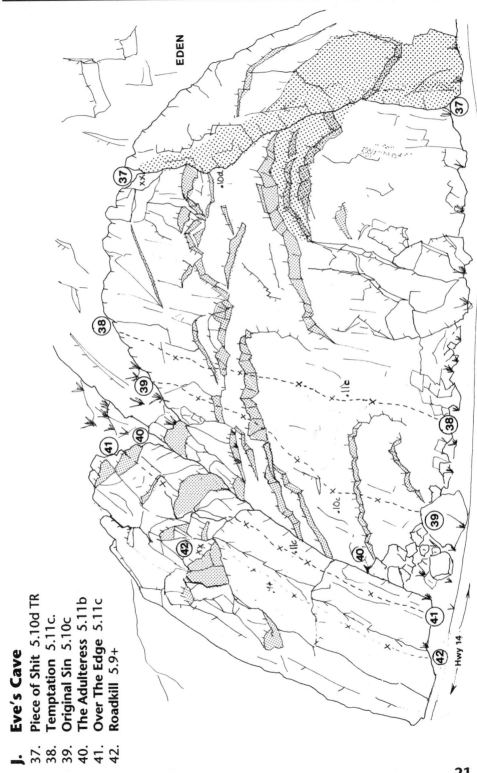

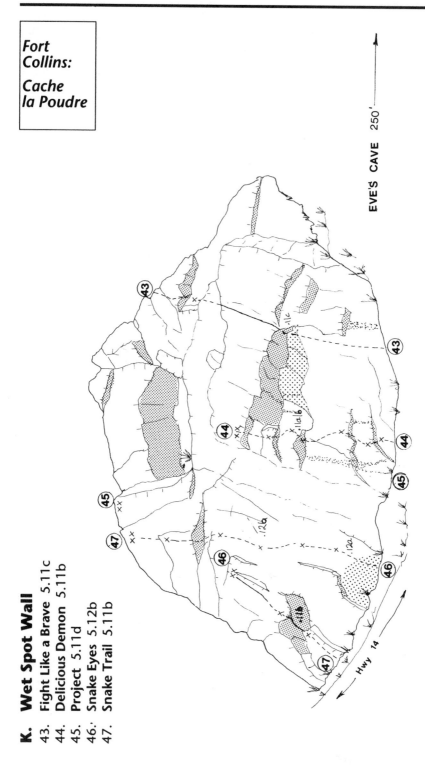

Fort
Collins:

*Cache
la Poudre*

EVE'S CAVE 250'

K. Wet Spot Wall

43. Fight Like a Brave 5.11c
44. Delicious Demon 5.11b
45. Project 5.11d
46. Snake Eyes 5.12b
47. Snake Trail 5.11b

22

Hwy 14

Scott Leonard on **Anarchy in the UK** 5.12b and Mia Axon on **Anarchy Rules** 5.12b, Clear Creek Canyon. Photo by Cameron M. Burns.

Big Thompson Canyon: Combat Rock

Combat Rock is located about 12 miles east of Estes Park off of Highway 24. It features some of the best face climbing in the Estes Park Area with micro edges and friction moves on its 70-80 degree face. Protection usually consists of bolts interspersed with flexible camming protection. There are also quite a few crack climbs, many of which are flared and discontinuous, with face climbing between crack systems. Many of the routes top out, but some just go up to a set of lowering anchors.

There are many climbs and climbing areas not listed in this guidebook due to lack of information. These will appear in the next edition of the guide.

Directions

To get there, take Highway 34 west from Highway 25 or east from Estes Park to the town of Drake. Turn right towards Glenhaven and go about .3 mile to a forest access road on the right. You are now facing Combat Rock. Follow this road past three switchbacks until you are directly across from the rock. Park and follow a trail that starts east of the pull-out and crosses the draw below the face. Contour up and west to the base of the rock. As you start down the trail, you cross below Elmer Fudd's Wok, the small slab with the tree on top.

To get to S&M Wall, follow the road past Combat Rock for about another .5 mile. The rock is located on your left. Park in a pull-out just past S&M Wall about 200 yards east. Beware of friable holds.

Considerations

In addition to climbing traffic, this area sees quite a lot of four-wheel-drive action. A popular 4x4 area is accessed by the same forest service road used by climbers. Consequently, there is a fair amount of trash on the road. Please take the time to pick this up as well as any trash you find at the base of the rock. Craig Luebben has bolted some of the lower grade climbs for the purpose of teaching beginning climbers. Please respect the effort he has put into this, not to mention time and expense. Leave the routes as you find them.

Camping and Recreation

In addition to climbing, Big Thompson Canyon also offers some excellent fishing, camping facilities, picnic areas, hiking

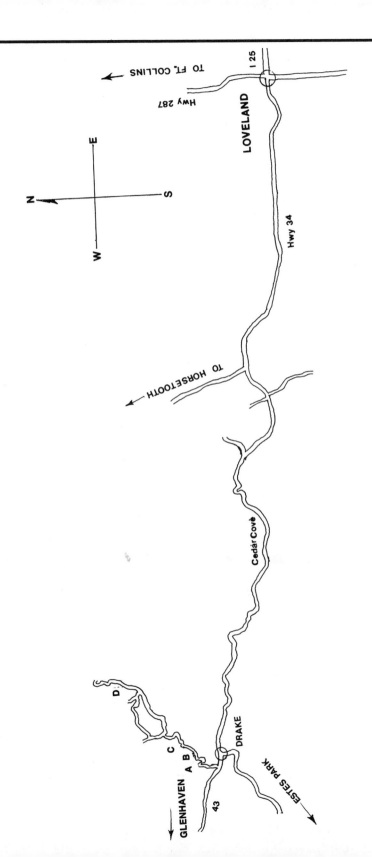

and mountain bike trails. For more information contact Colorado State Parks, 1313 Sherman Street, Room 618, Denver, CO 80203, (303)866-3437.

Emergency numbers

911

Estes-Poudre District Ranger
148 Remington St.
Ft. Collins, CO 80524
(303)482-3822

Larimer County Sheriff's Department
911 or (303)498-5100

Arapaho National Forest
(303)498-1100

Roosevelt National Forest
(303)498-1100

Big Thompson Canyon Rocks and Routes

A. Combat Rock:

1. **Arkansas Patriot** 5.9+   Pro: To 1".
2. **Rambo Santa** 5.7   Pro: To 2".
3. **Pop Off Route** 5.7 R   Pro: Miscellaneous to 2".
4. **Tree Roof** 5.7 or 5.8 (reach)   Pro: Miscellaneous to 2".
5. **Pearl Harbor** 5.10d   Pro: To 3".
6. **Eight Clicks to Saigon** 5.10d R   Pro: To 2.5".
7. **Saigon to Pearl Harbor Express** 5.10d   Combine pitch one of Eight Clicks and pitch two of Pearl Harbor. Pro: To 3".
8. **Ain't Nobody Here but Us Chickens** 5.11d Pro: To 3.5".
9. **Across Enemy Lines** 5.11b   Pro: To 2".
10. **Diagonal** 5.9   Pro: To 3.5".
11. **Battle of Evermore** 5.10b   Start with first pitch of Diagonal. Pro: To 3".
12. **Blood for Oil** 5.12b   Pro: To 1.5".
13. **No More War** 5.10a R   Pro: To 2.5".
14. **Front Line** 5.10d   Pro: To 2.5".
15. **Lizard Warrior** 5.11a/b A1   Pro: To 1.5".
16. **Camouflage** 5.9 R   Pro: To 3".
17. **GI Joe Does Barbie** 5.9+ R A1   Pro: To 1".
18. **Nuclear Polka** 5.10a   Pro: To 2".
19. **Monkey Lust** 5.9   Pro: To 3".

B. Elmer Fudd's Wok

20. **Silly Wabbit** 5.7 or 5.9-   Pro: Miscellaneous to 2".
21. **Fox Trot** 5.7 R   Pro: To 2".

C. S&M Wall (Billy Schott and Daryl Miller)

22. **Pop Rock (aka Fear of Feeling)** 5.11b   Pro: 3"-4" Friends for belay.

23. **I Love Little Girls** 5.10c/d R   Pro: 3"-4" Friends for belay.

24. **My Name Is Not Elvis (aka One Bolt Short)** 5.9 R   Pro: To 3".

D. Cedar Park Slab   No topo provided. Located at end of dirt road past S&M Wall. Cedar Park Slab is a 600 foot rock located on National Forest Land. The approach crosses private land, so ask permission first. There are two known routes on the slab, though due to the nature of the rock, many more are sure to exist.

25. **Slab Ants** 5.6 R   Start at the bottom of the main rock on ledge, left of **Dags in Beanland**. Go up slabs for 3 or 4 pitches, joining Dags in Beanland at the 4th pitch belay.

26. **Dags in Beanland** 5.8   Begin at the lowest section in the middle of the rock. 1. Follow a diagonal line past a bolt to a big ledge. 2. Follow bolts (6) past a roof to a double bolt belay. 3. Angle up and right to another ledge and belay. 4. Go up and left to a tree belay. 5. Face climb 5.6 past two more bolts and then take easier ground to the top.

A. Combat Rock

1. **Arkansas Patriot** 5.9+
2. **Rambo Santa** 5.7
3. **Pop Off Route** 5.7 R
4. **Tree Roof** 5.7 or 5.8 (reach)
5. **Pearl Harbor** 5.10d
6. **Eight Clicks to Saigon** 5.10d R

7. **Saigon to Pearl Harbor Express** 5.10d
8. **Ain't Nobody Here but Us Chickens** 5.11d
9. **Across Enemy Lines** 5.11b

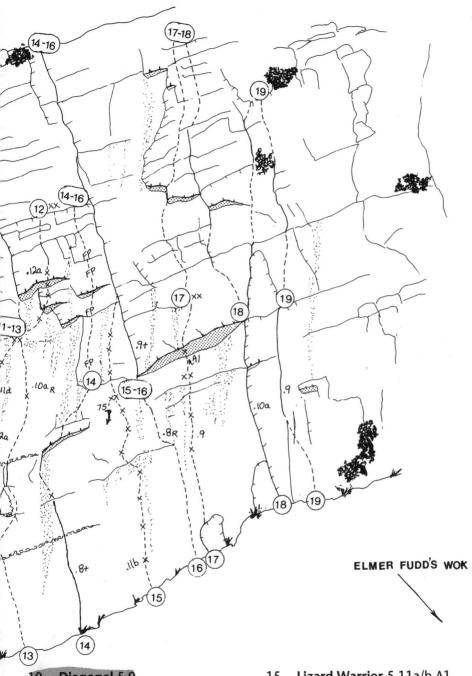

ELMER FUDD'S WOK

10. **Diagonal 5.9**
11. **Battle of Evermore** 5.10b
12. **Blood for Oil** 5.12b
13. **No More War** 5.10a R
14. **Front Line** 5.10d

15. **Lizard Warrior** 5.11a/b A1
16. **Camouflage** 5.9 R
17. **GI Joe Does Barbie** 5.9+ R A1
18. **Nuclear Polka** 5.10a
19. **Monkey Lust** 5.9

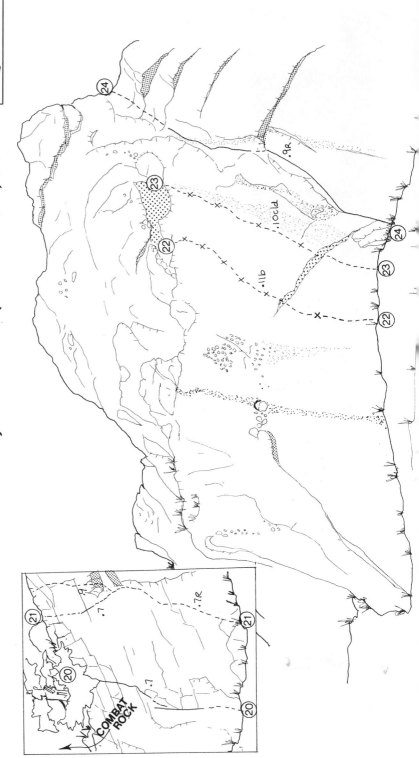

Fort Collins:

Big Thompson Canyon

B. Elmer Fudd's Wok
20. Silly Wabbit 5.7 or 5.9
21. Fox Trot 5.7 R

C. S&M Wall
22. Pop Rock (aka Fear of Feeling) 5.11b
23. I Love Little Girls 5.10c/d R
24. My Name Is Not Elvis (aka One Bolt Short) 5.9 R

Alvino Pon on **Too Many Puppies**, The Piz Badille. Photo by Ruel Chapman.

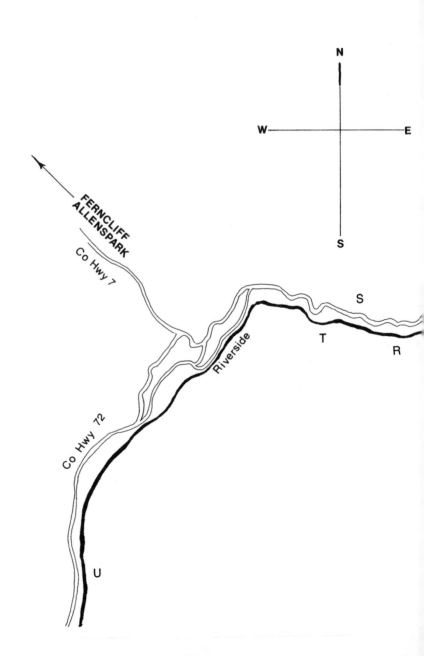

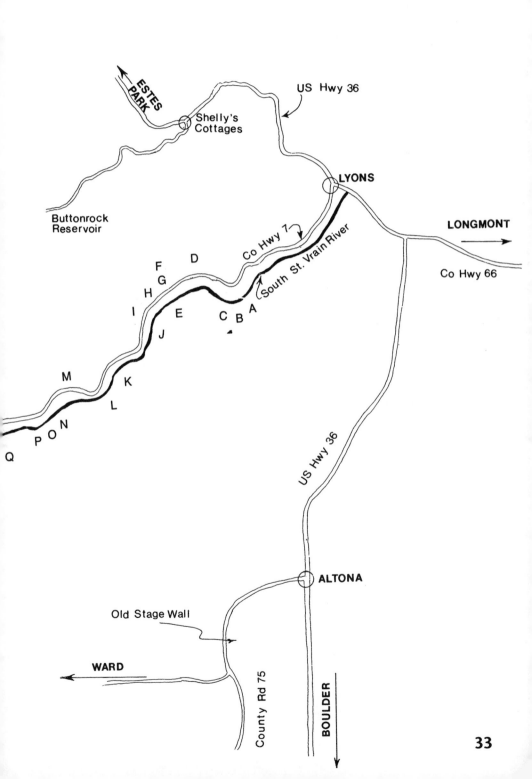

South St. Vrain

The rocks are located on either the right or left as you
drive up the canyon from Lyons.

0.0 miles; Light at the junction of Highways 36 and 7.

A. 3.4 miles; Guardian Rock
On left side just above the river. Known routes are on
the far west face.

B. 3.8 miles; The Mushroom Massif
The large, sprawling formation on the left about 700
feet above the river.

C. 3.85 miles; Des Dome
First separate formation west of The Mushroom
Massif, 1,000 feet above the river.

D. 4.3 miles; December Wall
Long formation on the right side, 800 feet above the
road. All known routes start left of the large corner
left of center (Winter Dream) and left of where the
rocks become broken up

E. 4.5 miles; The Sentinel
Just above the river on the left side.

F. 5.1 miles; Lower Infirmary Slabs
On the right side, but hard to see from the road.
These slabs are about 300 feet above the road directly
across from a small pull-out on the south side.

G. 5.1 miles; Upper Infirmary Slabs
300 feet above Lower Infirmary Slabs. Follow a trail
west around the base of the lower slabs to a break in
the rock band.

H. 5.3 miles; Observatory Rock
On the right side just past the road to the ranger
housing and immediately above a pull-out.

I. 5.4 miles; North Narrows Slabs
Five feet off the road on the right side.

J. 5.4 miles; South Narrows Slabs
Directly across the the river on the left.

K. 6.0 miles; The Spire
Obvious separate rock formation on the left side
above the river across from a large pull-out/camping
space.

L. 6.1 miles; Little Ogre
Large formation on left side immediately above the
river.

M. 6.6 miles; Monkey Skull
On the right side about 200 feet above the road, char-
acterized by the large right facing corner on the west
face (Sunshine Dihedral). Approach is best made from

the smaller pull-out on the right side below the indistinct east face.

N. 6.9 miles; Trojan Bunny Buttress–East Face
    Large formation with many roofs about 400 feet
    above the river on the left.

O. 6.9 miles; Trojan Bunny Buttress–West Face
    Gray slabs just around the corner facing west.

P. 6.9 miles; Leatherface
    150 feet farther, next west facing slab.

Q. 8.7 miles; Hideaway Dome
    Located up a valley about 1000 feet above the river on
    the left side.

R. 9.1 miles; The Fang
    Prominent buttress 600 feet above the river on the
    left side.

S. 9.6 miles; Violator Buttress
    100 feet off of the road on the right side immediately
    north of a two track pull-out and just before an abandoned cabin.

T. 10.5 miles; The Watchtower
    Last formation in the canyon on the left side.

U. The Piz Badille
    Located about 4.5 miles down Highway 72 (Peak to
    Peak Highway) on the left side just before you reach
    Peaceful Valley.

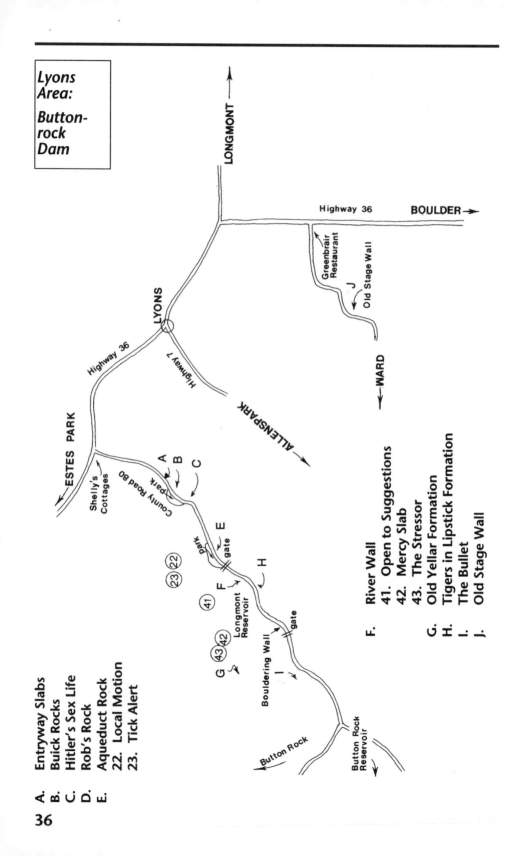

Lyons Area:
Button-rock Dam

LONGMONT

Highway 36   BOULDER →

Greenbriar Restaurant

J
Old Stage Wall

LYONS

Highway 36

Highway 7

ALLENSPARK

WARD

ESTES PARK

Shelly's Cottages

County Road 80

park

A
B
C

E

gate

park

23 22

H

F

41

Longmont Reservoir

G 43 42

Bouldering Wall

gate

I

Button Rock

Button Rock Reservoir

A.   Entryway Slabs
B.   Buick Rocks
C.   Hitler's Sex Life
D.   Rob's Rock
E.   Aqueduct Rock
22. Local Motion
23. Tick Alert

F.   River Wall
41. Open to Suggestions
42. Mercy Slab
43. The Stressor
G.   Old Yellar Formation
H.   Tigers in Lipstick Formation
I.   The Bullet
J.   Old Stage Wall

Lyons Area

Buttonrock Dam Area

The Buttonrock Dam area offers some of the most concentrated grouping of hard rock climbs in this guidebook as well as more moderate routes. With the exception of the Old Yellar Formation, and The Bullet, most climbs are within a 5-minute walk from your car.

The Buttonrock Dam area follows the North St. Vrain River and the climbing is on granite. The climbs at the beginning of the canyon are primarily crack climbs. The climbing farther up the canyon, with some exceptions, consists of hard face climbs.

Directions

To get there, go right at the junction of Highways 36 and 7 at the light in Lyons, heading towards Estes Park. After about 3.7 miles, turn left at the Shelly's Cottages sign (County Road 80). One-half mile after the turn are the Entryway Slabs on the left. Around the corner, .1 mile farther, are Buick Rocks and Hitler's Sex Life, also on the left. Continuing past Hitler's Sex Life for another 2.3 miles brings you to a steel gate and parking. Aqueduct Rock is on your left before crossing through the gate. River Wall is the formation immediately past the gate on the right. The best approach for River Wall (especially during times of high water), and the approach for the Old Yellar Formation, starts on the right, just before you cross the gate. Use the rappel bolts at the top of The Box to access River Wall. Continue up the trail above River Wall as it diagonals uphill to reach the Old Yellar Formation.

Three hundred feet past River Wall on the left, just off the road, is the small but pretty Tigers In Lipstick Formation. Two miles or so further past the second gate and about 60 yards uphill is The Bullet, where all but two of the climbs are crack climbs. Between The Bullet and River Wall is a nice bouldering wall on the right.

Duncan Ferquson, Paul Piana, George Bracksieck and Susanne Jackson as well as other climbers, were responsible for some of the first routes on Buick Rocks and Hitler's Sex Life. Mark Wilford and Steve Mammen put up routes such as Tick Alert and Local Motion as well as routes on the River Wall and The Bullet. Most of the climbs on River Wall were done in the late '80s by a virtual who's who of Boulder climbers as well as visiting Paul Piana,

Bob Horan, Rob Candeleria, Colin Lantz, Beth Wald, Harold Quib, Wolfgang Schweiger, Chip Ruckgraber, Jeff Gruenberg and the late Katherine Frier. Pat Adams was involved lately in one of the newer additions right of New Horizon. Steve Hong has been very active on the Old Yellar Formation.

Camping and Recreation

There is no camping or mountain biking at Buttonrock, but there is some excellent fishing in the North St. Vrain as well as some great hiking trails. Please keep the area as clean as you find it. The only trashed out spots are the parking areas beneath Entryway Slabs, Buick Rocks and Hitler's Sex Life areas.

Buttonrock Dam Rocks and Routes

A. Entryway Slabs

1. **Rock Biter** 5.3 (No pro.)
2. **First Door** 5.6   Pro: To 3".
3. **Joy** 5.7   Pro: To 5".

B. Buick Rocks (First buttress)

4. **Green Slab** 5.9+/5.10a
5. **The Buick** 5.10a   Pro: To 3".
6. **Fat Girls on Mopeds** 5.11d R   Pro: To 3".
7. **Pontiac** 5.11a   Pro: To 3".
8. **Veedub** 5.11a   Pro: To 3".

Buick Rocks (Second Buttress)

9. **Civic Minded** 5.8   Pro: To 3".
10. **Energon Cube** 5.9-   Pro: To 2.5".
11. **The Infamous Pink Thunderbird** 5.11b/c   Pro: To 3".
12. **Beamer Up, Scotty** 5.8   Pro: To 4".
13. **Pooh Belly** 5.7   Pro: To 3.5".
14. **Unknown Face** 5.10c/d   Pro: TCUs.
15. **Kiss Face** 5.10a   Pro: To 2.5".

C. Hitler's Sex Life

16. **Initial Route** 5.7   Pro: To 3.5".
17. **Top Rope** 5.11b/c   Very indistinct line, variations from 5.10a up.
18. **Gestapo Mega** 5.11d R   Pro: To 3.5".
19. **Hitler's Sex Life** 5.11c   Pro: To 2".

D. Rob's Rock (No topo.)

20. **Tain't No Crack** 5.10c   Free standing rock on left, follows seam with 3 bolts.

E. Aqueduct Rock

21. **The Pipeline** 5.12a R   Pro: To ¾".

The following two climbs are on the rocks to the right and up the hill, directly across from The Pipeline. No topos are provided.

22. **Local Motion** 5.11c/d   Overhanging fingers to thin hands crack. Pro: To 2".

23. **Tick Alert** 5.10c/d   Underclings for two pitches. Pro: 3".

F. River Wall
Best approach for River Wall and Old Yellar Formation: Follow trail on right side of parking before gate. There are two bolts on top of The Box to get to the base of River Wall. For Old Yellar, keep high on trail as it traverses the slope, staying quite a bit above River Wall and angling up to Old Yellar.

24. **Pooh Corner** 5.8   Pro: To 3".
25. **Dihedral** 5.8   Pro: To 4".
26. **Shades of Murky Depths** 5.10d   Pro: To 2.5".
27. **Neurosurgeon** 5.12a   Pro: To 2".
27a. **Direct** 5.11c/d R
28. **Le Diamant E'ternal (The Eternal Diamond)** 5.13a/b
29. **The Box** 5.7   Pro: To 3".
30. **Introducing Meteor Dad** 5.10d
31. **Live Wire** 5.10d   Pro: To 2".
32. **Escape From Alcatraz** 5.11b/c
33. **Red Neck Hero** 5.12a
34. **Big, Big Monkey Man** 5.12b
35. **Pocket Hercules** 5.12a   Pro: To 1.5".
36. **Big, Big Gunky Man** 5.12a R
37. **Brother From Another Planet** 5.13a/b
38. **Project**
39. **Lost Horizon** 5.13a/c   Pro: To 1.5".
40. **New Horizon** 5.12d
41. **Open to Suggestions** 5.11d   No topo. Thirtyfive-foot face on hill above New Horizon. Follows seam. Pro: To ¾".

The following two routes are located near the Old Yellar Formation, but not on it.

42. **Mercy Slab** 5.10c/d   No topo. Located slightly below and to the right of the Old Yellar Formation. Climb a 30 foot face to a right leaning corner. Pro: To 2.5".

43. **The Stressor** 5.11c/d   No topo. Takes the thin seam left of Mercy Slab. Pro: To 1.5".

G. Old Yellar Formation

44. Project
45. **Old Yellar** 5.13a
46. **Bambi** 5.12d
47. **Nuttin' but Button** 5.12c
48. Project

H. Tigers in Lipstick Formation (Located 300 feet past dam on left side of road.)

49. **Tigers in Lipstick** 5.10a   Pro: To 1.5".

I. The Bullet

50. **Spy Dust** 5.10d   Pro: To 3.5".
51. **Sharps 50** 5.12a/b
52. **Where Eagles Die** 5.10d   Pro: To 4.5", mostly big.
53. **Pretty Blue Gun** 5.10d   Pro: To 3".
54. **Finger Tattoo** 5.12a/b   Pro: To 1".

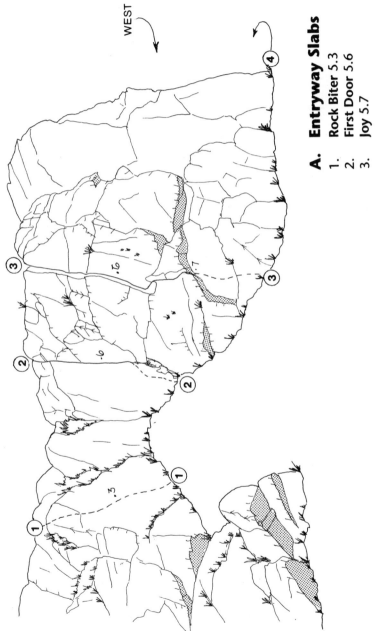

WEST

A. Entryway Slabs
1. Rock Biter 5.3
2. First Door 5.6
3. Joy 5.7

B. Buick Rocks (First buttress)
4. Green Slab 5.9+/5.10a

41

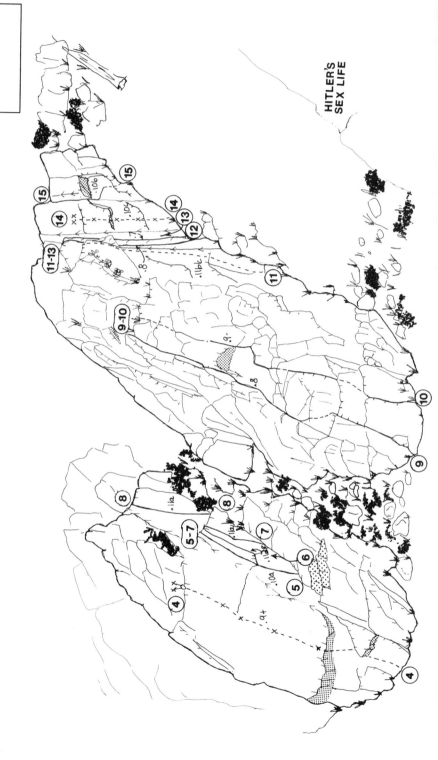

Lyons Area:

Button-rock Dam

HITLER'S SEX LIFE

B. Buick Rocks (First buttress)

4. Green Slab 5.9+/5.10a
5. The Buick 5.10a
6. Fat Girls on Mopeds 5.11d R
7. Pontiac 5.11a
8. Veedub 5.11a

Buick Rocks (Second Buttress)

9. Civic Minded 5.8
10. Energon Cube 5.9
11. The Infamous Pink Thunderbird 5.11b/c
12. Beamer Up, Scotty 5.8
13. Pooh Belly 5.7
14. Unknown Face 5.10c/d
15. Kiss Face 5.10a

Buick Rocks (Second Buttress)
10. Energon Cube 5.9-

C. Hitler's Sex Life
16. Initial Route 5.7
17. Top Rope 5.11b/c
18. Gestapo Mega 5.11d R
19. Hitler's Sex Life 5.11c

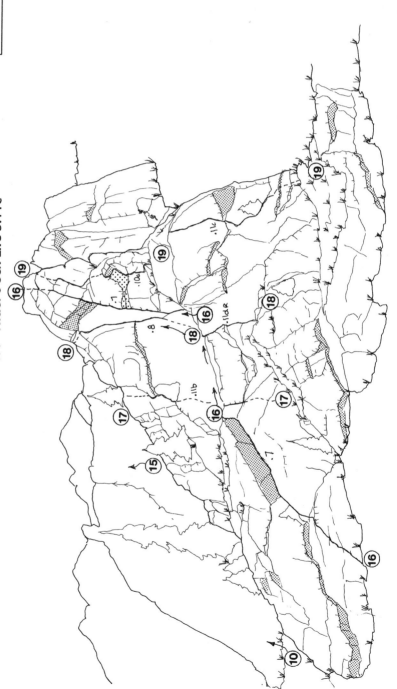

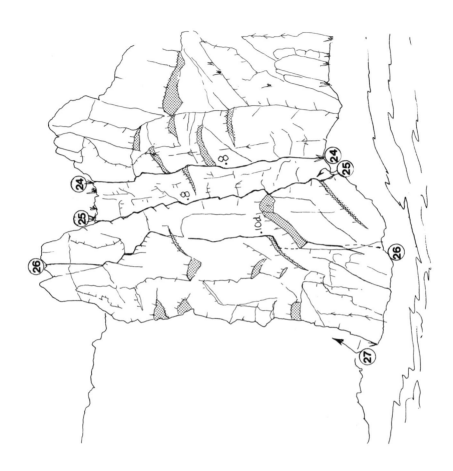

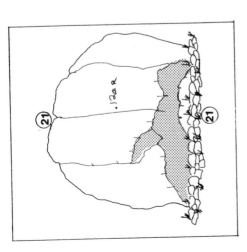

E.   Aqueduct Rock
21.   The Pipeline 5.12a R

F.   River Wall
24.   Pooh Corner 5.8
25.   Dihedral 5.8
26.   Shades of Murky Depths 5.10d
27.   Neurosurgeon 5.12a

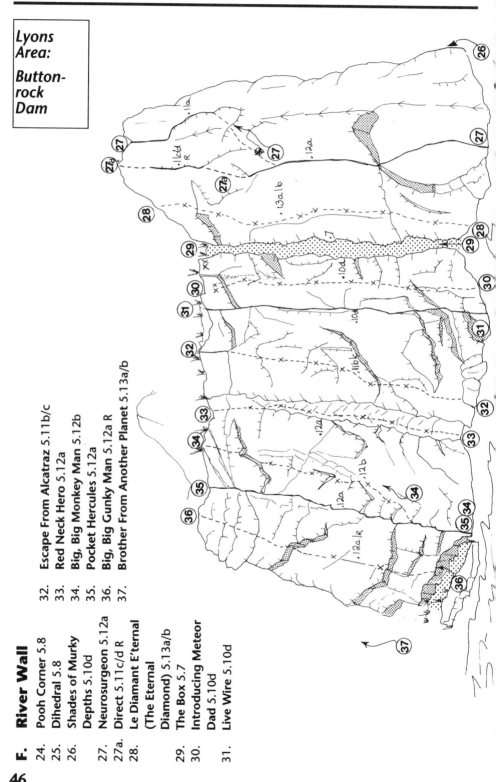

F. River Wall

24. Pooh Corner 5.8
25. Dihedral 5.8
26. Shades of Murky Depths 5.10d
27. Neurosurgeon 5.12a
27a. Direct 5.11c/d R
28. Le Diamant E'ternal (The Eternal Diamond) 5.13a/b
29. The Box 5.7
30. Introducing Meteor Dad 5.10d
31. Live Wire 5.10d
32. Escape From Alcatraz 5.11b/c
33. Red Neck Hero 5.12a
34. Big, Big Monkey Man 5.12b
35. Pocket Hercules 5.12a
36. Big, Big Gunky Man 5.12a R
37. Brother From Another Planet 5.13a/b

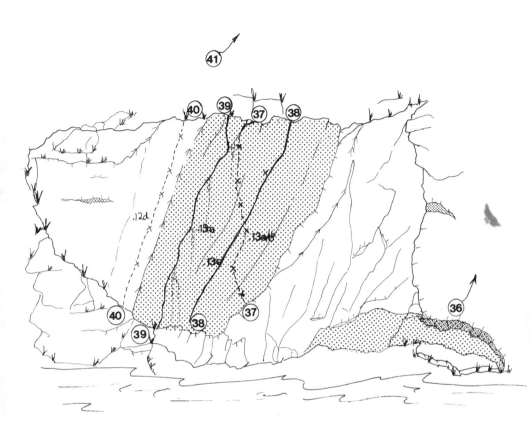

F. River Wall

36. **Big, Big Gunky Man** 5.12a R
37. **Brother From Another Planet** 5.13a/b
38. **Project**
39. **Lost Horizon** 5.13a/c
40. **New Horizon** 5.12d
41. **Open to Suggestions** 5.11d

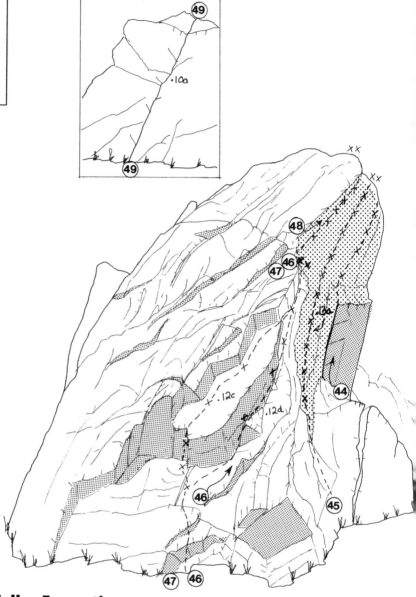

Lyons Area:

Buttonrock Dam

G. Old Yellar Formation

44. **Project**
45. **Old Yellar 5.13a**
46. **Bambi 5.12d**
47. **Nuttin' but Button 5.12c**
48. **Project**

H. Tigers in Lipstick Formation

49. **Tigers in Lipstick 5.10a**

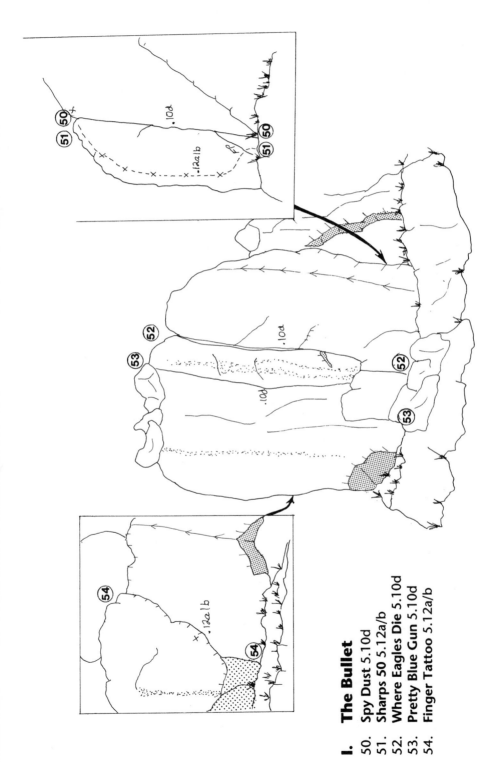

I. The Bullet

50. **Spy Dust** 5.10d
51. **Sharps 50** 5.12a/b
52. **Where Eagles Die** 5.10d
53. **Pretty Blue Gun** 5.10d
54. **Finger Tattoo** 5.12a/b

Old Stage Wall

Since the publication of Richard Rossiter's book *Boulder Climbs North*, this beautiful climbing area has been closed. This area is on private land and the landowner became worried about the liability issues, a prime and sad example of what is happening (at the rate of one closure per week) across the states. This area has been included for two reasons. 1. To give the Access Fund a little more ammunition in their efforts to reopen the area. 2. To make climbers more aware of the fact that this is, indeed, happening in Colorado. Please become involved with access issues, including crossing private land, trash, noise and disrupting traffic.

Old Stage Wall Rocks and Routes

1. **Dragon Lady** 5.12b/c
2. **Via Dolorosa (Sorrowful Road)** 5.11b/c A0
3. **Alex in Wonderland** 5.11d
4. **Trojan Crack** 5.11b   Pro: To 2.5".
5. **The Solstice** 5.13a
6. **Flying Saucers** 5.12a
7. **5.12** TR

Old Stage Wall

1. Dragon Lady 5.12b/c
2. Via Dolorosa (Sorrowful Road) 5.11b/c A0
3. Alex in Wonderland 5.11d
4. Trojan Crack 5.11b
5. The Solstice 5.13a
6. Flying Saucers 5.12a
7. 5.12 TR

South St. Vrain Canyon

South St. Vrain Canyon, located between Lyons and Allenspark on Highway 7 is an eleven-mile long canyon filled with granite cliffs from 40' to 400' high. The climbs range from 5.5 to mid-5.13 with a couple of 5.14 projects in the works. There is a wide variety of climbing here, from faces to cracks and roofs. Many of the older climbs are mid- to lower-end climbs that primarily follow crack systems. The newer climbs tend to be bolt protected thin cracks or faces.

A few of the obvious rock formations, some quite large, weren't listed simply because of lack of any available route information. Many of the rocks and climbs do not reflect the original names, but reflect only the currently available information. This is the first guidebook to be printed on this area, and errors and omissions may occur. The author extends his apologies, and would appreciate any first ascent information, rock and route name corrections, etc. Corrections will be included in the next edition.

Leonard Coyne, Roger and Bill Briggs, the Lowe Brothers, Gene Ellis, Steve Brodhead, Brett and Judy Rirckman and Tim Hunt were responsible for quite a few of the older routes listed. Mark Rolofson, Paul Gagner, Alvino Pon, Hank Caylor and others were responsible for many of the newer, harder climbs.

Emergency numbers

911
Larimer County Fire Department
586-2341
Larimer County Sheriff Department
586-4466

Camping and Recreation

South St. Vrain offers some good fishing and camping, along with some hiking trails. Also, there is information on South St. Vrain canyon in Mark Rolofson's new guidebook, *1993 Boulder Sport Climber's Guide*, as well as other sport climbing areas.

South St. Vrain Canyon Rocks and Routes

A. Guardian Rock
1. **Shuffling Madness** 5.11b   Pro: To 3".
2. **Stone Knives** 5.12a   Pro: To 3".

B. The Mushroom Massif (Note: Due to some inconsistent and incomplete information on this rock, climbs here should be treated as first ascents and bolt gear is advisable. Anchors may or may not be where indicated and ratings may be different than shown.)
3. **Unknown**
4. **Unknown** 5.9   Pro: To 4".
5. **Unknown** 5.7   Pro: To 4".
6. **Unknown** 5.8   Pro: To 4".
7. **Unknown** 5.7   Pro: To 4".
8. **The Mushroom** 5.8   Pro: Miscellaneous to 2".
9. **Unknown**
10. **Unknown**
11. **Unnamed** 5.7   Pro: To 2.5".
12. **Unnamed** 5.8   Pro: To 3".

The following two routes are located in a corridor on the southeast corner, and are best approached from Routes 5 through 10, then rappelling down to the base of the climbs.
13. **Unnamed** 5.8   Four bolts to 2 bolt anchors.
14. **Unnamed** 5.11   Five bolts to 2 bolt anchors.
15. **Unknown**

C. Des Dome
16. **Desdoma** 5.11a   Pro: To 4".

D. December Wall (Note: All known climbs start from the large corner left of center, and left of where the rock becomes broken up. Due to some inconsistent and incomplete information on this rock, climbs here should be treated as first ascents and bolt gear is advisable. Anchors may or may not be where indicated and ratings may be different than shown.)
17. **Winter Dreams (aka Gene and George's Excellent Adventure)** 5.10c   Pro: To 4", extra 2"-4".
18. **Ranklands of Infinity** 5.10b   Pro: To 4", extra 3"- 4".
19. **Caesar's Crack** 5.10b   Pro: To 4", extra 3"-4".
20. **I'm Camming, I'm Camming** 5.9   Pro: To 4".
21. **Short Takes** 5.9   Pro: To 4".
22. **Great Tree Route** 5.8+   Pro: To 4".
23. **I Promise Not to Cam In Your Mouth** 5.10b   Pro: To 4".

E.   **The Sentinel** Very old routes and haven't seen much traffic.
24.   **Spy Story** 5.8/5.9   Pro: To 4".
25.   **I Spy** 5.8+ R   Pro: To 3.5".
26.   **Unknown** 5.9-   Pro: To 4".
27.   **Roundabout** 5.9-   Pro: To 3".
28.   **Tapestry** 5.10   Pro: To 3".

F.   **Lower Infirmary Slabs**
29.   **Morning Oyster** 5.6   Pro: Miscellaneous to 2.5".
30.   **Plague Boys** 5.7
31.   **Acts of Contrition** 5.8

G.   **Upper Infirmary Slabs**
32.   **Panic in the Gray Room** 5.9+/5.10a
32a.   **I.V. League** 5.7   Pro: To 4".
32b.   **Emergency Entrance** 5.6+   Pro: To 3".
33.   **Remission** 5.7+
33a.   **Admission Crack** 5.7   Pro: To 4".

H.   **Observatory Rock**
34.   **Original Route** 5.8   Pro: To 4".
35.   **Variation** 5.8   Pro: To 4".

I.   **The Narrows Slabs (North)**
36.   **The Hitcher** 5.12b
37.   **Crack** 5.10d   Pro: To 3".
38.   **Death Tongue** 5.11d/5.12a or 5.10a A1   Pro: To 3".
39.   **Death Tongue Variation** 5.11d/5.12a or 5.10a A1   Pro: To 3".
40.   **Flash Flood** 5.12a
41.   **Climb to Safety** 5.9   Pro: To 2.5".
42.   **Cling to Safety** 5.11b   Pro: Miscellaneous to 2.5".
43.   **Unknown**
44.   **Unknown**
45.   **Unknown**
46.   **Alley Cat Street** 5.10a

J.   **The Narrows Slabs (South)**
47.   **Sidetrack** 5.6   Pro: To 1".
48.   **Pon Scum** 5.12a/b
49.   **Bullfight** 5.13a
49a.   **Vrain Dead** 5.8+   Pro: To 4".
49b.   **Vrain Child** 5.11c/d or 5.11a

K.   **The Spire**
50.   **Dire Spire** 5.9-   Pro: To 3".
51.   **Unknown** 5.8   Pro: To 3".
52.   **Unknown** 5.8   Pro: To 3".

L. Little Ogre

53. **The Giveaway** 5.10c/d   Pro: To 4".
54. **Unknown** (project?)

M. Monkey Skull

55. **Unknown**   Corner.
56. **Unknown**   Pro: Bolts and anchors.
57. **Summit Block** 5.10a   Pro: To 2".
58. **Fever Dance Variation** 5.9   Pro: To 3.5".
59. **Fever Dance** 5.10c   Pro: To 2.5".
60. **Upside The Cranium** 5.10a/b
61. **Alvino's Variation** 5.9   Pro: To 4".
62. **Sunshine Dihedral** 5.10a/b   Pro: To 4".
63. **Hollow Be Thy Name** 5.10d/5.11a (reach)   Pro: To 2.5".
64. **Fringe Dweller** 5.10c   Pro: #0 or #1 TCU.
65. **Casual Corner** 5.8+   Pro: To 2".
66. **Amy, Good Gorilla** 5.10b/c   Pro: To 2".
67. **Crack** 5.9-   Pro: To 2.5".

N. Trojan Bunny Buttress (East Face)

68. **Project** (?)

O. Trojan Bunny Buttress (West Face)

69. **Lick My Plate** 5.8+
70. **Streatch** 5.9+
71. **Dog Will Hunt** 5.10b
72. **Unknown**   Very clean crack through roofs.

P. Leatherface

73. **Project** (Fingercrack)
74. **Vrain Storm** 5.9 R/X   Pro: To 1.5".
75. **Pondemonium** 5.10d
76. **Unknown** 5.8   Pro: To 3".
77. **Unknown** 5.7   Pro: To 3".

Q. Hideaway Dome (Located high up in a valley facing west on the south side of river.)

78. **Gumbi Parade** 5.11a   Pro: To 3.5".
79. **Hidden Pleasures** 5.8+   Pro: To 4".

R. The Fang

80. **The Turning Point** 5.11c   Pro: To 2.5".
81. **Stiletto** 5.13d/5.14a (Project)
82. **Project** 5.13b
83. **Jugular Vein** 5.12b/c   Pro: To 2.5".
84. **Warm Up Climb** 5.10c   Pro: To 3".
85. **Witch Doctor** 5.13 (Project)

86. **Goldfinger** 5.12a   Pro: To 3".
87. **Perfect Stemetry** 5.12c/d
88. **Belligerent Buttress** 5.12b

S.   Violator Buttress

89. **The Violator** 5.10a   Pro: To 4".
90. **Trespassers Will Be Violated** 5.11b/c   Pro: To 2.5".

T.   The Watchtower

91. **The Corner** 5.9-   Pro: To 4".
92. **Highway Robbery** 5.12a
92a. **Business Loop** 5.11b

U.   The Piz Badille

93. **The Ridge** 5.6   Pro: To 4".
94. **Unknown**
95. **Unknown**
96. **Reusable Love Bag** 5.9+   Pro: To 2".
97. **Too Many Puppies** 5.9-   Pro: To 2".
98. **Unknown**
99. **Sympathetic Mind Fuck** 5.6

A. Guardian Rock, West Face

1. **Shuffling Madness** 5.11b
2. **Stone Knives** 5.12a

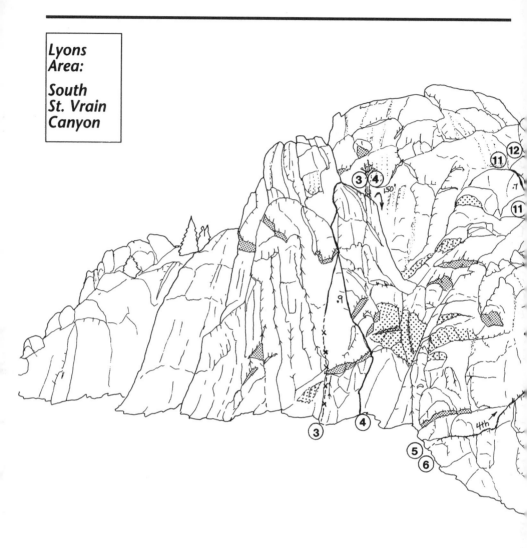

B. The Mushroom Massif

3.	Unknown	10.	Unknown
4.	Unknown 5.9	11.	Unnamed 5.7
5.	Unknown 5.7	12.	Unnamed 5.8
6.	Unknown 5.8	13.	Unnamed 5.8
7.	Unknown 5.7	14.	Unnamed 5.11
8.	The Mushroom 5.8	15.	Unknown
9.	Unknown		

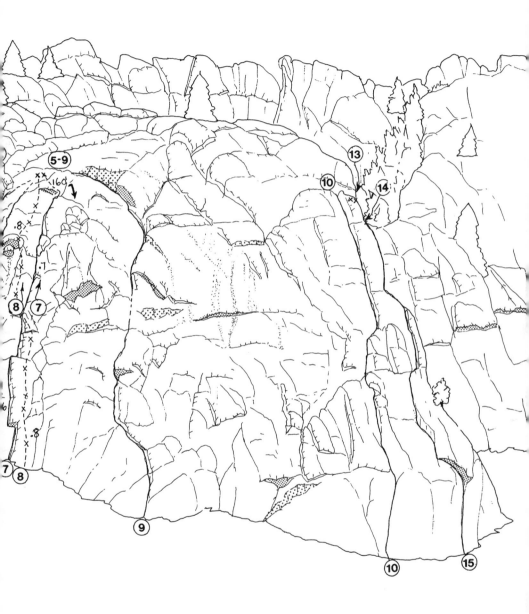

C. Des Dome

16. Desdoma 5.11a

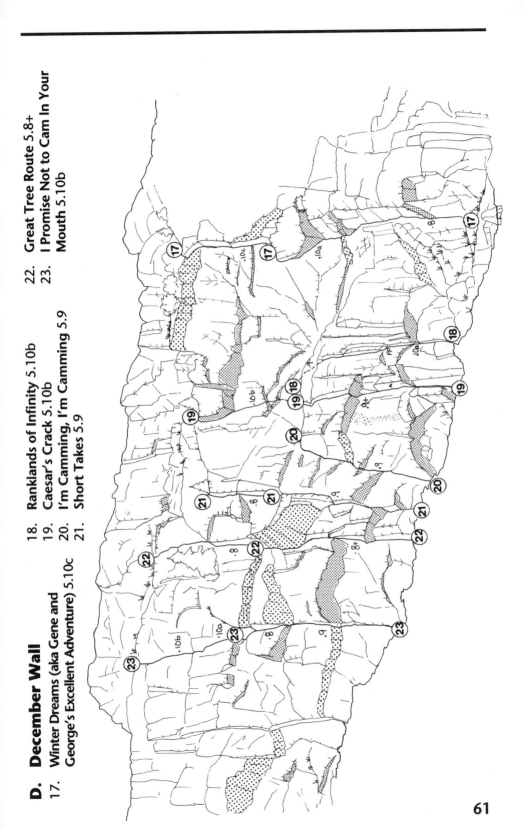

D. December Wall

17. Winter Dreams (aka Gene and George's Excellent Adventure) 5.10c
18. Ranklands of Infinity 5.10b
19. Caesar's Crack 5.10b
20. I'm Camming, I'm Camming 5.9
21. Short Takes 5.9
22. Great Tree Route 5.8+
23. I Promise Not to Cam In Your Mouth 5.10b

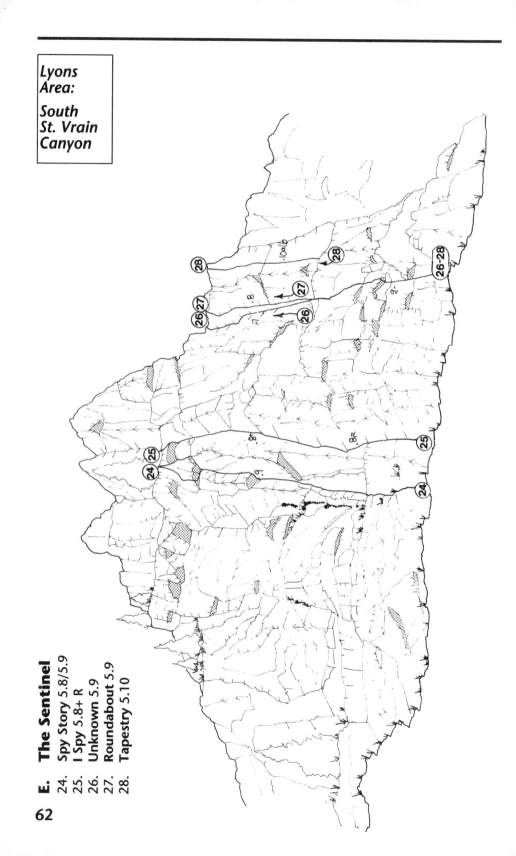

E. The Sentinel
24. Spy Story 5.8/5.9
25. I Spy 5.8+ R
26. Unknown 5.9
27. Roundabout 5.9
28. Tapestry 5.10

F. Lower Infirmary Slabs

29. Morning Oyster 5.6
30. Plague Boys 5.7
31. Acts of Contrition 5.8

G. Upper Infirmary Slabs

32. Panic in the Gray Room 5.9+/5.10a

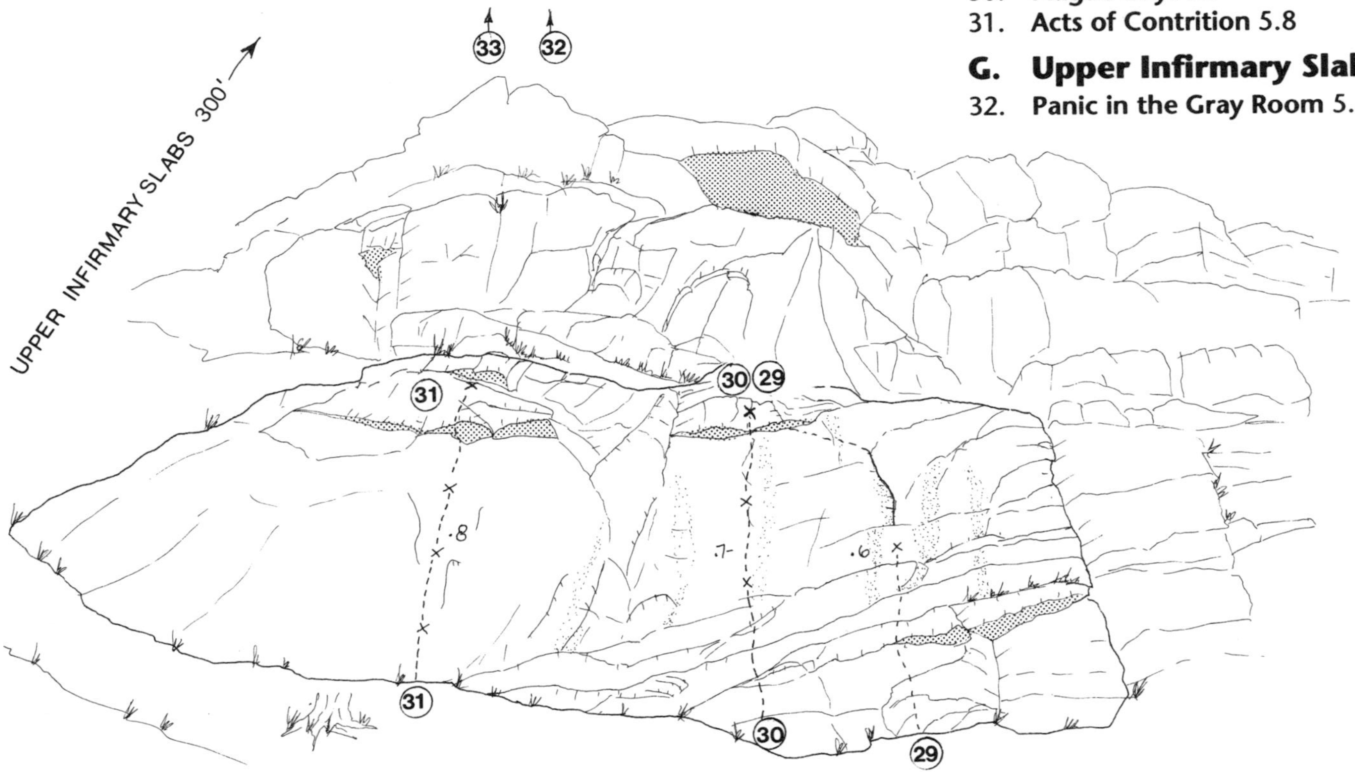

UPPER INFIRMARY SLABS 300'

G. Upper Infirmary Slabs

32. Panic in the Gray Room 5.9+/5.10a
32a. I.V. League 5.7
32b. Emergency Entrance 5.6+
33. Remission 5.7+
33a. Admission Crack 5.7

Lyons
Area:

South
St. Vrain
Canyon

H. Observatory Rock
34. Original Route 5.8
35. Variation 5.8

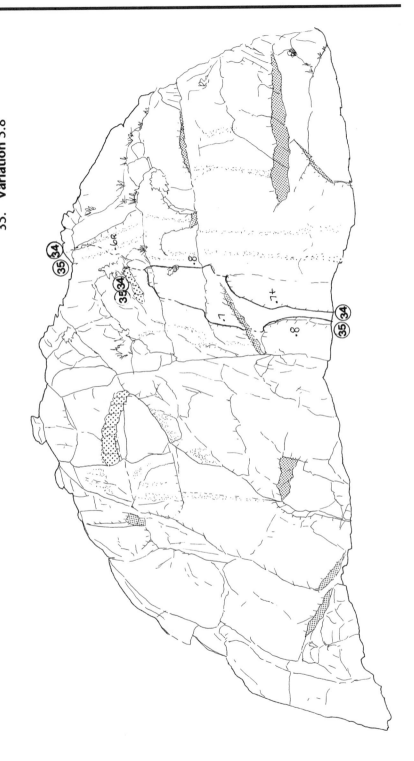

I.   The Narrows Slabs (North)

36. The Hitcher 5.12b
37. Crack 5.10d
38. Death Tongue 5.11d/5.12a or 5.10a A1
39. Death Tongue Variation 5.11d/5.12a or 5.10a A1
40. Flash Flood 5.12a
41. Climb to Safety 5.9
42. Cling to Safety 5.11b
43. Unknown
44. Unknown
45. Unknown
46. Alley Cat Street 5.10a

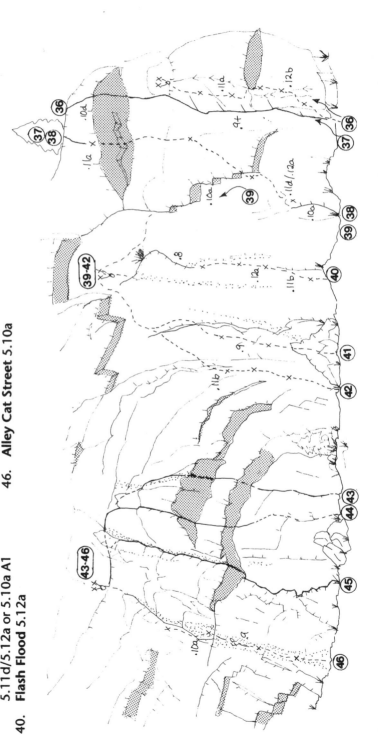

J. The Narrows Slabs (South)

47. Sidetrack 5.6
48. Pon Scum 5.12a/b
49. Bullfight 5.13a
49a. Vrain Dead 5.8+
49b. Vrain Child 5.11c/d or 5.11a

Located 200 feet west and 300 feet uphill from Narrows Slabs, on the same side of the road.

49a. **Vrain Dead** 5.8+
49b. **Vrain Child** 5.11c/d or 5.11a

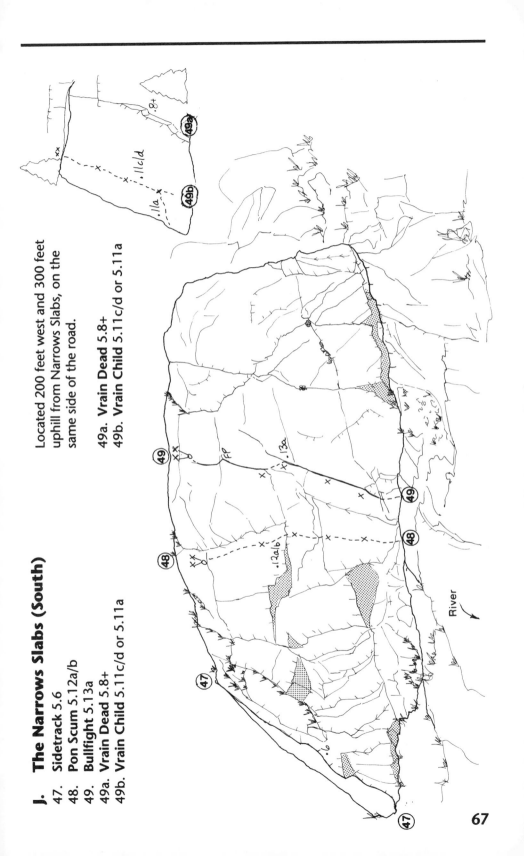

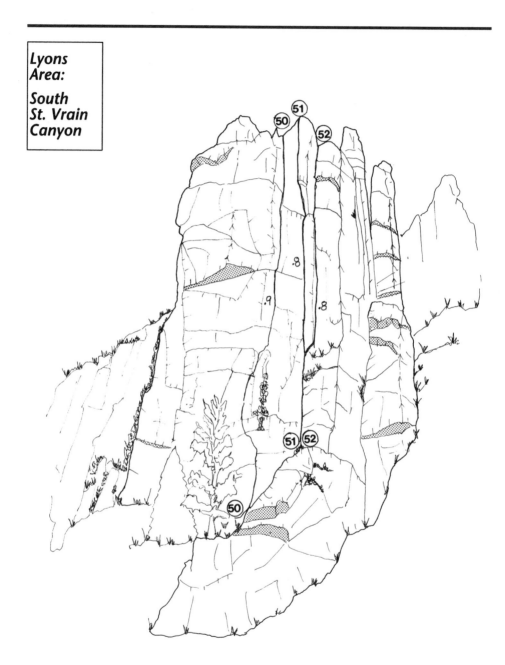

K. The Spire
50. **Dire Spire** 5.9
51. **Unknown** 5.8
52. **Unknown** 5.8

68

L. Little Ogre

53. The Giveaway 5.10c/d
54. Unknown (project?)

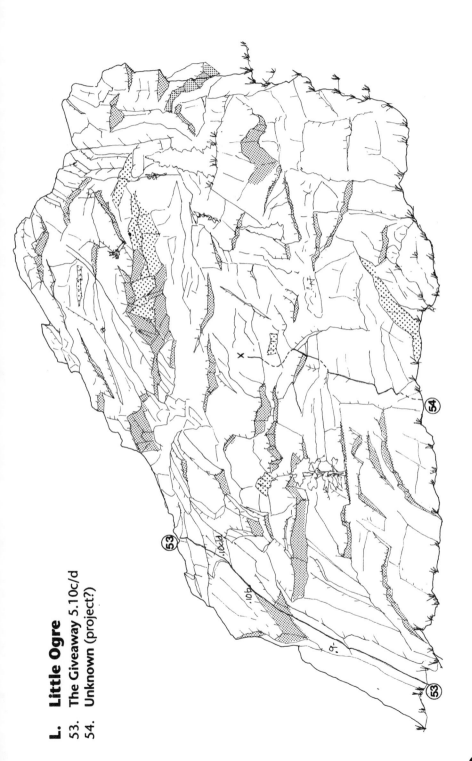

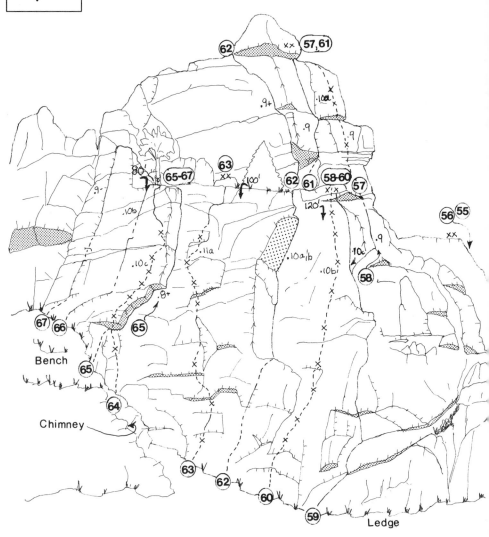

Bench

Chimney

Ledge

M. Monkey Skull

55. Unknown
56. Unknown
57. Summit Block 5.10a
58. Fever Dance Variation 5.9
59. Fever Dance 5.10c
60. Upside The Cranium 5.10a/b
61. Alvino's Variation 5.9
62. Sunshine Dihedral 5.10a/b
63. Hollow Be Thy Name 5.10d/5.11a (reach)
64. Fringe Dweller 5.10c
65. Casual Corner 5.8+
66. Amy, Good Gorilla 5.10b/c
67. Crack 5.9-

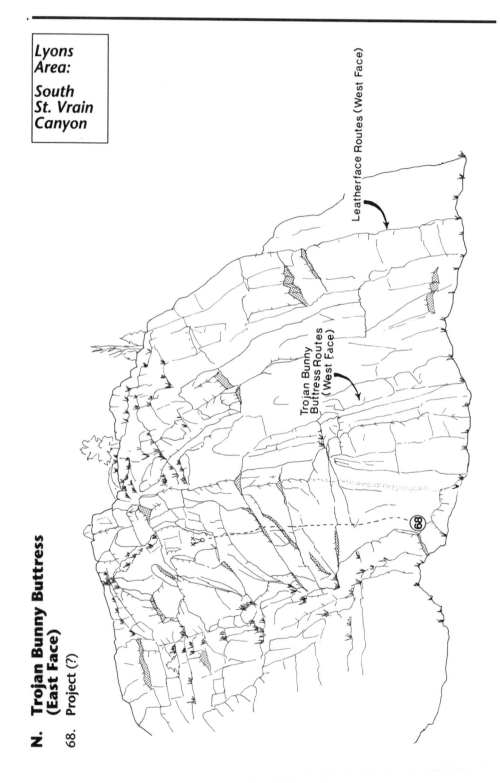

Leatherface Routes (West Face)

Trojan Bunny
Buttress Routes
(West Face)

N. Trojan Bunny Buttress (East Face)

68. Project (?)

N. Trojan Bunny Buttress (East Face)
68. Project (?)

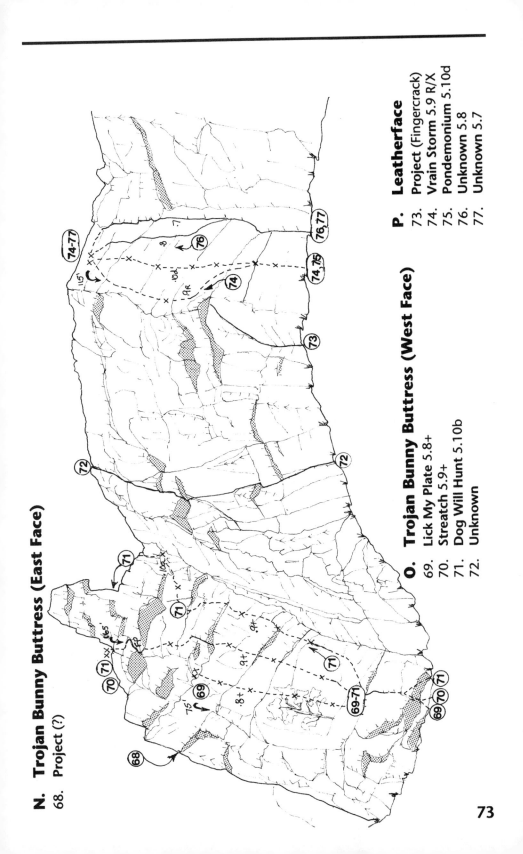

O. Trojan Bunny Buttress (West Face)
69. Lick My Plate 5.8+
70. Streatch 5.9+
71. Dog Will Hunt 5.10b
72. Unknown

P. Leatherface
73. Project (Fingercrack)
74. Vrain Storm 5.9 R/X
75. Pondemonium 5.10d
76. Unknown 5.8
77. Unknown 5.7

73

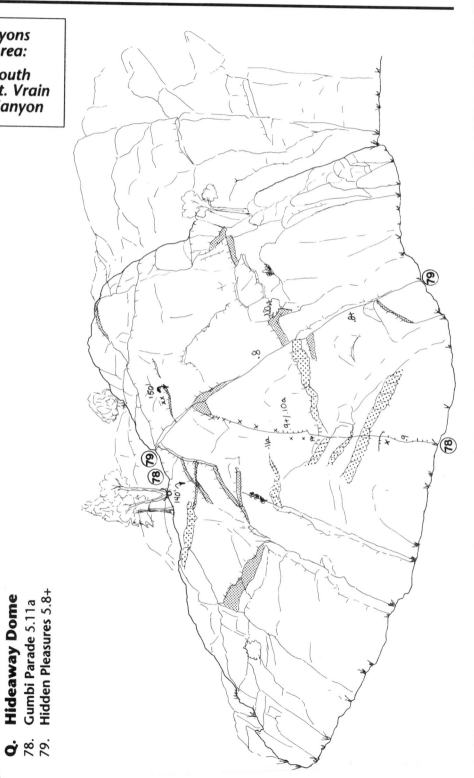

Q. Hideaway Dome

78. Gumbi Parade 5.11a
79. Hidden Pleasures 5.8+

Lyons Area:

South St. Vrain Canyon

R. The Fang

80. The Turning Point 5.11c
81. Stiletto 5.13d/5.14a (Project)
82. Project 5.13b
83. Jugular Vein 5.12b/c
84. Warm Up Climb 5.10c
85. Witch Doctor 5.13 (Project)
86. Goldfinger 5.12a
87. Perfect Stemetry 5.12c/d
88. Belligerent Buttress 5.12b

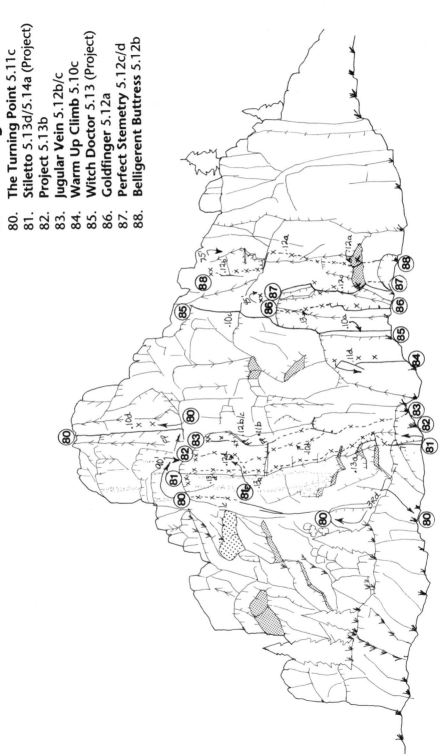

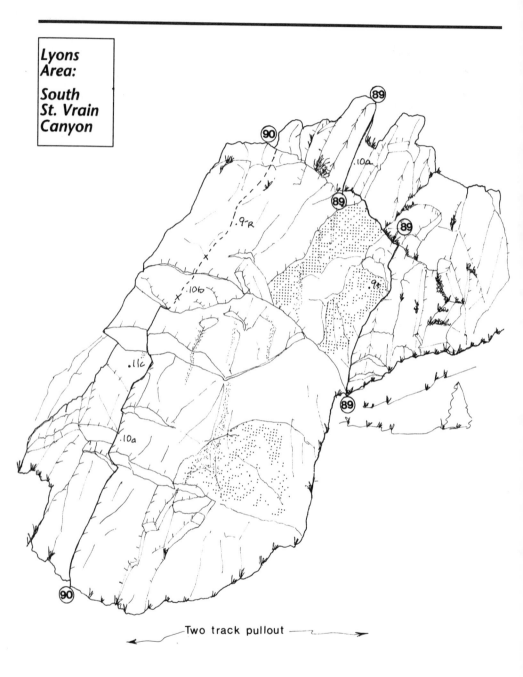

Two track pullout

S. Violator Buttress
89. The Violator 5.10a
90. Trespassers Will Be Violated 5.11b/c

T. The Watchtower
91. The Corner 5.9-
92. Highway Robbery 5.12a
92a. Business Loop 5.11b

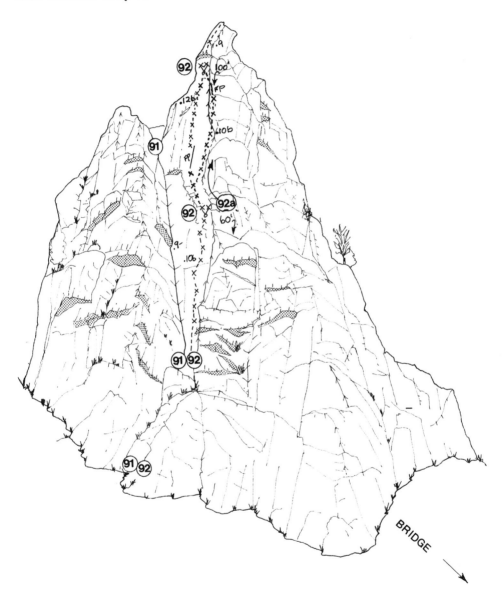

U. The Piz Badille

93. The Ridge 5.6
94. Unknown
95. Unknown
96. Reusable Love Bag 5.9+
97. Too Many Puppies 5.9-
98. Unknown
99. Sympathetic Mind Fuck 5.6

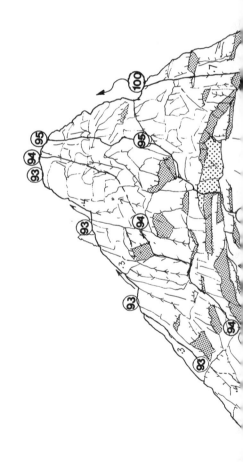

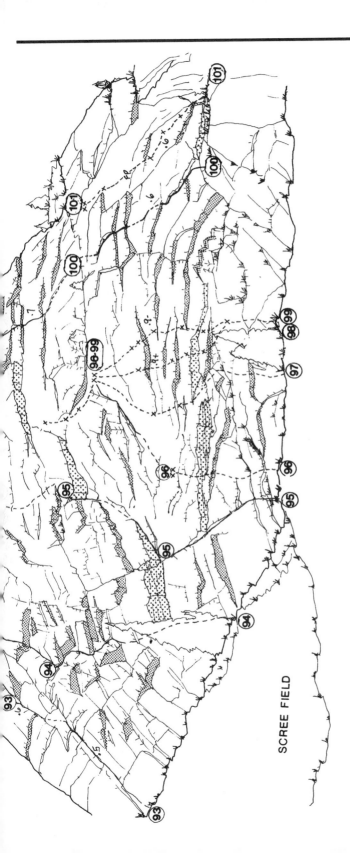

SCREE FIELD

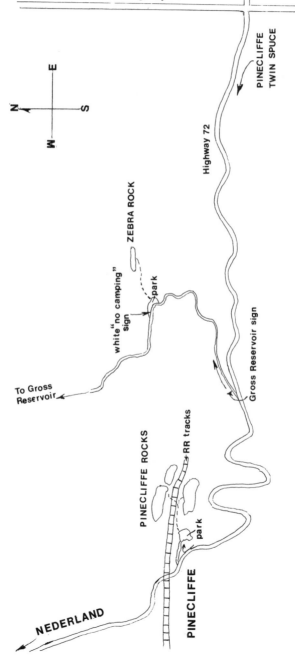

Gross Reservoir: Zebra Rock

BOULDER ← Highway 93 → DENVER

PINECLIFFE TWIN SPUCE

Highway 72

ZEBRA ROCK

park

white "no camping" sign

To Gross Reservoir →

Gross Reservoir sign

PINECLIFFE ROCKS

RR tracks

park

NEDERLAND

PINECLIFFE

N E S W

80

Gross Reservoir

Zebra Rock and Pinecliffe

These two areas are located just south of Boulder and west on Highway 72. Most of the climbs are on granite formations about 100 feet high. The granite, as a whole, is pretty good and provides a mix of both crack and face climbs. To get to Zebra Rock, drive to the junction of Highway 93 and 72. Follow Highway 72 towards Pinecliffe and Twin Spruce for 8 miles to Gross Reservoir. Turn right and drive an additional 3.2 miles until you see a white "No Camping" sign on your right. Park and follow a faint trail past the sign northeast for about 300 feet. Zebra Rock is on the east side of the ridge facing south.

For Pinecliffe, follow Highway 72 an additional 5 miles past Gross Reservoir. Just after crossing the bridge east of Pinecliffe, turn right onto a dirt road that parallels the railroad tracks to a parking area. The main climbing rock is visible about 400 yards east on the north side of the tracks.

Dave Rice and Chris Scanlon were responsible for discovering, cleaning and climbing the climbs on Zebra Rock in 1988. John Loren and Les Schafer put up the early routes on Pinecliffe in 1987 with Alvino Pon, Eddie Pain and Z. Pomtier putting in the newer, harder routes.

Camping and Recreation

Camping is restricted around Gross Reservoir to specified sites. Some of the best mountain biking trails in this guide are to be found in the Walker Ranch areas as well as some very nice hiking trails. Excellent fishing can be found around the Pinecliffe area in the river that runs through town.

Gross Reservoir Rocks and Routes

A. Zebra Rock
1. **Earthbound Misfit 5.11a**   Pro: To 4".
2. **Zebra Crack (aka Glitter Leopard) 5.11c**   Pro: To 2".

B. Pinecliffe Area (North Side cliffs)
3. **Hardman Jr. 5.11b/c**   Four bolts to 2-bolt anchor.
4. **Knuckle Sandwich 5.10+**   Face to crack, clip first bolt on Pica. Pro: 1"-3".
5. **Pica 5.12**   Four bolts to 2-bolt anchor.

6. **End of the Line** 5.9   Leads to **Don't Blame the Youth.** Pro: To 2.5".
8. **Don't Blame the Youth** 5.12/5.13? (Project)
7. **Grimlock** 5.9+   Pro: To 2.5".
9. **Unnamed** 5.6   Leads to **Nocturnal Leg Muscle Cramp.** Pro: To 2".
10. **Nocturnal Leg Muscle Cramp** 5.11a/b   One-pin, 4 bolts to 2-bolt anchor.
11. **Blaster** 5.11a   Pro: To 2".
12. **Project**
13. **Frenzy** 5.10a   Pro: To 3.5".
14. **Crescent Moon** 5.8   Pro: To 3".
15. **Longhaired Freaky People** 5.10a   Five bolts to 2-bolt anchor.

The following two routes are located on the cliff south of the railroad tracks but are not shown in topo format.

16. **Wimpy I** 5.7 R   Follows left to right diagonal weakness. Pro: To 3".
17. **Percepter** 5.9   Cross overhang to a large flake, follow finger crack through roof. Pro: To 2.5".

82

A. Zebra Rock
1. Earthbound Misfit 5.11a
2. Zebra Crack (aka Glitter Leopard) 5.11c

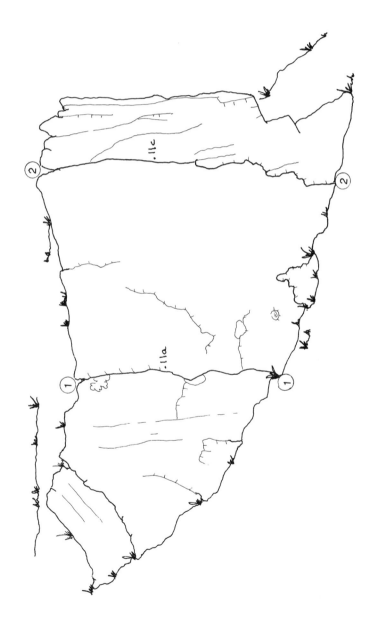

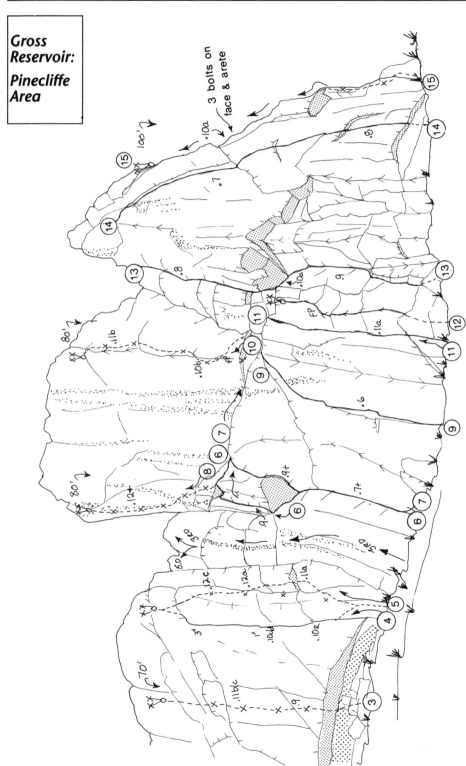

3 bolts on face & arete

.10a

(15) 100'

.7

.8

(14)

(15)

(14)

.8

(13)

.10a

.9

(13)

XX

(11)

FP

.11a

(12)

.11b

80'

(10)

(11)

.10b

(9)

(9)

.6

(7)

80'

(6)

.7+

(9)

(8)

.12+

.9+

(7)

(6)

(6)

.9

GRD

GRD

.11a

(5)

.12c

.12a

3"

(4)

.10d

1"

.10a

60'

70'

.11b/c

(3)

.9

B. Pinecliffe Area (North Side cliffs)

3. Hardman Jr. 5.11b/c
4. Knuckle Sandwich 5.10+
5. Pica 5.12
6. End of the Line 5.9
8. Don't Blame the Youth 5.12/5.13? (Project)
7. Grimlock 5.9+
9. Unnamed 5.6
10. Nocturnal Leg Muscle Cramp 5.11a/b
11. Blaster 5.11a
12. Project
13. Frenzy 5.10a
14. Crescent Moon 5.8
15. Longhaired Freaky People 5.10a

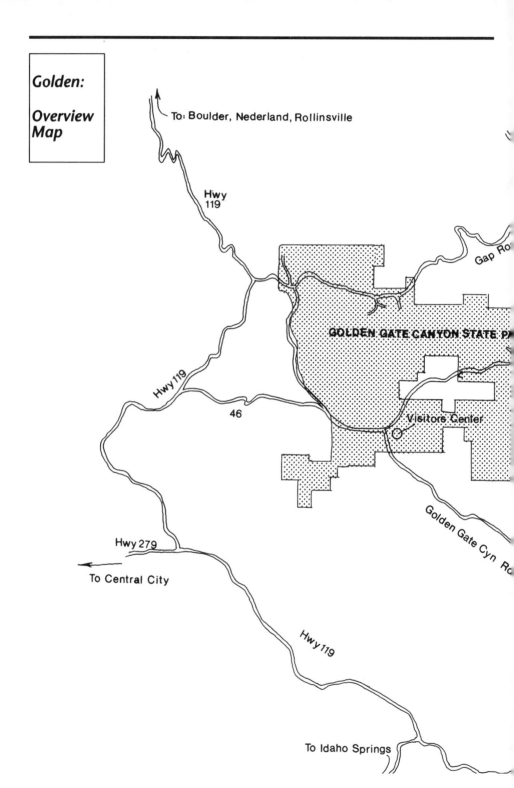

Golden:

Overview
Map

To: Boulder, Nederland, Rollinsville

Hwy
119

Hwy 119

GOLDEN GATE CANYON STATE P

Gap Ro

46

Visitors Center

Golden Gate Cyn Rd

Hwy 279

To Central City

Hwy 119

To Idaho Springs

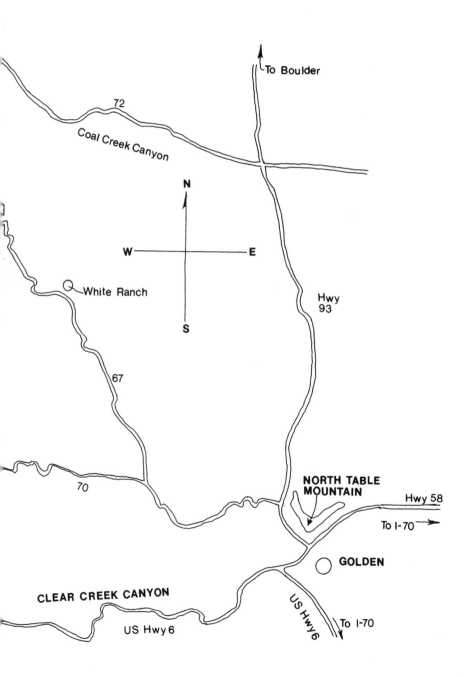

Golden Gate Canyon State Park

Golden Gate Canyon State Park, west of Golden, is filled with a multitude of granite outcroppings ranging in height from 150' to 400'. The granite is the same as Boulder Canyon, but tends to be rougher and of a more alpine nature. Most of the climbing is at a fairly high elevation; 8,000' to 10,000', making this a good summer climbing area.

Only a few of the many formations that abound in Golden Gate are shown in this guidebook due to the lack of available information. People have been climbing in this canyon for many years, starting in the late 1950s, and climbs exist on almost every rock. The majority of the climbs follow natural crack lines; but there are a few bolted-face routes. There is evidence of previous ascents as witnessed by the occasional fixed pin and pin scars. Treat these fixed pins with suspicion, they have been know to come out in your hand! As of this printing, climbs range in difficulty level from 5.2 to 5.11.

Many of the rocks require approaches, some up to an hour long. Allow time for this as well as changes in the weather.

It is wise to check out the rocks through binoculars if you are approaching an unfamiliar formation. The rock quality differs drastically from rock to rock.

Directions

From the junction of Colorado Highway 58 and I-70, go west on Hwy 58, passing underneath North Table Mountain on the right, to a junction with Colorado Highway 93 and US Hwy 6. Turn right (north) on Hwy 93 for 1.4 miles. Turn left (west) on Golden Gate Canyon Road and follow it for 15 miles to the park entrance. From Boulder, take Hwy 93 south and follow Golden Gate Canyon Road right (west). A $3.00 admission fee is required, or a state park pass.

Camping and Recreation

Mountain biking and hiking trails, fishing and cross-country skiing, along with many picnic areas (with water fountains), make this a nice place to bring non-climbers. There are many campsites, including some backcountry sites.

This park is also very clean and well maintained. Please help keep it this way by doing minor trail repair where needed and picking up trash.

Restrictions

Golden Gate Canyon State Park currently has the same bolting restrictions in effect as Eldorado Canyon State Park and Castlewood Canyon State Park.

Son of Ralson

1. Nomad's Land 5.7+   Pro: To 3.5".
2. Unknown

Ralston Roost

3. Unknown
4. Unknown
5. Rain Fuck 5.11a/b   Pro: To 4".
6. Unknown
7. Unnamed 5.9+/5.10a   Pro: To 3", extra 2"-3".
8. Unnamed 5.11b R   Pro: To 3".
9. West Face Route 5.7   Pro: To 3".

Mount Thoridin

Turn right at Kriley Pond and follow the signs to Panorama Point. Park at Panorama Point and take the Racoon Trail from Panorama Point to an obvious switchback on the valley floor. Follow a faint trail left (west) directly off the switchback until you reach a faint open area, directly underneath the Second Buttress. Take this trail, following cairns and markings, straight uphill to reach the Second Buttress.To reach the First Buttress, go right at the bottom of the scree field, contouring around to the right and uphill. An alternative is to drive about ½ mile father to the Racoon Trail. Take the trail as it drops into the valley heading west until you reach the switchback (see above). Continue straight at the switchback. This approach, although somewhat longer, avoids an uphill return tip to Panorama Point, as well as deadfall and underbrush. Both approaches take about an hour from the car.

First Buttress

10. Twin Cracks 5.8   Pro: To 4".

Second Buttress

11. Pope on a Rope 5.10a/b R   Pro: To 3".
12. Mr. Misty 5.10a   Pro: To 3.5".
13. Papal Bull 5.9+   Pro: To 3".
14. CMC Route 5.6+/5.7   Pro: To 4".
15. For Love of Mother Not 5.9   Pro: Miscellaneous to 3".
16. Outland 5.9+   Pro: For first pitch: miscellaneous to 3"; for second pitch, extra ½" to ¾".

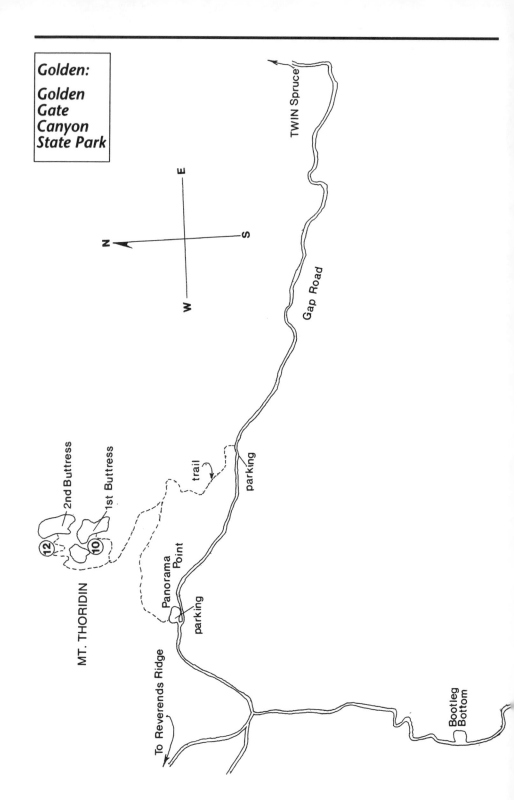

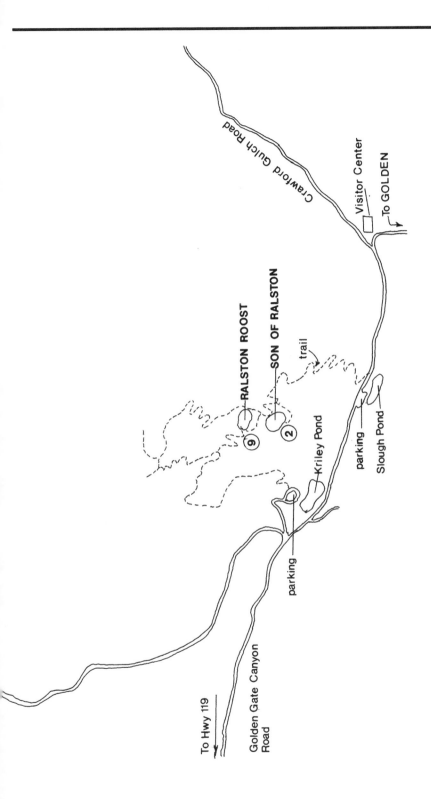

Son of Ralson

1. Nomad's Land 5.7+
2. Unknown

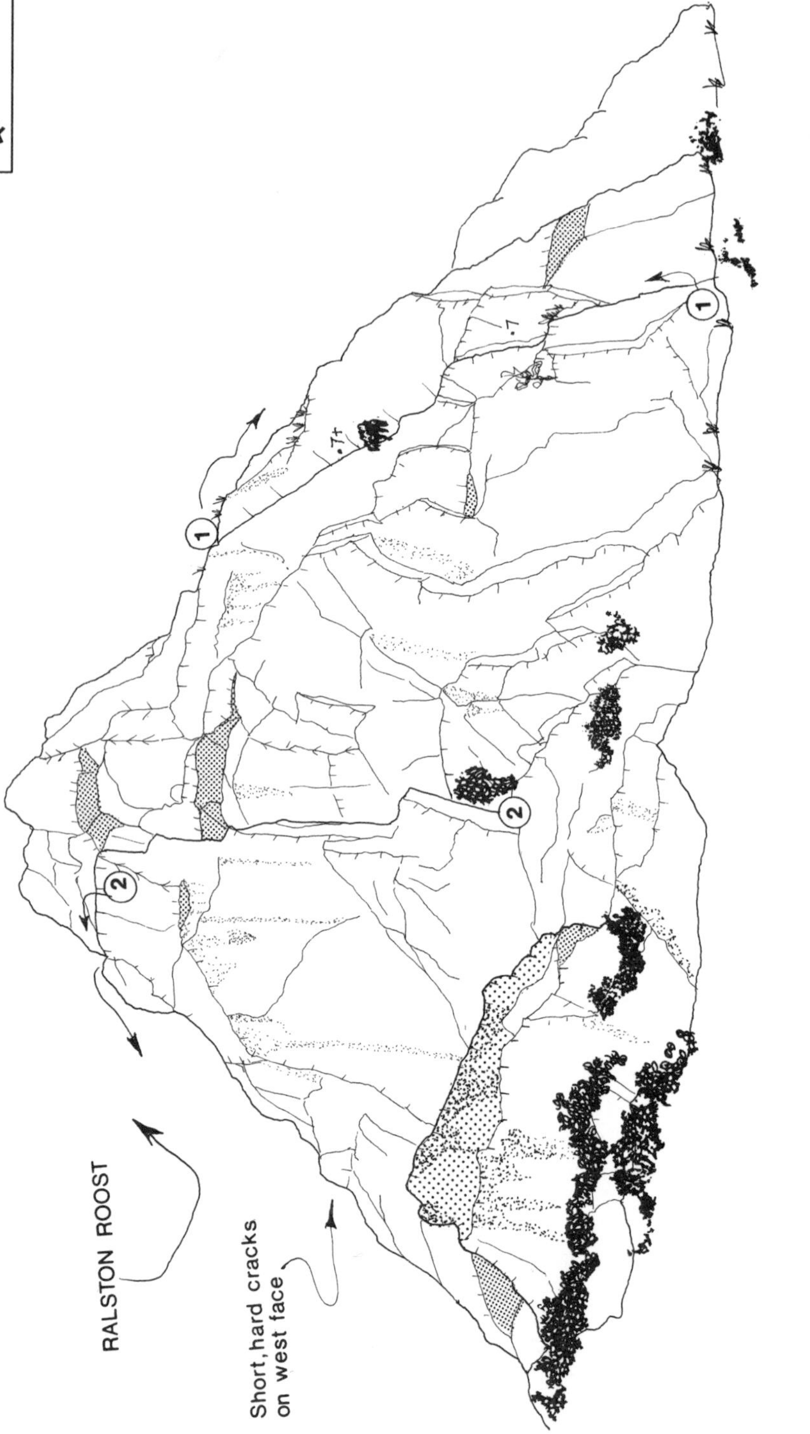

Golden:

Golden
Gate
Canyon
State Park

RALSTON ROOST

Short, hard cracks
on west face

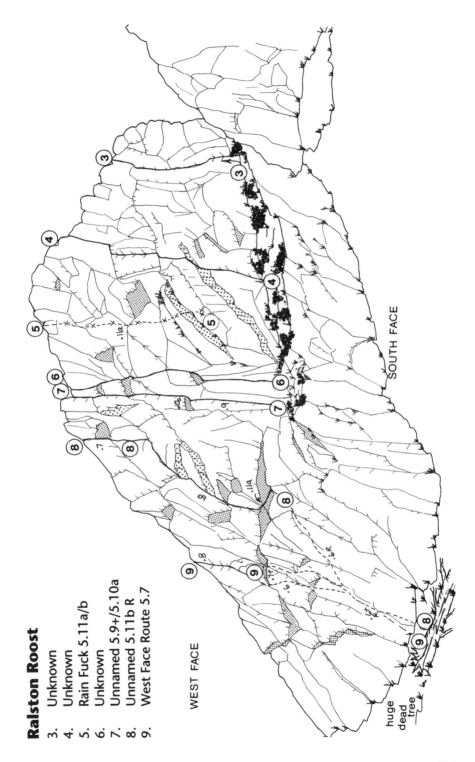

Ralston Roost

3. Unknown
4. Unknown
5. Rain Fuck 5.11a/b
6. Unknown
7. Unnamed 5.9+/5.10a
8. Unnamed 5.11b R
9. West Face Route 5.7

WEST FACE

SOUTH FACE

huge
dead
tree

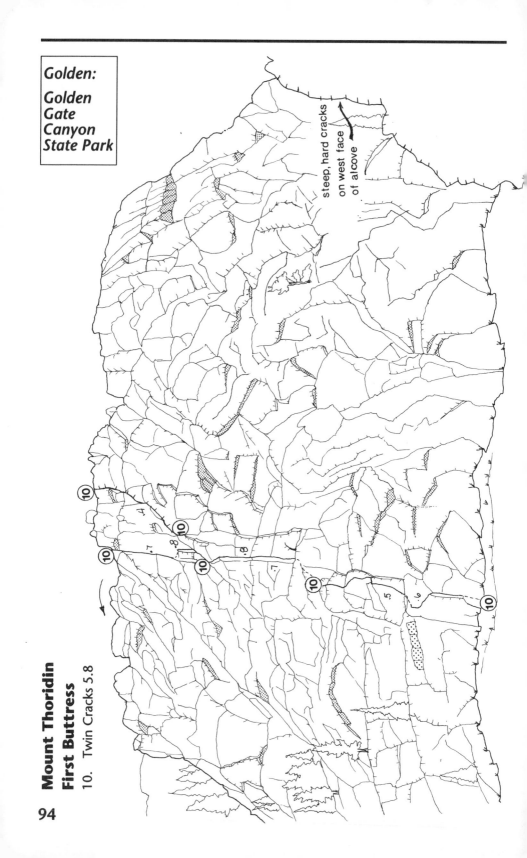

Golden:

Golden
Gate
Canyon
State Park

steep, hard cracks
on west face
of alcove

Mount Thoridin
First Buttress
10. Twin Cracks 5.8

94

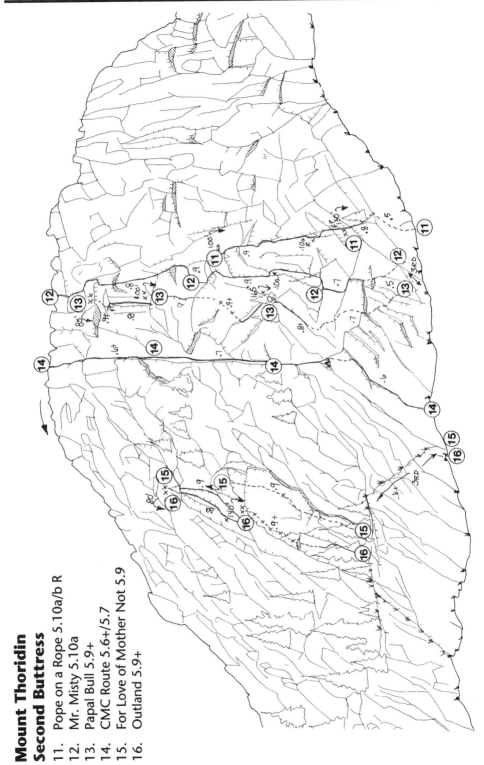

Mount Thoridin
Second Buttress

11. Pope on a Rope 5.10a/b R
12. Mr. Misty 5.10a
13. Papal Bull 5.9+
14. CMC Route 5.6+/5.7
15. For Love of Mother Not 5.9
16. Outland 5.9+

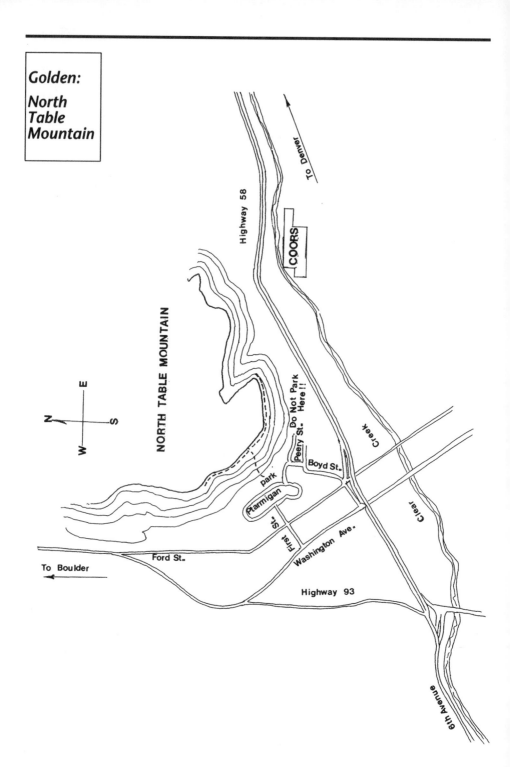

Golden:
North Table Mountain

NORTH TABLE MOUNTAIN

Highway 58

To Denver

COORS

Creek

Clear

Do Not Park
Here!!

Peery St.

Boyd St.

Park

Ptarmigan

First St.

Washington Ave.

Ford St.

To Boulder

Highway 93

6th Avenue

N
E
S
W

North Table Mountain

North Table Mountain is the basalt capped mesa overlooking Highway 58 and Coors Brewery on the north side of the highway. This basalt, though lacking in large overhangs, lends itself to short, thin, vertical face cruxes well-protected by bolts. This is also one of the few areas covered in this guide to offer a selection of lower end bolted sport routes. (Castlerock, the basalt formation on the south side of Highway 58, once offered some climbing but the routes and access information are unavailable.) Most of the crack climbs that divide the bolted areas and faces have been done. The majority of these climbs are in the 5.7-5.9 range and vary from fingers to chimneys.

Climbing started here in about 1950 and remained somewhat sporadic until being rediscovered in 1982 by Robert and Scott Berk. Ken Trout's mini guide in *Rock and Ice* a few years later opened climber's eyes to the accessibility of the climbs and the new route potential to be had here. Ken Trout, Alan Nelson, Guy Lord, Tod Anderson, Alvino Pon, Mark Rolofson and many others increased the number of climbs to over 200. Information was available on only about 150 at this time.

Considerations

This land is privately owned by two corporations: Argentine Mining and Mobile Pre-Mix. Liability issues have already caused the closure of this area once. The Access Fund was able to reopen the area, but access still depends on the continuing cooperation of the local landowners, who have posted "Walk at your own risk" signs, but still allow access across their land.

Please do not park on Peery Street! Parking on Peery Street has caused some of the locals to become rather irate. Instead, park on Ptarmigan Street or in the parking area off Ptarmigan Street. Failure to do this could result in another closure.

There are some hazards to be aware of, but these are few. Rattlesnakes sun themselves on rocks at the base of the routes in summer and fall. There are some loose blocks perched on ledges and at the top of some of the routes. The trail can be slippery. There are unwelded cold shuts on some of the climbs. Also, there are some peregrine falcon nests located along the cliffs. Please respect these raptors and their nesting sites.

There are two last considerations: please pick up any trash and keep the area as clean as possible. The last consideration is underage drinkers who tend to congregate at the oak trees below the eastern end of the cliffs. This is a concern of the local land owners, so please notify the police if you see this happening.

Remember—a closure closes the area to everyone.

Emergency numbers

911 or Jefferson County Sheriff's Department (303)271-5304.

Camping and Recreation

There is no camping at North Table, but there are some fine hiking trails that follow paths around the mesa.

Golden Area Rocks and Routes
Pinnacle Area
1. **Catching the Quarry** 5.11a
2. **Cracking Up** 5.11b   Pro: Miscellaneous small to 2".

Risk Area
3. **Almost Left Out** 5.8   Pro: To 4".
4. **Big Red Catcher's Mitt** 5.10c/d
4a. **Mama Midget** 5.10b
4b. **Daddy Dwarf** 5.10d
5. **This Bolt's for You** 5.11b
6. **5.8+**   Pro: To 4".
6a. **The Perfect Ten** 5.10a
6b. **Not** 5.10b
7. **Serendipity** 5.9-   Pro: To 3".
8. **Risk of Injection** 5.11b/c".
9. **5.7+**   Pro: To 5".
10. **Baby Beeper** 5.10b
11. **Sinister Minister of Evil** 5.11c/d TR
12. **Rope Trick** 5.10c/d

Winterfest Wall Area
13. **5.9+**   Pro: To 3".
14. **Photo Art** 5.11a R   Pro: RPs.
15. **Sunset Arête** 5.11a
16. **5.8+**   Pro: To 3".
17. **Too Dumb to Sleep In** 5.8   Pro: To 5".
18. **Rebel Yell** 5.11b
19. **Driving Over Stella** 5.11b/c
20. **5.9**   Pro: To 3".
21. **5.9**   Pro: To 2.5".
22. **Interstellar Overdrive** 5.11a/b
23. **Variation** 5.11a   Pro: To 2.5".
24. **Pseudo Bullet (aka Stronger than Pride)** 5.12a/b

25.   **Bush Loves Detroit** 5.8   Pro: To 3".
26.   **Variation** 5.9-
27.   **Crawling up Roseanne's Belly** 5.11a/b
28.   **Bimbo in Limbo** 5.10a
29.   **Abortion Control** 5.7   Pro: To 4".
30.   **Killian's Red** 5.11d
31.   **Silver Bullet** 5.10c
32.   **Anartichoke** 5.10d
33.   **5.10a**   Pro: To 2.5".
33a.   **Bimbos in Limbo** 5.10a   Pro: To 3".
34.   **Under the Wire** 5.10a/b
35.   **Back to the Bayou (aka Leaning Pillar)** 5.10c/d
36.   **5.9+/5.10a**   Pro: To 3.5".
37.   **The Resolution** 5.11c
38.   **Jello Brand Napalm** 5.9+ R
39.   **Whole Lotta Drunk** 5.10d

Hot Spot Area
40.   **5.8+/5.9-**   Pro: To 3".
41.   **Dumb Politician** 5.10a   Pro: To 3".
42.   **A Quark for Quail** 5.9+   Pro: To 3.5".
43.   **The Crack and Face Route** 5.10d R   Pro: Stoppers to #3 Friend.
44.   **Widespread Selfishness** 5.12a
45.   **The World Through a Bottle** 5.10a   Pro: To 2.5".
46.   **5.9**   Pro: To 3".

Cold Shut Area
46a.   **Nine to Five** 5.9+
46b.   **Unknown** 5.10a or 5.11a
47.   **Rummies and Reporters** 5.8   Pro: To 3".
47a.   **Unknown** 5.9
48.   **Shut Down, Plugged Up and Cold to Boot** 5.9- Pro: To 2.5".
49.   **5.7**   Pro: To 4".
50.   **5.7 Crack**   Pro: To 3".
51.   **5.10a**   Pro: To 2".
52.   **5.7**   Pro: To 3".

Fence Area
53.   **5.10d/5.11a** Pro: To 1".
54.   **Pass the Basalt, Please** 5.10b   Pro: To 1.5".
55.   **Winter Warmer** 5.10d   Pro: Long slings.
56.   **Winter Warmer variation** 5.11a
57.   **Fenced In** 5.9+   Pro: To 3".
58.   **No Gumbies** 5.10d
59.   **5.9-**   Pro: To 5".
60.   **Basalt and Battery** 5.10c   Pro: To 1".
60a.   **Disappearing Man** 5.10d
61.   **Unknown** 5.10b/c?
62.   **Klimbink is Verbolten** 5.11c
63.   **Electrocuticles** 5.12a
64.   **5.9**   Pro: To 5".

64a. **Solar Panel** 5.13 Project
65. **G-Spot 5.8+**   Pro: Wires to #.4.
66. **Power of Tower 5.10d/5.11a**   Pro: Wires to #.4.
67. **Abortion Central** 5.7+ R

Twelve-Pack Wall

68. **5.9+**   Pro: To 3".
69. **Briefcase Fulla Blues** 5.9+   Pro: To 2".
70. **Raw Fish and Rice** 5.10b   Pro: To 3".
71. **Honey, I Shrunk the Hemorrhoids** 5.8   Pro:
     Miscellaneous to 1.5".
71a. **Unknown** 5.8
72. **Love, Sex and the IRS** 5.8   Pro: To 4".
73. **Chunky Monkey** 5.10a
74. **Spitfires and Funeral Parlors** 5.9- R
75. **Pump You Up** 5.9-   Pro: To 4".
76. **5.8**   Pro: To 3".
77. **5.8+**   Pro: To 3".

Industrial Buttress

78. **5.8**   Pro: To 5".
79. **Belly Up** 5.8-   Pro: To 4".
80. **Toure Koundra variation** 5.10a   Pro: To 5".
81. **Heidi Hi** 5.8   Pro: To 3".
82. **Politicians, Priests and Body Bags** 5.10a
83. **Fast Boat to China** 5.8   Pro: To 2".
84. **Noodle Factory** 5.9   Pro: To 3".
85. **Salad Bar** 5.10a/b
86. **The John Roskelly Show** 5.9+   Pro: To 3".
87. **Nipple Phyle** 5.6   Pro: To 4".
88. **Left Hand Monkey Wrench** 5.7   Pro: To 4".
89. **Polyvinylchloride** 5.9+   Pro: To 3".
90. **Blow Chow** 5.7+   Pro: To 4".
91. **Flight 67 to Stockholm** 5.11a R
92. **Industrial Disease (aka Dead Moonies Don't Sell
     Flowers)** 5.11c   Pro: Medium stopper.
93. **Thunderbird and Light Beer** 5.8   Pro: To 3".
94. **5.7**   Pro: To 3".
95. **5.11a/b** TR?
96. **Sick Minds Think Alike** 5.8+   Pro: To 4".
97. **5.7**   Pro: To 5".
98. **Feeding Frenzy** 5.11d/5.12a
98a. **Shark Infested Waters** 5.10d
99. **Mournful Mullet** 5.8+   Pro: To 5".
100. **Major Bolt Achievement** 5.11a/b   Pro: To 2".
101. **Mandela (aka Leaning Pillar)** 5.8+
102. **Brain Cloud** 5.9
103. **Shadow of a Hangdog (aka Fat Fingers)** 5.10a/b   Pro:
     To 2".
103a. **Table Manners** 5.11c   Pro: #1 TCU.

104. **Stoney Middleton** 5.8   Pro: To 4".
105. **5.9-**   Pro: To 3".
106. **5.8+**   Pro: To 3".
107. **Meat is Murder** 5.8   Pro: To 3.5".

Overhang Area
108. **Table Top** 5.10a/b   Pro: To #1.5 Friend.
109. **5.7+**   Pro: To 5".
110. **Sleeper** 5.8+   Pro: To 4".
111. **Let's Wake Up Ronnie and Barb** 5.9-   Pro: To 3.5".
112. **Umph** 5.6   Pro: Miscellaneous to 3".
113. **Drinking Wine with the Chinese** 5.9   Pro: To 3".
114. **Lying on the Ground** 5.11d/5.12a
115. **Don't Pout 'cause yer Down 'n Out** 5.8+/5.9- Pro: To 3".
116. **The Ground Doesn't Lie** 5.10c/d
117. **TR** (face?)
118. **Beer Barrel Buttress** 5.10c/d
119. **Beer Drinker and Hell Raisers** 5.8+   Pro: To 4".
120. **Corniche** 5.8   Pro: To 4".
121. **Mr. Squirrel Places a Nut** 5.11c/d
122. **Tora, Tora, Tora** 5.11c   Pro: To 2".
123. **Mr. Coors Contributes to the Pink Stain** 5.9+ Pro: To 4".
124. **Mrs. Hen Places a Peck** 5.11d/5.12a
125. **Hell Raiser** 5.9   Pro: To 3.5".
126. **Hellbound II** 5.9+/5.10a   Pro: To 4".
127. **This Ain't Naturita, Pilgrim** 5.9
128. **Natural Fact** 5.7   Pro: To 3".
128a. **Another Unnamed Billy Bob Route** 5.8
128b. **Pack o' Bobs** 5.8
129. **The Fabulous Flying Carr's Route** 5.11a/b

Brown Cloud Crags
130. **Deck Chairs on the Titanic** 5.10a/b
130a. **5.9 Variation**   Pro: To 2".
131. **Killian's Dead** 5.6   Pro: To 3".
132. **John Adams' Adams Apple** 5.8   Pro: To 3".
133. **Bullet the Brown Cloud** 5.11a
134. **Tenacious** 5.9+/5.10a
135. **Interface** 5.8   Pro: Bring #1 or #1.5 Camalot.
136. **Lemons, Limes and Tangerines** 5.8 Pro: Misc. to 2".
137. **Big Dihedral** 5.8   Pro: To 4".
138. **5.11a/b TR**
139. **Thick Crust** 5.7   Pro: To 4".
140. **New River Gorge Homesick Blues** 5.11b/c
141. **Kid's Climb** 5.9+
142. **Thelma** 5.7
143. **Louise** 5.8 or 5.10a
144. **Monkey Puzzle** 5.12c
144a. **Parental Abuse** 5.11c
145. **Carolina Direct** (Alternate start)

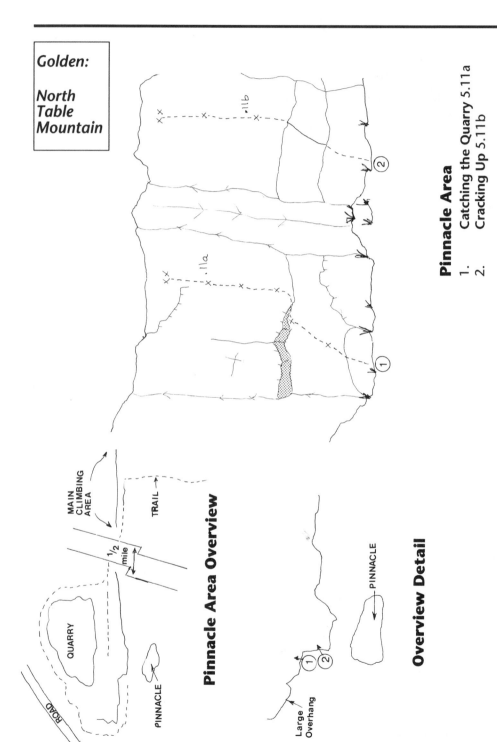

Golden:

*North
Table
Mountain*

Pinnacle Area Overview

MAIN
CLIMBING
AREA

TRAIL →

½ mile

QUARRY

ROAD

PINNACLE

Overview Detail

PINNACLE

Large
Overhang

Pinnacle Area

1. Catching the Quarry 5.11a
2. Cracking Up 5.11b

Risk Area

3. **Almost Left Out** 5.8
4. **Big Red Catcher's Mitt** 5.10c/d
5. **This Bolt's for You** 5.11b

6. **5.8+**
7. **Serendipity** 5.9
8. **Risk of Injection** 5.11b/c.

9. **5.7+**
10. **Baby Beeper** 5.10b
11. **Sinister Minister of Evil** 5.11c/d

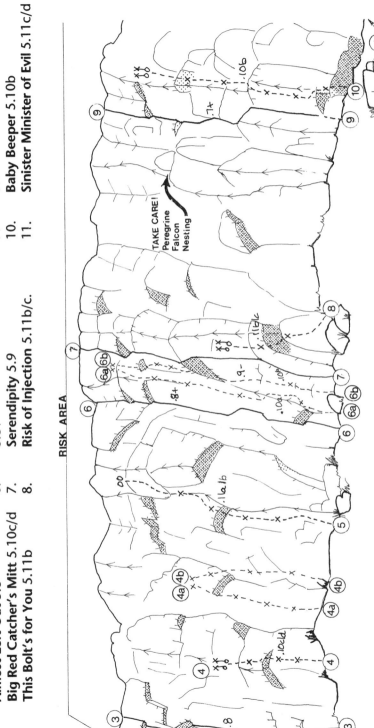

Golden:

*North
Table
Mountain*

WINTERFEST WALL

RISK AREA

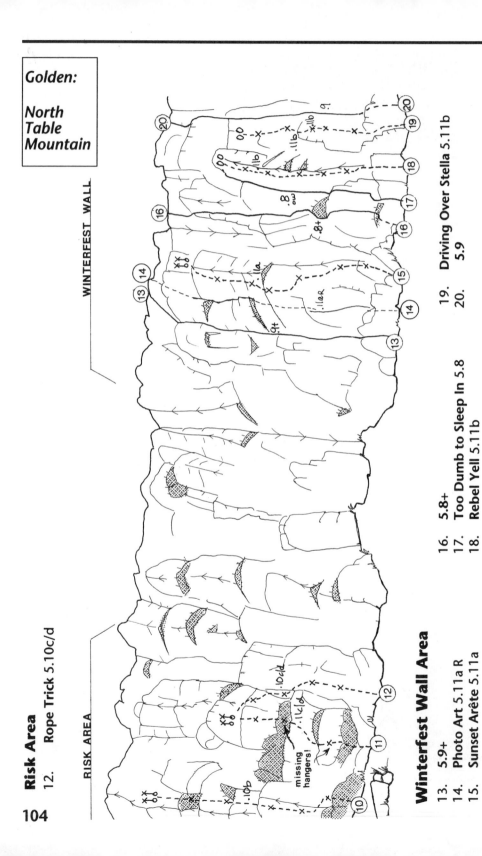

Risk Area

12. Rope Trick 5.10c/d

Winterfest Wall Area

13. 5.9+
14. Photo Art 5.11a R
15. Sunset Arête 5.11a

16. 5.8+
17. Too Dumb to Sleep In 5.8
18. Rebel Yell 5.11b

19. Driving Over Stella 5.11b
20. 5.9

Alvino Pon on **Monkey Puzzle** 5.12c/d, North Table Mountain. Photo by Ruel Chapman.

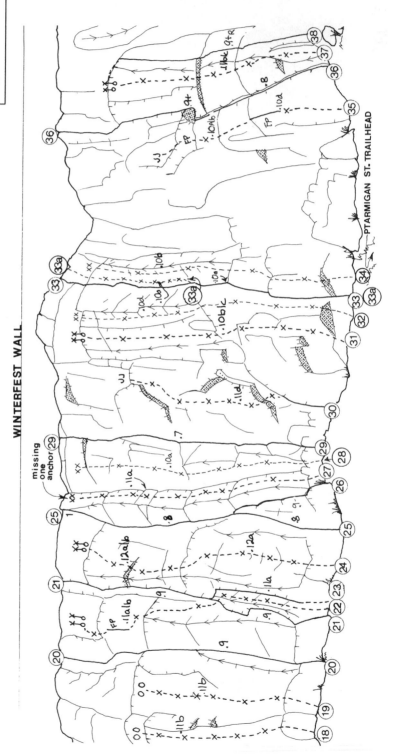

WINTERFEST WALL

PTARMIGAN ST. TRAILHEAD

Winterfest Wall Area

18. Rebel Yell 5.11b
19. Driving Over Stella 5.11b
20. 5.9
21. 5.9
22. Interstellar Overdrive 5.11a/b
23. Variation 5.11a
24. Pseudo Bullet (aka Stronger than Pride) 5.12a/b
25. Bush Loves Detroit 5.8
26. Variation 5.9-
27. Crawling up Roseanne's Belly 5.11a
28. Bimbo in Limbo 5.10a
29. Abortion Control 5.7
30. Killian's Red 5.11d
31. Silver Bullet 5.10c
32. Anartichoke 5.10d
33. 5.10a
33a. Bimbos in Limbo 5.10a
34. Under the Wire 5.10a/b
35. Back to the Bayou (aka Leaning Pillar) 5.10c/d
36. 5.9+/5.10a
37. The Resolution 5.11c
38. Jello Brand Napalm 5.9+ R

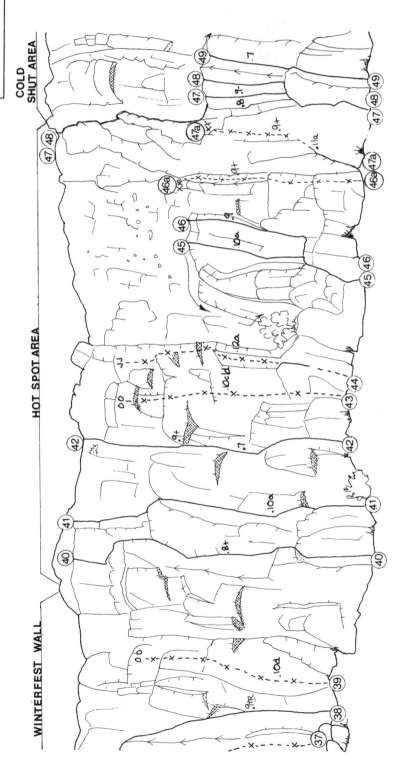

COLD SHUT AREA

HOT SPOT AREA

WINTERFEST WALL

Winterfest Wall Area

37. The Resolution 5.11c
38. Jello Brand Napalm 5.9+ R
39. Whole Lotta Drunk 5.10d

Hot Spot Area

40. 5.8+/5.9
41. Dumb Politician 5.10a
42. A Quark for Quail 5.9+
43. The Crack and Face Route 5.10d R
44. Widespread Selfishness 5.12a
45. The World Through a Bottle 5.10a
46. 5.9

Cold Shut Area

46a. Nine to Five 5.9+
46b. Unknown 5.10a or 5.11a
47. Rummies and Reporters 5.8
47a. Unknown 5.9
48. Shut Down, Plugged Up and Cold to Boot 5.9-
49. 5.7

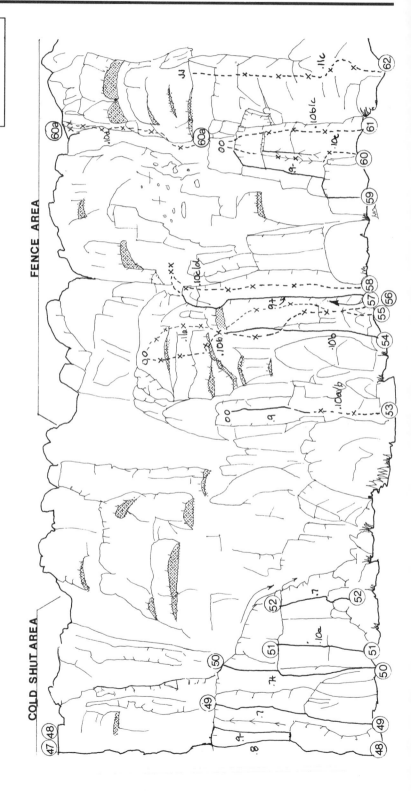

Cold Shut Area

46a. Nine to Five 5.9+
46b. Unknown 5.10a or 5.11a
47. Rummies and Reporters 5.8
47a. Unknown 5.9
48. Shut Down, Plugged Up and Cold to Boot 5.9-
49. 5.7
50. 5.7 Crack
51. 5.10a
52. 5.7

Fence Area

53. 5.10d/5.11a
54. Pass the Basalt, Please 5.10b
55. Winter Warmer 5.10d
56. Winter Warmer variation 5.11a
57. Fenced In 5.9+
58. No Gumbies 5.10d
59. 5.9-
60. Basalt and Battery 5.10c
60a. Disappearing Man 5.10d
61. Unknown 5.10b/c?
62. Klimbink is Verbolten 5.11c

Golden:

North Table Mountain

Fence Area

62. **Klimbink is Verbolten** 5.11c
63. **Electrocuticles** 5.12a
64. **5.9**

64a. **Solar Panel** 5.13 Project
65. **G-Spot** 5.8+
66. **Power of Tower** 5.10d/5.11a
67. **Abortion Central** 5.7+ R

FENCE AREA

112

Fence Area

67. Abortion Central 5.7+ R

Twelve-Pack Wall

68. 5.9+
69. Briefcase Fulla Blues 5.9+

TWELVE-PACK WALL

Twelve-Pack Wall

68. 5.9+
69. Briefcase Fulla Blues 5.9+
70. Raw Fish and Rice 5.10b
71. Honey, I Shrunk the Hemorrhoids 5.8
71a. Unknown 5.8
72. Love, Sex and the IRS 5.8
73. Chunky Monkey 5.10a
74. Spitfires and Funeral Parlors 5.9- R
75. Pump You Up 5.9-
76. 5.8
77. 5.8+

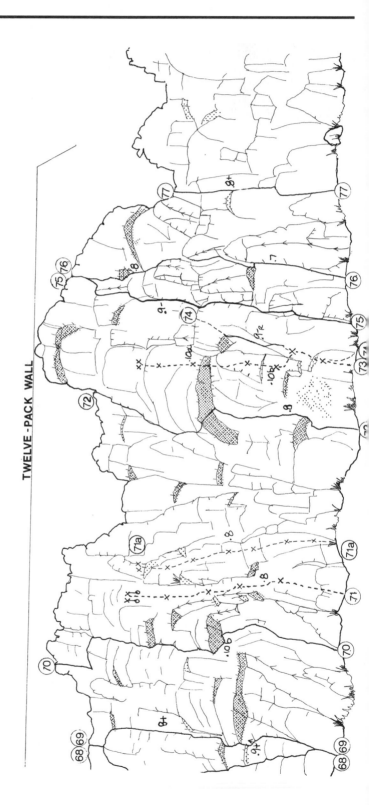

TWELVE - PACK WALL

Alvino Pon on **Dreidle**, Rebel Wall 5.10b. Photo by Ruel Chapman.

Golden:

**North
Table
Mountain**

INDUSTRIAL BUTTRESSES

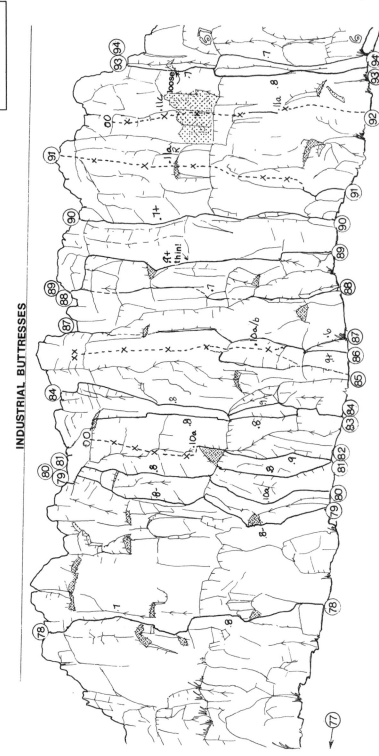

116

Twelve-Pack Wall

77. 5.8+

Industrial Buttress

78. 5.8
79. Belly Up 5.8-
80. Toure Koundra variation 5.10a
81. Heidi Hi 5.8
82. Politicians, Priests and Body Bags 5.10a
83. Fast Boat to China 5.8
84. Noodle Factory 5.9
85. Salad Bar 5.10a/b
86. The John Roskelly Show 5.9+
87. Nipple Phyle 5.6
88. Left-Hand Monkey Wrench 5.7
89. Polyvinylchloride 5.9+
90. Blow Chow 5.7+
91. Flight 67 to Stockholm 5.11a R
92. Industrial Disease (aka Dead Moonies Don't Sell Flowers) 5.11c
93. Thunderbird and Light Beer 5.8
94. 5.7

Industrial Buttress

92. Industrial Disease (aka Dead Moonies Don't Sell Flowers) 5.11c
93. Thunderbird and Light Beer 5.8
94. 5.7
95. 5.11a/b TR?
96. Sick Minds Think Alike 5.8+
97. 5.7
98. Feeding Frenzy 5.11d/5.12a
98a. Shark Infested Waters 5.10d
99. Mournful Mullet 5.8+

OLD PEERY ST. TRAILHEAD (LEFT)

118

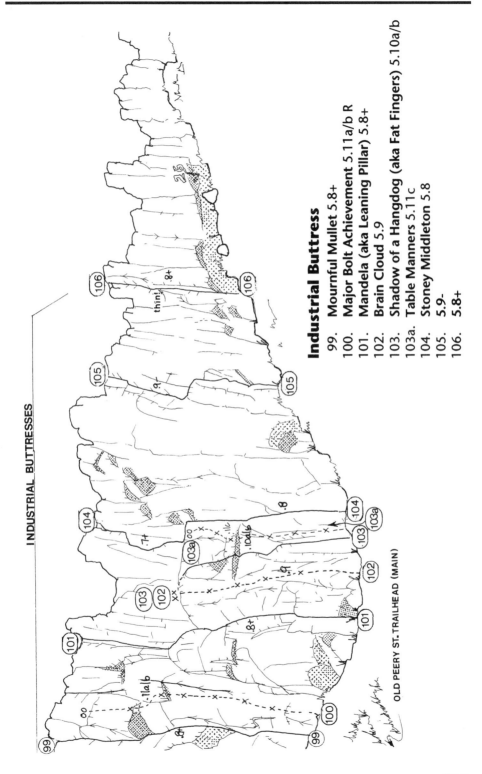

Industrial Buttress

99. **Mournful Mullet** 5.8+
100. **Major Bolt Achievement** 5.11a/b R
101. **Mandela (aka Leaning Pillar)** 5.8+
102. **Brain Cloud** 5.9
103. **Shadow of a Hangdog (aka Fat Fingers)** 5.10a/b
103a. **Table Manners** 5.11c
104. **Stoney Middleton** 5.8
105. 5.9-
106. 5.8+

INDUSTRIAL BUTTRESSES

OLD PEERY ST.TRAILHEAD (MAIN)

Industrial Buttress

105. 5.9-
106. 5.8+
107. Meat is Murder 5.8

Golden:

North Table Mountain

Overhang Area

108. Table Top 5.10a/b
109. 5.7+
110. Sleeper 5.8+
111. Let's Wake Up Ronnie and Barb 5.9-

OVERHANG AREA

75'

120

Overhang Area

108. **Table Top** 5.10a/b
109. 5.7+
110. **Sleeper** 5.8+
111. **Let's Wake Up Ronnie and Barb** 5.9
112. **UMph** 5.6
113. **Drinking Wine with the Chinese** 5.9
114. **Lying on the Ground** 5.11d/5.12a
115. **Don't Pout 'cause yer Down 'n Out** 5.8+/5.9-
116. **The Ground Doesn't Lie** 5.10c/d
117. **TR** (face?)
118. **Beer Barrel Buttress** 5.10c/d

OVERHANG AREA

Overhang Area

118. Beer Barrel Buttress 5.10c/d
119. Beer Drinker and Hell Raisers 5.8+
120. Corniche 5.8
121. Mr. Squirrel Places a Nut 5.11c/d
122. Tora, Tora, Tora 5.11c
123. Mr. Coors Contributes to the Pink Stain 5.9+
124. Mrs. Hen Places a Peck 5.11d/5.12a
125. Hell Raiser 5.9

OVERHANG AREA

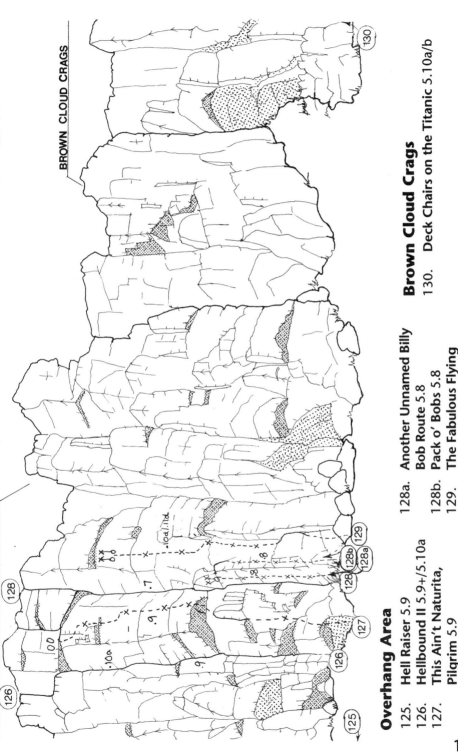

BROWN CLOUD CRAGS

Overhang Area

125. **Hell Raiser** 5.9
126. **Hellbound II** 5.9+/5.10a
127. **This Ain't Naturita,**
      Pilgrim 5.9
128. **Natural Fact** 5.7

128a. **Another Unnamed Billy**
       Bob Route 5.8
128b. **Pack o' Bobs** 5.8
129. **The Fabulous Flying**
       Carr's Route 5.11a/b

Brown Cloud Crags

130. **Deck Chairs on the Titanic** 5.10a/b

123

Brown Cloud Crags

130. Deck Chairs on the Titanic 5.10a/b
130a. 5.9 Variation
131. Killian's Dead 5.7
132. John Adams' Adams Apple 5.8
133. Bullet the Brown Cloud 5.11a
134. Tenacious 5.9+/5.10a
135. Interface 5.8
136. Lemons, Limes and Tangerines 5.8

BROWN CLOUD CRAGS

loose anchor!

Brown Cloud Crags

130. Deck Chairs on the Titanic 5.10a/b
131. Killian's Dead 5.7
132. John Adams' Adams Apple 5.8
133. Bullet the Brown Cloud 5.11a
134. Tenacious 5.9+/5.10a
135. Interface 5.8
136. Lemons, Limes and Tangerines 5.8
137. Big Dihedral 5.8
138. 5.11a/b TR
139. Thick Crust 5.7
140. New River Gorge Homesick Blues 5.11b/c
141. Kid's Climb 5.9+
142. Thelma 5.7
143. Louise 5.8 or 5.10a

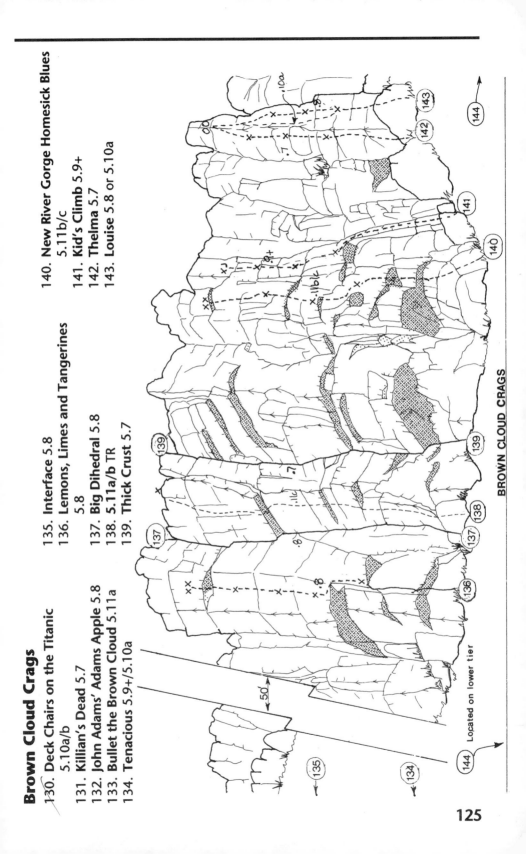

BROWN CLOUD CRAGS

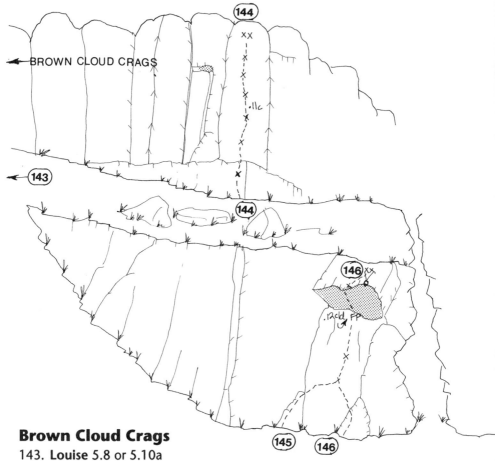

Brown Cloud Crags
143. **Louise** 5.8 or 5.10a
144. **Parental Abuse** 5.11c
145. **Monkey Puzzle** 5.12c
146. **Carolina Direct** (Alternate start)

Clear Creek Canyon

Clear Creek Canyon, located west of Golden on Highway 6, was long viewed as merely an alternative approach to I-70 and the sight of a few moderate ice climbs. This all changed in 1989 when the bolting ban in Boulder Mountain Parks caused climbers to look at the rock in Clear Creek with a slightly different viewpoint.

The result has been some of the most diverse sport climbs in the Front Range. The routes range from 5.5 to 5.13 and feature slabs, steep to overhanging face climbs, crack climbs of all difficulty levels, pocket climbs and roofs. Though most of the climbs are bolt-protected sport routes, many climbs are traditional routes, and many others require some gear in addition to bolts.

History

Some climbing was done in the canyon in the '50s and '60s, but information on these climbs is sadly lacking at this time. Many of the newer routes can be attributed to Mike Pont, Peter Zoller, Eric Johnson, Alvino Pon, Alan Nelson, Jimmy Surrette, Ken Trout, Kurt Smith, Eddie Pain and many other.

Many of the routes listed are noted as being "projects." Please respect the effort and expense, both in time and money, of the climbers working on these routes. Also, please don't steal hangers off existing routes or projects.

Considerations

Clear Creek Canyon suffers from being too close to the road, with the attendant trash problems. There is a serious trash problem in Clear Creek! Please take a little extra time to pick up any trash you come across and leave the area in better condition than when you found it. Clear Creek was by far the worst area for trash of any researched in this book.

Emergency numbers

911 or Jefferson County Sheriff's Dept. (303)271-5304.

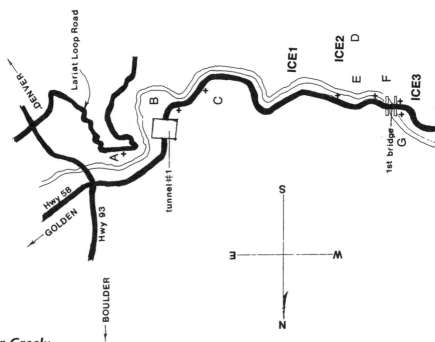

Clear Creek:

A.	Lookout Mountain Crag	G.	Red Slab (aka Rainbow Wall)
B.	Sport Crag	ICE3	Third Winter Ice
C.	Stumbling Block Area parking on right.	H.	New River Wall
ICE1	First Winter Ice	I.	Evil Cave
ICE2	Second Winter Ice	J.	River Wall
D.	Piledriver Buttress	K.	Twitch
E.	Rainy Day Rock	L.	High Wire Crag
F.	Little Eiger	M.	Wall of Justice
		N.	Wall of the '90s

128

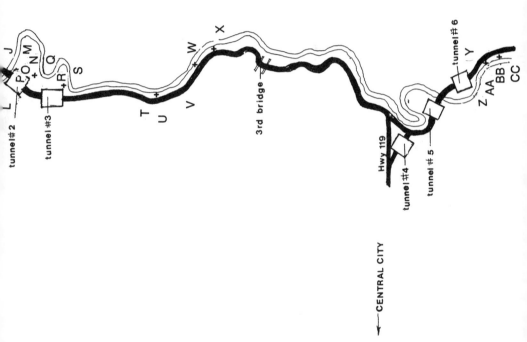

O.	Monkey House	W.	A Little Piece of South Dakota
P.	Death Rock	X.	High Profile Wall
Q.	Mission Wall	Y.	Kayak Wall
R.	Anarchy Wall	Z.	The Armory
S.	Kool Krag	AA.	Crystal Tower
T.	Pete's Wicked Cave	BB.	Primo Wall
	(aka Sex Cave)	CC.	Nomad's Cave
U.	Rebel Wall		
V.	Nightworm Pinnacle		

Clear Creek Canyon

A.   Lookout Mountain Crag
     From Highway 6 take Lookout Mountain Road 1.7 miles to a
     parking pull-out on the right side. Follow a trail east of the
     parking area for about 100 feet and down to the base of the
     rock.
     0.0 miles; Junction of Highways 6, 58 and 93 at the light.
     1.0 miles; Tunnel #1
B.   1.1 miles; Sport Crag on left.
     1.2 miles; Sport Crag parking on right.
C.   1.5 miles; Stumbling Block Area parking on right.
     1.6 miles; Stumbling Block Area (including, The Blond
     Formation, Skinny Legs Formation and Stumbling Block) on
     right.
ICE1 2.8 miles; First Winter Ice on left.
ICE2 3.9 miles; Second Winter Ice on left.
D.   3.9 miles; Piledriver Buttress on left.
E.   4.1 miles; Rainy Day Rock on left.
F.   4.1 miles; Little Eiger on left.
G.   4.1 miles; Red Slab (aka Rainbow Wall) on right.
     4.15 miles; First bridge and parking areas on both sides of
     the bridge and the road. To approach Rainy Day Rock, fol-
     low the trail on the south side of Clear Creek for about 300
     feet east. Rainy Day Rock is immediately above the trail on
     the right. For climbs on the Second Winter Ice formation
     and Piledriver Buttress, continue along the trail for about
     another .2 mile. The ice climb is quite obvious (in winter,
     anyway). The approach trail to Piledriver Buttress stays to
     the right side of the gully.
ICE3 4.3 miles; Third Winter Ice on left.
H.   5.7 miles; New River Wall on right.
     Parking for New River Wall, Evil Cave, Twitch, High Wire
     Crag, walk toward the tunnel (west), High Wire Crag is
     directly in front and if you turn back east, Twitch is located
     above and slightly to the left behind a big tree. Continue
     along the trail to New River Wall.
     For Evil Cave, cross the road from the parking area and fol-
     low a steep, loose and sometimes wet trail up to the cave.
     Wall of Justice is a hidden, southeast-facing wall located left
     of the tunnel and 200' above Clear Creek. To get there, walk
     left (south) from the tunnel to a shoulder with large pines
     on it at the base of the upper wall. Wall of Justice is directly
     downhill from the trees. Approach along a sloping ledge
     system, called Death Row, from the north. Anchor bolts are
     located along this ledge and the routes are numbered from
     south to north.
     To approach River Wall, head toward the tunnel, cross the
     road to the east end of the guardrail.
I.   5.8 miles; Evil Cave high on hill to left.
J.   5.8 miles; River Wall on right by river.

K. 5.8 miles; Twitch on right.
    5.9 miles; Tunnel #2
L. High Wire Crag on right.
M. Wall of Justice on left.
    6.1 miles; Parking on left for Wall of the '90s, Monkey House
    and Death Rock.
N. Wall of the '90s
O. Monkey House
P. Death Rock (Above and to the left of Monkey House, direct-
    ly above the tunnel.)
Q. Mission Wall (West across from Wall of the '90s and across
    Clear Creek.)
    6.3 miles; Tunnel #3
    6.4 miles; Parking on left for Anarchy Wall and Kool Krag.
R. Anarchy Wall
S. Kool Krag (Across Clear Creek from Anarchy Wall.)
T. 7.1 miles; Pete's Wicked Cave (aka Sex Cave) on right.
    7.2 miles; Parking for Pete's Wicked Cave and Rebel Wall.
    Rebel Wall is directly across from the large black boulder in
    the parking area. Follow a trail that starts behind a small
    tree.
U. Rebel Wall
V. Nightworm Pinnacle, 200 yards around corner west of Rebel
    Wall, 30 feet up from road on the right side.
W. 8.1 miles; A Little Piece of South Dakota on left.
    8.2 miles; Parking for A Little Piece of South Dakota and
    High Profile Wall.
X. High Profile Wall on left.
    10.8 miles; Junction with Highway 119.
    11.0 miles; Stop sign and Tunnel #4 on right.
    11.4 miles; Tunnel #5
    11.9 miles; Tunnel #6
    12.0 miles; Parking for Kayak Wall, Nomad's Cave, Primo
    Wall, Crystal Tower, and The Armory. To approach all but
    Kayak Wall, cross the river at the fourth telephone pole
    from the tunnel upstream from obvious large boulder on
    opposite bank.
Y. Kayak Wall This rock is located about 200 yards uphill and
    south of the tunnel. It is not visible from the road or from
    where you park. To approach Kayak Wall, follow the line of
    least resistance on the opposite side of the road from where
    you cross the stream for Nomad's Cave. Kayak Wall may be
    seen from the first curve west of the tunnel looking back
    east.
Z. The Armory
AA. Crystal Tower
BB. Primo Wall
CC. Nomad's Cave

Clear Creek Rocks and Routes

A. Lookout Mountain Crag

1. **5.7 Crack**
2. **5.8 Crack**
2a. **Unnamed** 5.10a (face)
3. **5.9+ Crack**
4. **5.9 Face**
5. **5.8** Crack

B. Sport Crag

6. **5.6 Route**   Pro: To 3".
7. **5.8+**   Pro: To 3.5".
8. **The Happiness of Pursuit** 5.10b   Pro: To 1".
9. **5.8 R**   Pro: To 3".
10. **5.9-**   Pro: To 3.5".
11. **Generation Gap** 5.10a   Pro: Miscellaneous to 1.5".
12. **Balkan Dirt Driving** 5.12a   Pro: Miscellaneous to 1".
13. **Pet Semetary** 5.11b   Pro: Miscellaneous to 1.5".
14. **Coffin Crack** 5.9   Pro: To 3".
15. **Olaf's Roof** 5.11b   Pro: To 3".
16. **Rufus' Roof** 5.12b TR
17. **Rufus' Roof variation** 5.10c   Pro: To 3".

C. The Stumbling Block Area

The Blond Formation

18. **The Blond Leading the Blonde** 5.10b/c R
18a. **Blond Man's Bluff** 5.11b   Five bolts to 2-bolt anchor.
Skinny Legs Formation
19. **Skinny Legs 'n All** 5.12b/c   Pro: Miscellaneous to 1".
Stumbling Block
20. **Gniess Cleavage** 5.11b   Pro: To 2.5".
21. **Sabaki** 5.11b   Pro: RPs to #0 TCU.
22. **Décolletage** 5.12b/c   Pro: To ¾".
23. **Naked Kill** 5.12b   Pro: To 1½".
24. **Razor Blade Tittilation** 5.11d R   Pro: To 3".
25. **Lips Against the Steel** 5.11b   Pro: To 3".
26. **Fickle Finger of Fate** 5.8 X

D. Piledriver Wall

27. **Piledriver** 5.12c   Pro: Miscellaneous to 1.5".

E. Rainy Day Rock

28. **Rainy Day Twelve-A** 5.12a

F. Little Eiger

29. **Black Hole** 5.11b R   Pro: To 3".

30. **Black Haul** 5.10d   Pro: To 3".
31. **Bonehead** 5.10c
32. **Conehead** 5.11b
33. **Headline** 5.10a   Pro: To 2.5".
34. **Eiger Sanction** 5.10d
34a. **Unknown** 5.10d
36. **Natural Selection** 5.11b

G. The Red Slab (aka Rainbow Wall)

37. **Snakes for Snacks** 5.10a
38. **MK-74** 5.9   Pro: To 2".
39. **Slip and Slide** 5.10d
40. **Pink Slip** 5.12d
41. **Diamondback** 5.10c
42. **Spring Fever** 5.10c
43. **Wicked Game** 5.10d
44. **Trundelero** 5.10c
45. **Vapor Trail** 5.10a/b
46. **Bumblies for Breakfast** 5.10a
47. **Crack Climb** 5.8   Pro: To 4".
48. **Slip It In** 5.11b
49. **Fun 'n Games** 5.9-   Hard route in winter conditions.
    Pro: To 4".
50. **The Corner** 5.8+   Pro: To 4".

H. New River Wall

51. **Public Enemy** 5.13b
52. **Sonic Youth** 5.12d
53. **Beta Test** 5.11b
54. **Master Beta** 5.12a
54a. **Merlin** 5.11d
55. **5.10c** TR

I. Evil Cave

56. **Evil** 5.13a

J. River Wall

57. **Unknown**
58. **Unknown** 5.9 A2/A3?
59. **Bad Old Days** 5.10b   Pro: To 3".
60. **Kor Route** (?)

K. Twitch Area

61. **Twitch** 5.12d/13a

L. High Wire Crag

62. **Idiot Savant** 5.12a
63. **Project**
64. **Idiot's Roof** 5.12c   Pro: Wires to TCUs.

65. **Hip at the Lip** 5.12a   Pro: To 2.5".
66. **Power Play** 5.12a   Pro: To 2.5".

M. **Wall of Justice** (Routes are listed from south to north.)

67. **Testify** 5.12b   Five bolts, overhanging face/crack.
68. **Test a Fly** 5.12d/5.13a   Six bolts, overhanging face/crack.
69. **Justify** 5.12b   Six bolts, Goldshuts, overhanging face/crack.
70. **Criminal Mischief** 5.11c   Six bolts, Goldshuts, 25-foot roof crack.
71. **Miss Trial** 5.11c   Six bolts, 20-foot roof crack.
72. **Officer Friendly** 5.11c   Five bolts, Goldshuts, 15-foot face/roof.
73. **LA Law** 5.10a   Three bolts, Goldshuts, dihedral with roof.
74. **Lawsuit** 5.10b   Three bolts, Goldshuts, face to jug roof.
75. **Countersuit** 5.9   Face to roof bypass to Lawsuit anchors. Pro: To 3".

N. **Wall of the '90s (aka Roadrunner Buttress)**

76. **Instellar Overdrive** 5.13a/b   Pro: To 4".
77. **Thirty-Aught-Six**   Extra hands/fist. Pro: To 5".
78. **Roadrunner** 5.12a   Pro: To 4".
79. **Casual Gods** 5.11b   Pro: To 3".
80. **Stone Free** 5.11b   Pro: To 2.5".
81. **Unknown**

O. **Monkey House**

82. **Psycho Hose Beast** 5.11a
83. **Punishment for Shoplifting** 5.10d/5.11a TR
84. **Schwing Salute** 5.11c
85. **Monkey See, Monkey Do** 5.12a/b
86. **Monkey Pause** 5.12a
87. **Monkey Puzzle** 5.10d
88. **Unknown** 5.11a R   Pro: Small wires.

P. **Death Rock**

89. **The Sprawl** 5.12b
90. **Homeboy Bonanza** 5.12d/5.13a

Q. **Mission Wall**

91. **Project**
92. **Project**
93. **Project**
94. **Surrette's Route** 5.13c   Pro: To 2".
95. **Project**

R. Anarchy Wall

96. **Halloween** 5.9   South of approach to Anarchy Wall.
97. **Question Authority** 5.12a/b
98. **Chaos** 5.12d/5.13a
99. **Project** 5.13b/c
100. **Anarchitect** 5.12d
101. **Maestro** 5.12d
102. **Presto** 5.12c
103. **Matriarch** 5.12d   To **Presto** Finish.
104. **Monkey Wrench** 5.11c
105. **Monkey Rules** 5.12b   **Monkey Wrench** to **Anarchy Rules**.
106. **Monkey in the UK** 5.12b/c   **Monkey Wrench** to **Anarchy in the UK**.
107. **Anatomic** 5.12c   **Monkey Wrench** to **Hazardous Waste**.
108. **Anarchy Rules** 5.12b
109. **Rules in the UK** 5.12b   **Anarchy Rules** to **Anarchy in the UK**.
110. **Hazardous Rules** 5.12b/c   **Anarchy Rules** to **Hazardous Waste**.
111. **Anarchy in the UK** 5.12a/b
112. **Hazardous Anarchy** 5.12b   **Anarchy in the UK** to **Hazardous Waste**.
113. **Hazardous Waste** 5.11d

S. Kool Krag

114. **Kool Thing** 5.12c   Across Clear Creek from Anarchy Wall.

T. Pete's Wicked Cave (aka Sex Cave)

115. **Rubble** 5.13c
116. **Stone Cold Modern** 5.13b
117. **Head like a Hole** 5.12d

U. Rebel Wall

118. **Floppy Boot Stomp** 5.8+   Pro: To 3".
119. **Down to the Wire** 5.11d R   Pro: Small wires to ½".
120. **Last Chance to Dance** 5.12a   Pro: QDs, #1.5 Friend.
121. **Bust a Move** 5.11d
122. **Winter Kill** 5.13a TR
123. **Piedmont Boulder Toad** 5.10b
124. **Shane's Addiction** 5.11a   Pro: To 2.5".
125. **Siouxnami** 5.12c   Finishes on **Shane's Addiction**. Pro: To 2.5".
126. **Dreidel** 5.10b   Pro: Miscellaneous to1.5".
127. **Only the Strong** 5.11c   Pro: To 1.5".
128. **Jump Start** 5.11c R   Pro: Miscellaneous to 1.5".

129. **Make It Go** 5.9 R
130. **Make It So** 5.9   Pro: Miscellaneous to 1".
131. **Upper Cut** 5.10b   Pro: To 3".
132. **Body English** 5.9   Pro: To 3".
133. **Epidot** 5.11c   Pro: Miscellaneous to 3".
134. **The Curse of Eve** (Project)
135. **Mama Said Knock You Out** 5.11a   Pro: To 3".
136. **Large Crack** 5.9   Pro: Miscellaneous to 3".
137. **Learner's Permit** 5.5   Pro: To 3".
138. **Whistlin' Dixie** 5.6   Not shown. Face and slab downhill and east of main cliff. Follow a line in cliff just left of giant roof.

V. Nightworm Pinnacle
139. **Nightingale** 5.8   Pro: To 3".
140. **Nightcrawler** 5.9   Pro: To 2.5".

W. A Little Piece of South Dakota
141. **A Little Piece of South Dakota** 5.9 R   Pro: Miscellaneous to 2.5".
142. **Bugsy** 5.9-   Pro: To 4".
143. **Red's** 5.8   Pro: To 4".

X. High Profile Wall
144. **Puppy Chow** 5.1c TR
145. **Project** 5.13a/b
146. **Hungry Wolf** 5.12d/5.13a

Y. Kayak Wall
147. **Paddle Me Baby** 5.8+/5.9-   Pro: To 3".
148. **Splinter in the Mind's Eye** 5.11c TR

Z. The Armory
149. **Project** 5.12b?
150. **Semi-automatic** 5.11d   Pro: To 2.5".
151. **Bar Stangled Spanner** 5.12a/b TR

AA. Crystal Tower
152. **Project** 5.12a/b?
153. **Project** 5.12a/b TR
154. **Quartz Spots** 5.12b
155. **Mineral Museum** 5.9

BB. Primo Wall
156. **Hangman** 5.12b
157. **Suspended Sentence** 5.12b
158. **Moving Out** 5.12b
159. **Project**
160. **Groan Up** 5.11c

161. **Breakfast Club** 5.12a
162. **Flying Cowboys** 5.12d
163. **Suburban Cowgirls** 5.11c
164. **City Slickers** 5.12a
165. **Project** 5.13
166. **Sucking My Will to Live** 5.12d
167. **Mirthmobile** 5.10a
168. **Mildage** 5.11c/d

CC. Nomad's Cave

169. **Pizza Dick (aka It's Not Nice To Fool Mother Nature)** 5.12b
170. **Project** 5.13d
171. **Predator-X** 5.13a
172. **Predator** 5.12b
173. **Pro-Choice (aka Bad Day Mining)** 5.12c/d
174. **Express Yourself** 5.12d/5.13a

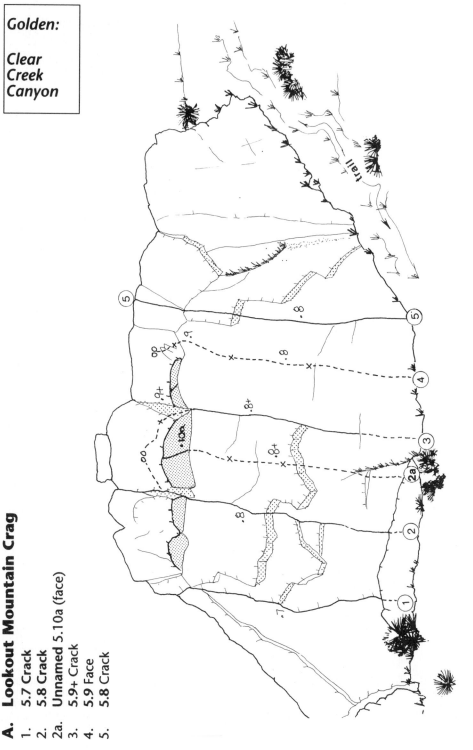

A. Lookout Mountain Crag

1. **5.7 Crack**
2. **5.8 Crack**
2a. **Unnamed 5.10a (face)**
3. **5.9+ Crack**
4. **5.9 Face**
5. **5.8 Crack**

Clear Creek Canyon, Colorado. Photo by Cameron A. Burns.

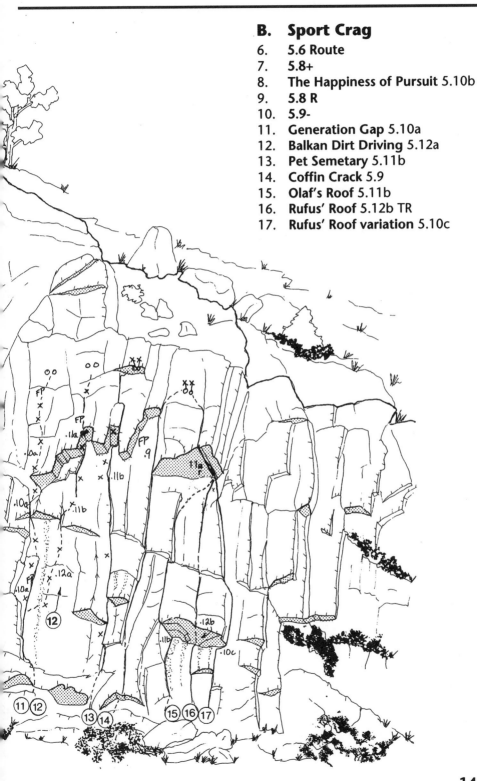

B. Sport Crag

6. **5.6 Route**
7. **5.8+**
8. **The Happiness of Pursuit** 5.10b
9. **5.8 R**
10. **5.9-**
11. **Generation Gap** 5.10a
12. **Balkan Dirt Driving** 5.12a
13. **Pet Semetary** 5.11b
14. **Coffin Crack** 5.9
15. **Olaf's Roof** 5.11b
16. **Rufus' Roof** 5.12b TR
17. **Rufus' Roof variation** 5.10c

C. The Stumbling Block Area

Skinny Legs Formation

19. Skinny Legs 'n All 5.12b/c

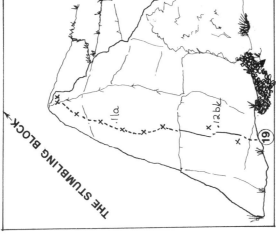

C. The Stumbling Block Area

The Blond Formation

18. The Blond Leading the Blonde 5.10b/c R
18a. Blond Man's Bluff 5.11b

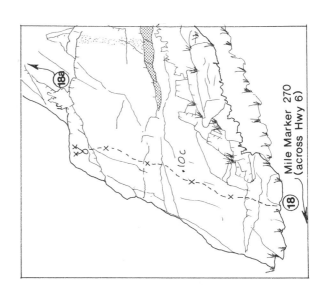

142

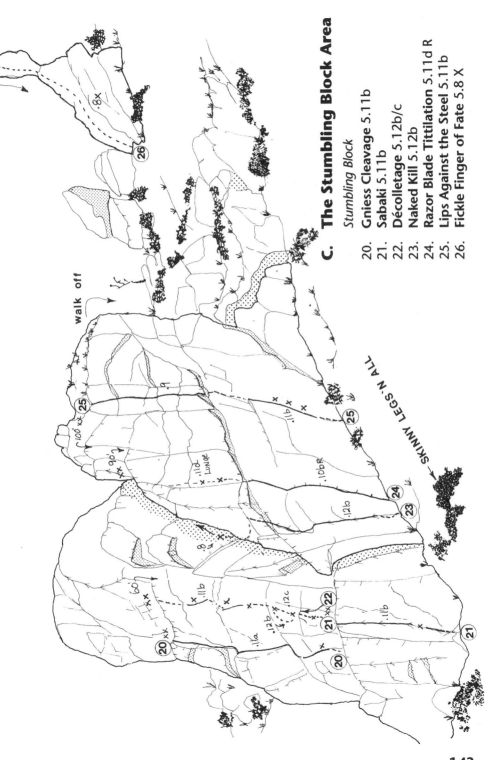

C. The Stumbling Block Area

Stumbling Block

20. **Gniess Cleavage** 5.11b
21. **Sabaki** 5.11b
22. **Décolletage** 5.12b/c
23. **Naked Kill** 5.12b
24. **Razor Blade Tittilation** 5.11d R
25. **Lips Against the Steel** 5.11b
26. **Fickle Finger of Fate** 5.8 X

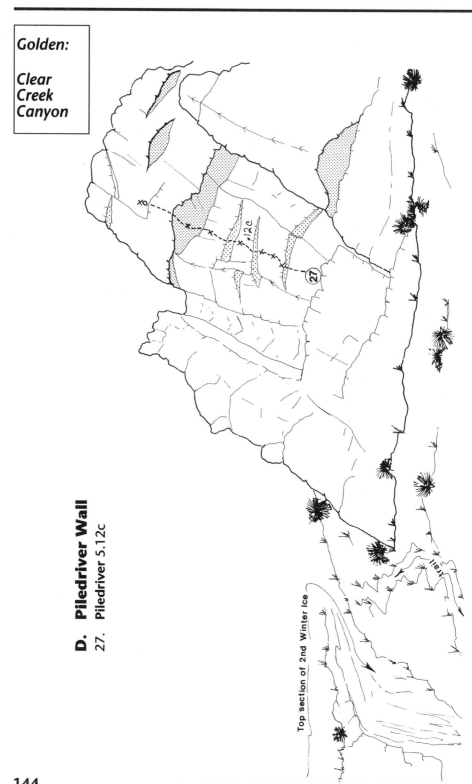

D. Piledriver Wall
27. Piledriver 5.12c

E. Rainy Day Rock

28. Rainy Day Twelve-A 5.12a

F. Little Eiger

29. Black Hole 5.11b R
30. Black Haul 5.10d
31. Bonehead 5.10c
32. Conehead 5.11b
33. Headline 5.10a
34. Eiger Sanction 5.10d
34a. Unknown 5.10d
36. Natural Selection 5.11b

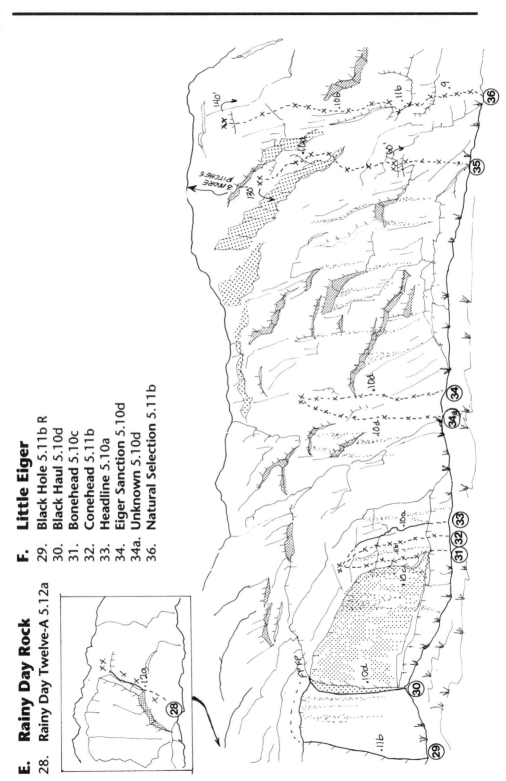

G. The Red Slab (aka Rainbow Wall)

37. Snakes for Snacks 5.10a
38. MK-74 5.9
39. Slip and Slide 5.10d
40. Pink Slip 5.12d
41. Diamondback 5.10c
42. Spring Fever 5.10c
43. Wicked Game 5.10d
44. Trundelero 5.10c
45. Vapor Trail 5.10a/b
46. Bumblies for Breakfast 5.10a
47. Crack Climb 5.8
48. Slip It In 5.11b
49. Fun 'n Games 5.9-

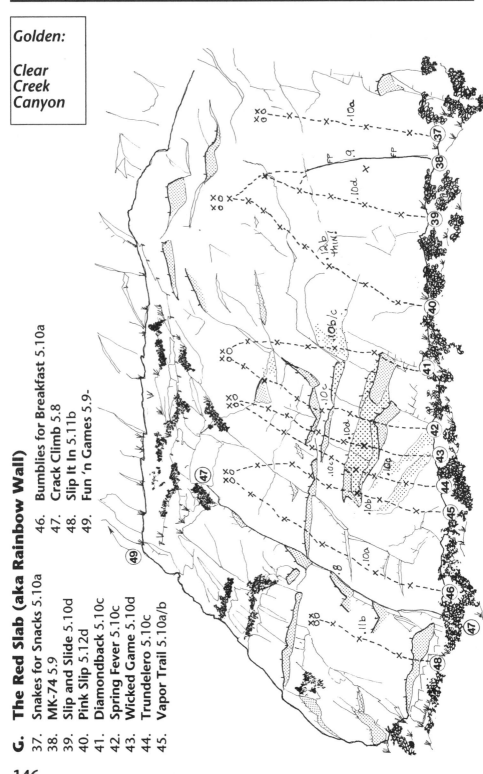

G. The Red Slab (aka Rainbow Wall)

49. Fun 'n Games 5.9
50. The Corner 5.8+

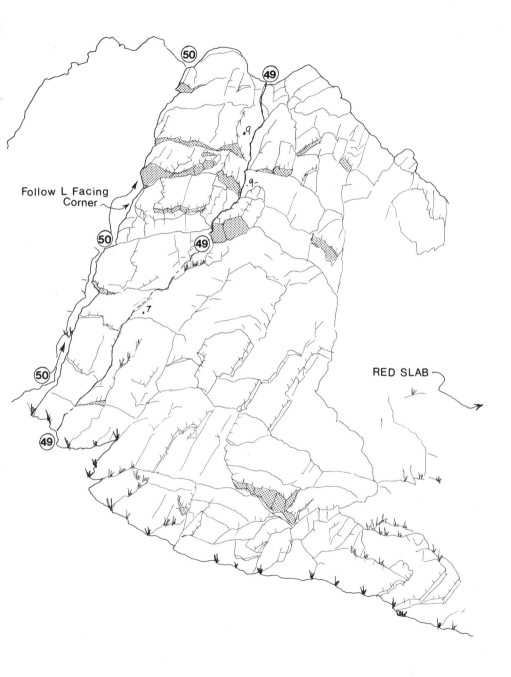

Follow L Facing
Corner

RED SLAB

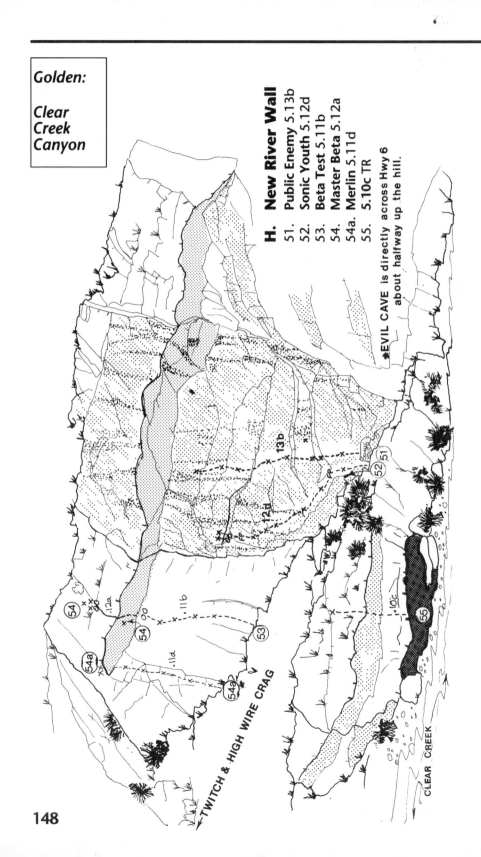

Golden:

Clear
Creek
Canyon

H. New River Wall
51. Public Enemy 5.13b
52. Sonic Youth 5.12d
53. Beta Test 5.11b
54. Master Beta 5.12a
54a. Merlin 5.11d
55. 5.10c TR

EVIL CAVE is directly across Hwy 6 about halfway up the hill.

TWITCH & HIGH WIRE CRAG

CLEAR CREEK

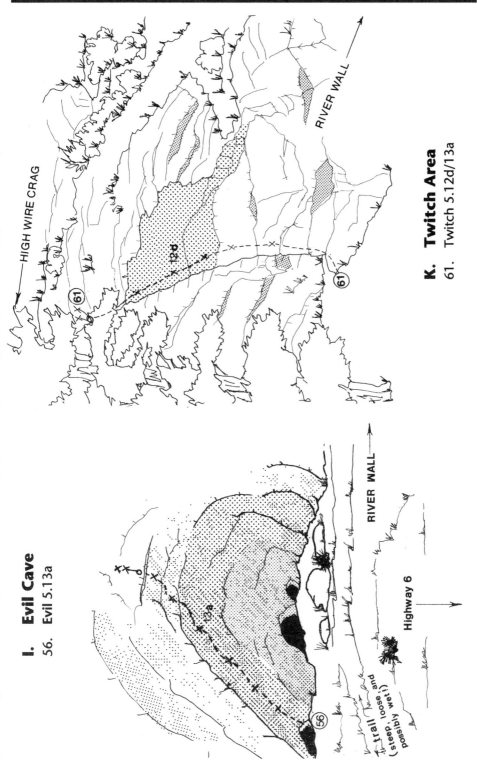

I. Evil Cave
56. Evil 5.13a

K. Twitch Area
61. Twitch 5.12d/13a

HIGH WIRE CRAG

RIVER WALL

RIVER WALL

Highway 6

trail (steep, loose, and possibly wet!)

149

J.   River Wall

57. Unknown
58. Unknown 5.9 A2/A3?
59. Bad Old Days 5.10b
60. Kor Route (?)

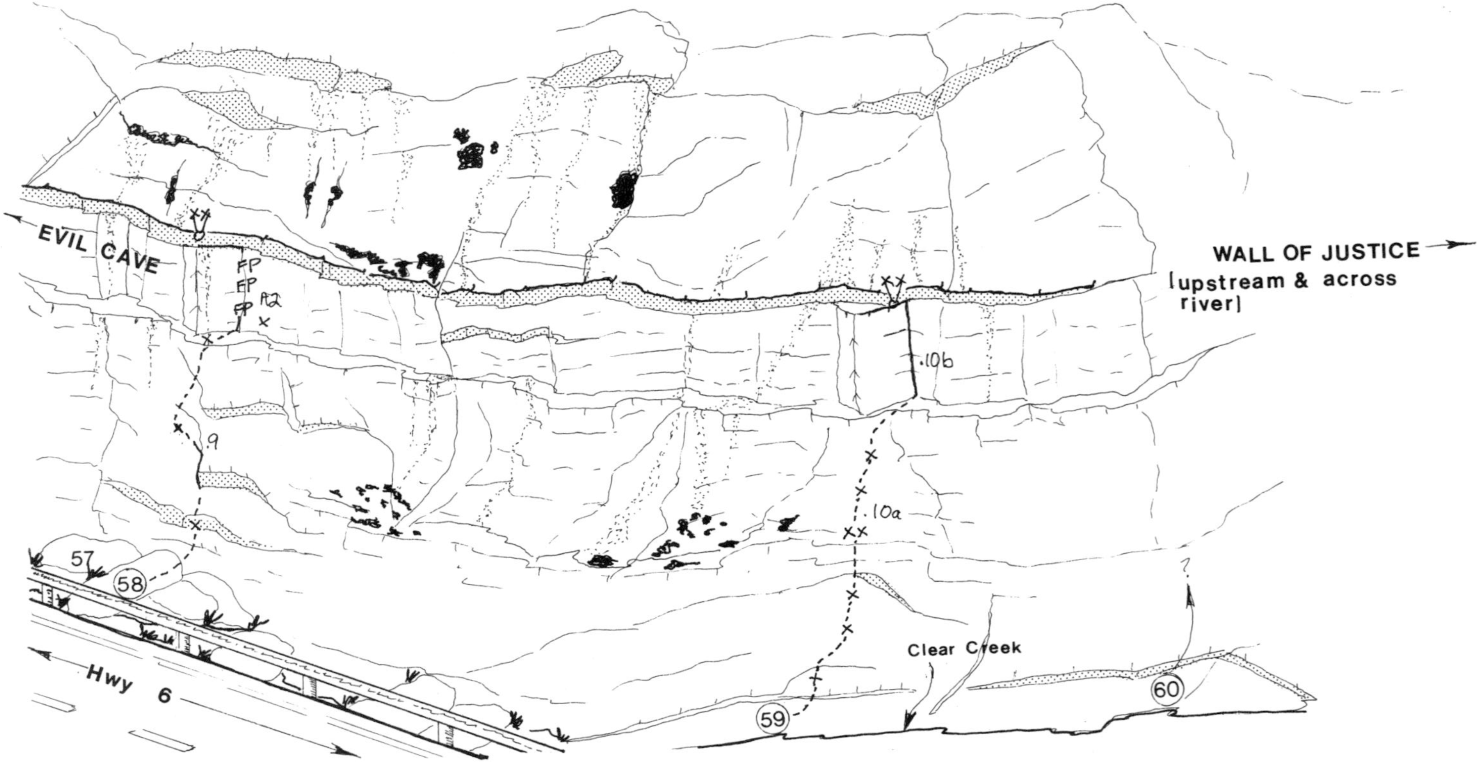

150

WALL OF JUSTICE
[upstream & across river]

Clear Creek

60

59

58

57

.10b

.10a

.9

EVIL CAVE

FP
FP
FP

Hwy 6

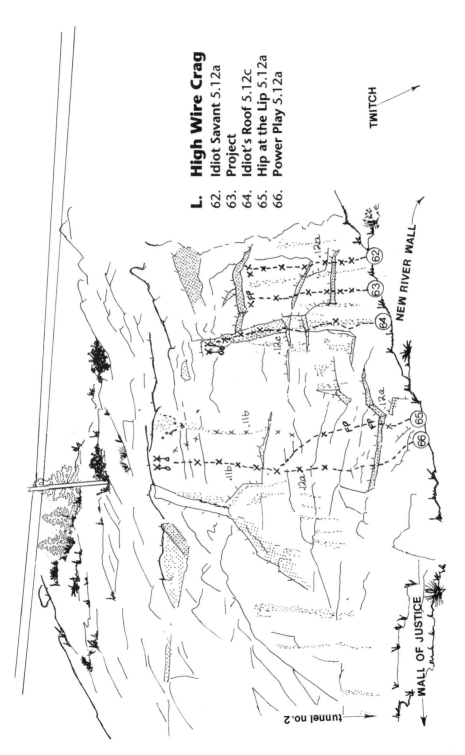

L. High Wire Crag

62. Idiot Savant 5.12a
63. Project
64. Idiot's Roof 5.12c
65. Hip at the Lip 5.12a
66. Power Play 5.12a

TWITCH

NEW RIVER WALL

WALL OF JUSTICE

tunnel no. 2

151

M. Wall of Justice

67. Testify 5.12b
68. Test a Fly 5.12d/5.13a
69. Justify 5.12b
70. Criminal Mischief 5.11c
71. Miss Trial 5.11c

72. Officer Friendly 5.11c
73. LA Law 5.10a
74. Lawsuit 5.10b
75. Countersuit 5.9

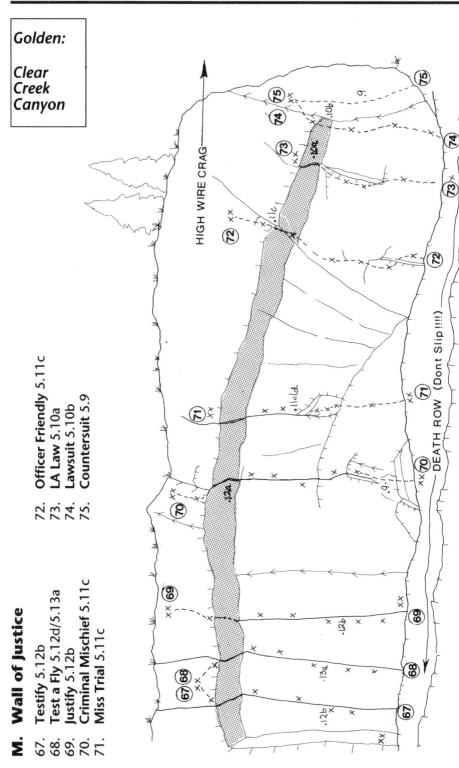

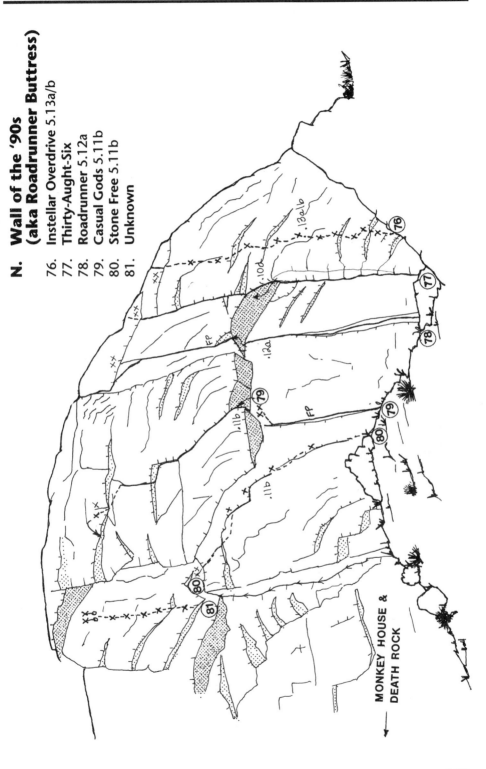

N. Wall of the '90s (aka Roadrunner Buttress)

76. Instellar Overdrive 5.13a/b
77. Thirty-Aught-Six
78. Roadrunner 5.12a
79. Casual Gods 5.11b
80. Stone Free 5.11b
81. Unknown

MONKEY HOUSE & DEATH ROCK

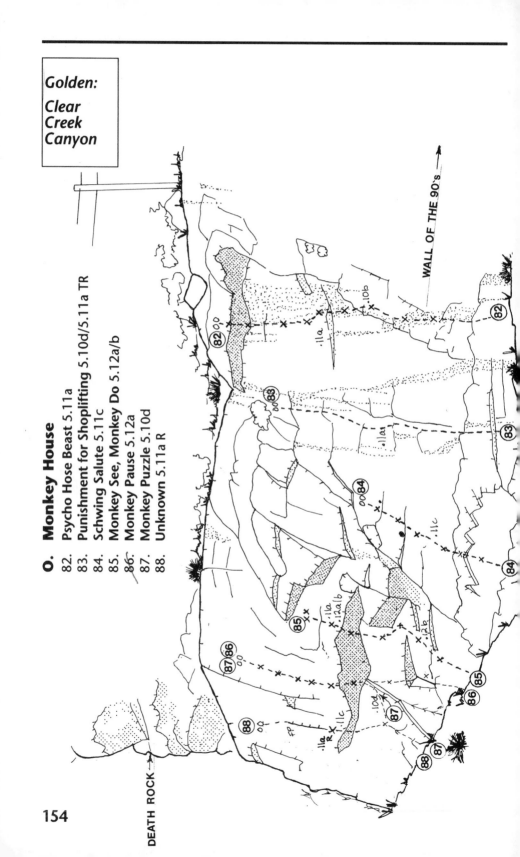

Golden:

Clear Creek Canyon

O. Monkey House

82. Psycho Hose Beast 5.11a
83. Punishment for Shoplifting 5.10d/5.11a TR
84. Schwing Salute 5.11c
85. Monkey See, Monkey Do 5.12a/b
86. Monkey Pause 5.12a
87. Monkey Puzzle 5.10d
88. Unknown 5.11a R

WALL OF THE 90's

DEATH ROCK

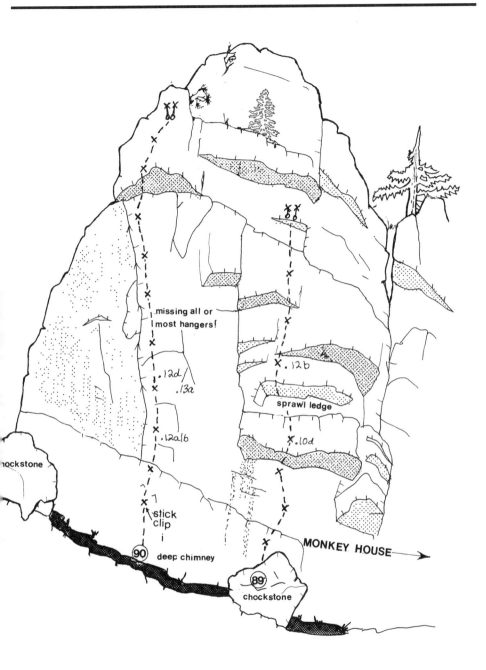

missing all or
most hangers!

.12d/
.13a

.12a/b

stick
clip

deep chimney

.12b

sprawl ledge

.10d

MONKEY HOUSE ⟶

chockstone

chockstone

90

89

P. Death Rock
89. **The Sprawl** 5.12b
90. **Homeboy Bonanza** 5.12d/5.13a

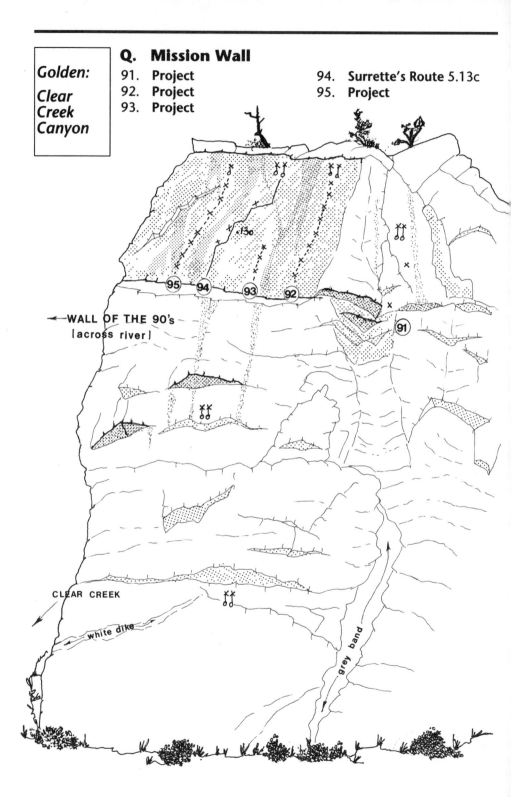

Q. Mission Wall

Golden:
Clear
Creek
Canyon

91. Project
92. Project
93. Project

94. Surrette's Route 5.13c
95. Project

.13o

95 94 93 92

←WALL OF THE 90's
(across river)

91

CLEAR CREEK

white dike

grey band

R. Anarchy Wall
96. Halloween 5.9
97. Question Authority 5.12a

S. Kool Krag
114. Kool Thing 5.12c   Across Clear Creek from Anarchy Wall.

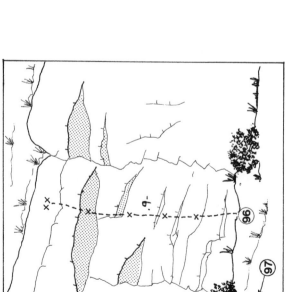

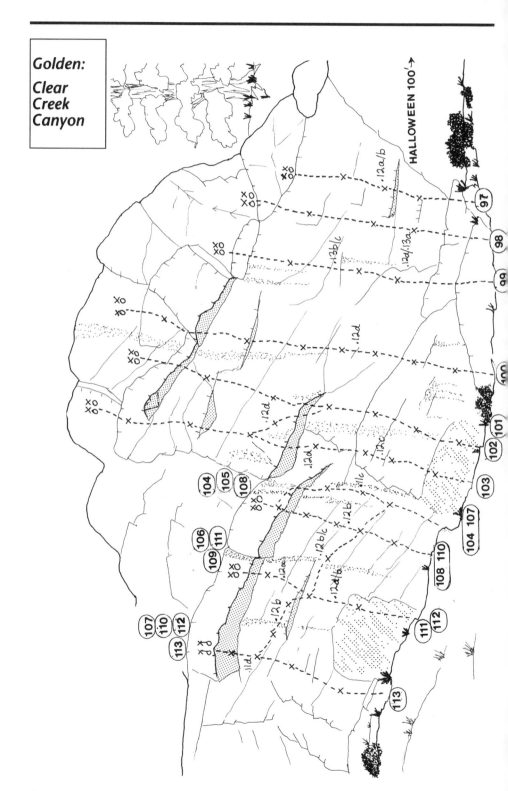

Golden:
Clear
Creek
Canyon

HALLOWEEN 100'→

158

R. Anarchy Wall

97. **Question Authority 5.12a/b**
98. **Chaos 5.12d/5.13a**
99. **Project 5.13b/c**
100. **Anarchitect 5.12d**
101. **Maestro 5.12d**
102. **Presto 5.12c**
103. **Matriarch 5.12d**
104. **Monkey Wrench 5.11c**
105. **Monkey Rules 5.12b**
106. **Monkey in the UK 5.12b/c**
107. **Anatomic 5.12c**
108. **Anarchy Rules 5.12b**
109. **Rules in the UK 5.12b**
110. **Hazardous Rules 5.12b/c**
111. **Anarchy in the UK 5.12a/b**
112. **Hazardous Anarchy 5.12b**
113. **Hazardous Waste 5.11d**

Golden:

Clear
Creek
Canyon

T. Pete's Wicked Cave
    (aka Sex Cave)

115. Rubble 5.13c
116. Stone Cold Modern 5.13b
117. Head like a Hole 5.12d

trail

115

116

117

13c

13b

12d

REBEL WALL

W. A Little Piece of South Dakota

141. A Little Piece of South Dakota 5.9 R
142. Bugsy 5.9-
143. Red's 5.8

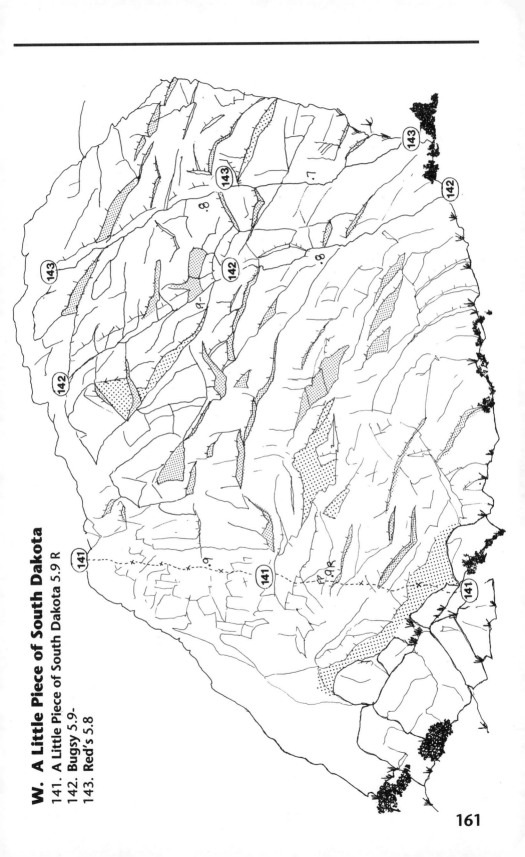

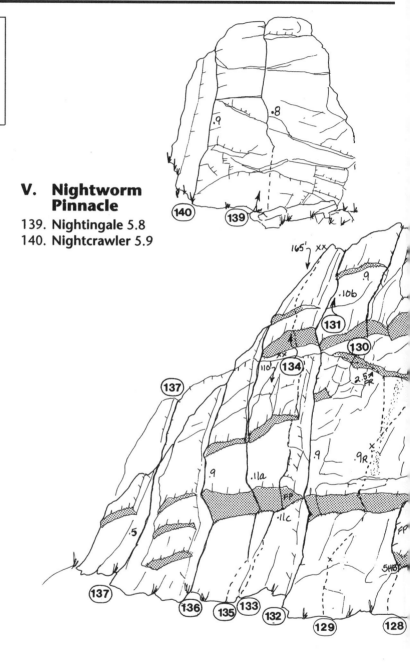

V. Nightworm Pinnacle

139. Nightingale 5.8
140. Nightcrawler 5.9

U. Rebel Wall

118. **Floppy Boot Stomp** 5.8+
119. **Down to the Wire** 5.11d R
120. **Last Chance to Dance** 5.12a
121. **Bust a Move** 5.11d
122. **Winter Kill** 5.13a TR

123. **Piedmont Boulder Toad** 5.10b
124. **Shane's Addiction** 5.11a
125. **Siouxnami** 5.12c
126. **Dreidel** 5.10b
127. **Only the Strong** 5.11c

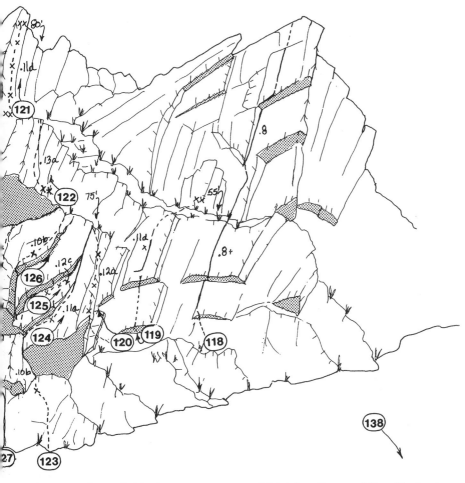

128. **Jump Start** 5.11c R
129. **Make It Go** 5.9 R
130. **Make It So** 5.9
131. **Upper Cut** 5.10b
132. **Body English** 5.9
133. **Epidot** 5.11c

134. **The Curse of Eve** (Project)
135. **Mama Said Knock You Out**
     5.11a
136. **Large Crack** 5.9
137. **Learner's Permit** 5.5
138. **Whistlin' Dixie** 5.6

X. High Profile Wall

Golden:

Clear
Creek
Canyon

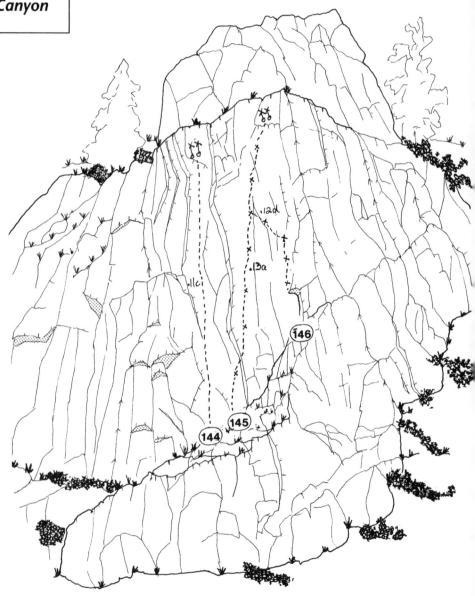

Y. Kayak Wall

147. Paddle Me Baby 5.8+/5.9-
148. Splinter in the Mind's Eye 5.11c TR

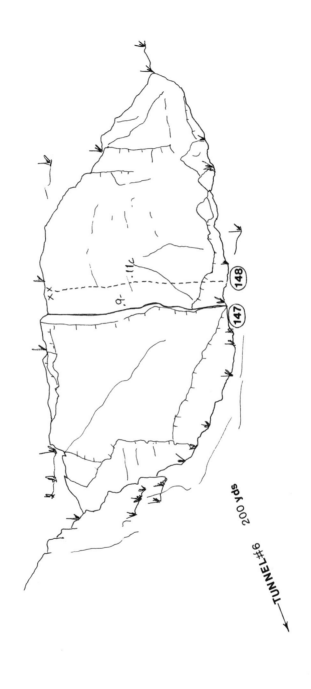

148

147

200 yds

←TUNNEL #6

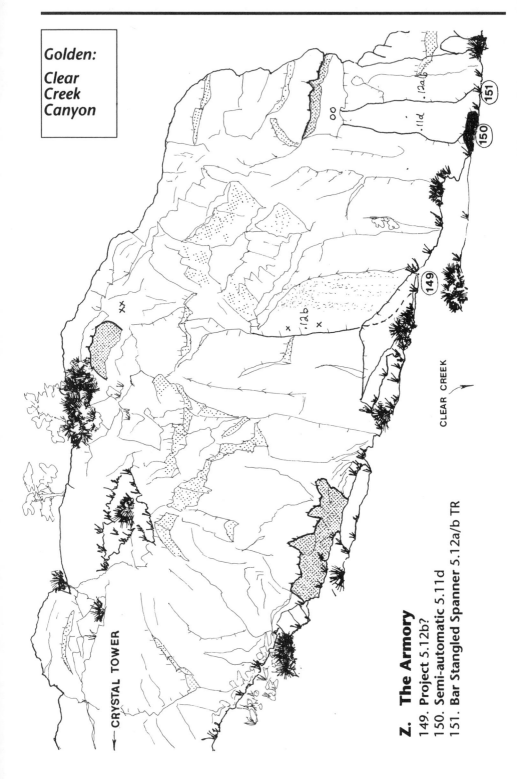

Golden:

Clear
Creek
Canyon

151
150
149

CLEAR CREEK

CRYSTAL TOWER

Z.   The Armory
149. Project 5.12b?
150. Semi-automatic 5.11d
151. Bar Stangled Spanner 5.12a/b TR

166

AA. Crystal Tower

152. **Project** 5.12a/b?
153. **Project** 5.12a/b TR
154. **Quartz Spots** 5.12b
155. **Mineral Museum** 5.9

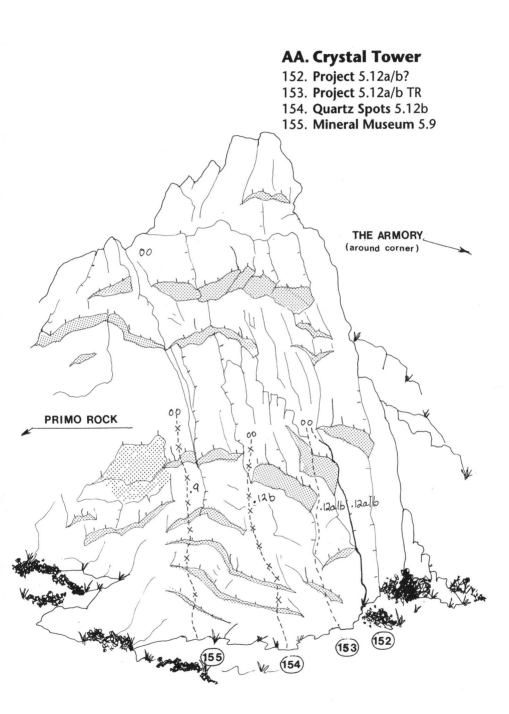

BB. Primo Wall

156. Hangman 5.12b
157. Suspended Sentence 5.12b
158. Moving Out 5.12b
159. Project
160. Groan Up 5.11c

161. Breakfast Club 5.12a
162. Flying Cowboys 5.12d
163. Suburban Cowgirls 5.11c
164. City Slickers 5.12a
165. Project 5.13

166. Sucking My Will to Live 5.12d
167. Mirthmobile 5.10a
168. Mildage 5.11c/d

Golden:
Clear
Creek
Canyon

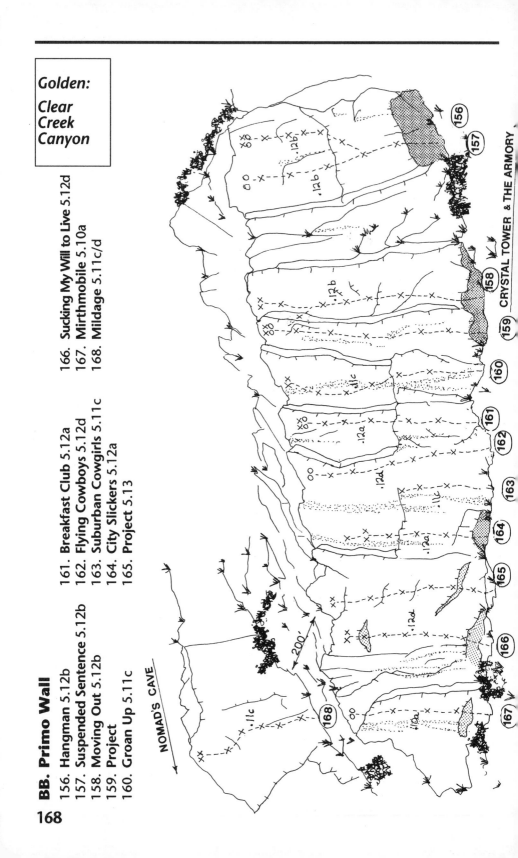

CRYSTAL TOWER & THE ARMORY

NOMAD'S CAVE

CC. Nomad's Cave

169. Pizza Dick
 (aka It's Not Nice To Fool Mother Nature) 5.12b
170. Project 5.13d
171. Predator-X 5.13a
172. Predator 5.12b
173. Pro-Choice (aka Bad Day Mining) 5.12c
174. Express Yourself 5.12d/5.13a

MILDAGE

PRIMO WALL ⟶

CRYSTAL TOWER
and THE ARMORY

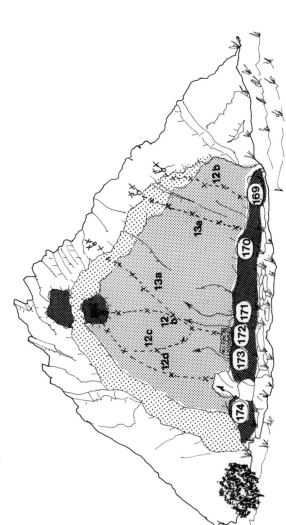

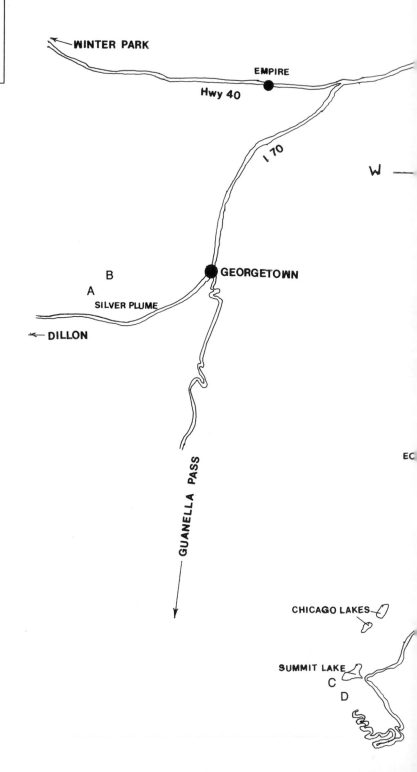

Mt. Evans
Area:

Overview
map

WINTER PARK

EMPIRE

Hwy 40

I 70

W

B

A

GEORGETOWN

SILVER PLUME

DILLON

GUANELLA PASS

EC

CHICAGO LAKES

SUMMIT LAKE

C

D

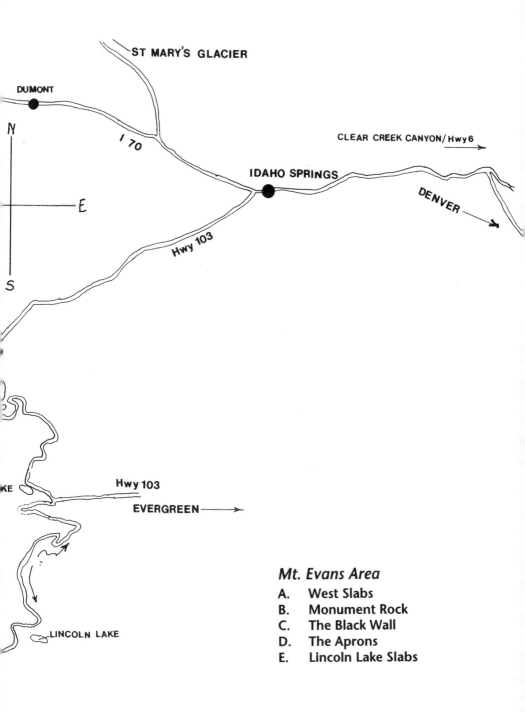

Mt. Evans Area
A. West Slabs
B. Monument Rock
C. The Black Wall
D. The Aprons
E. Lincoln Lake Slabs

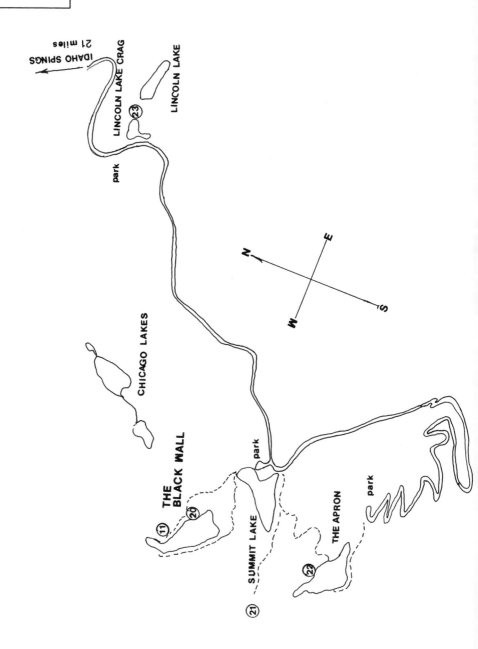

Mt. Evans Area:

Overview map

21 miles

IDAHO SPINGS

LINCOLN LAKE CRAG

LINCOLN LAKE

23

park

N
E
W
S

CHICAGO LAKES

THE BLACK WALL

11
20

SUMMIT LAKE

park

THE APRON

park

22

21

172

Mt. Evans Area

The Monument Rock area, located above the town of Silver Plume west of Idaho Springs on I-70, offers some fine granite climbing, both sport and traditional. At 9,500 feet, it is one of the cooler areas in the Front Range for summer climbs. Little is known about some of the earlier ascents, especially on Monument Rock itself, but there is a picture of Pat Ament climbing on Monument Rock on the back cover of one of his early guidebooks to the Boulder area, dating back to the early '70s.

Directions

The first area, and the lowest, is the West Slabs, which is above and west of the gully just west of the mine. To approach them, park in a pull-out off of the paved road and, staying off of the mining company's property, cross the gully to pick up an old mining road that winds uphill to the base of the slabs. Most of the climbs are located on the south or southwest face. There is a lot of potential for easier climbs on the right hand slabs. Kurt Smith and friends are responsible for most of the routes to date on this rock.

Monument Rock is higher up and on the right (east) side of the gully. There are about three different ways to approach. Follow the gully up and traverse right toward the top of the gully; follow the trail/road to West Slabs and cross the gully above the waterfall; and follow old roads and trails, staying to the right of the mine, up to the rock.

Much of the climbing here is on discontinuous cracks to very fine grained granite face climbing. It would be a good idea to approach Monument Rock as if you were going to do a first ascent.

A word of caution: These climbs may or may not be on private land. Although there have been no negative reports of landowner hassles, please keep a low profile, and respect the "No Trespassing" signs where you find them. Also, the tailings from the old mines are very loose. There is also some danger from the open mine shafts–you don't want to fall in one.

There are some ice climbs here, the most popular being the waterfall at the top of the gully just below Monument Rock. Another is located about a quarter-mile west on the same side of the road, but it is not as good.

The Mt. Evans Area is the highest area covered in this guide. The summit of Mt. Evans is above 14,000 feet high with all of the weather and problems associated with climbs at this altitude. For climbs on Mt. Evans it is wise to bring bivy and/or some basic survival gear, including a full set of winter type outer wear. It is not unusual for it to snow (and snow hard!) in July. Be prepared. Retreat is also a problem due to the overhanging nature of many of the routes. Keep this in mind before starting to climb.

To approach Good Evans or Road Warrior, it is best to go to the top and rappel the Rappel Route. For the other climbs, approach from the col just north of the Summit Lake parking and around to the base of the wall. If you need to cross the snowfield, make sure you have an ice axe and crampons as the runout is very bad. The rappels down the Rappel Route also require an additional 30 feet of rope to tie off the large boulder at the top. Another word of caution: It is wise to fix an escape rope to the top anchors of the route you are doing to facilitate retreat in case of bad weather.

Just above Summit Lake and facing the parking area is a large snowfield with some smaller gullies on either side of it. This offers some excellent low angle alpine ice climbs and even some mixed climbs depending on the time of year and conditions. Excellent summer skiing can be found in these same gullies as well as on the east face of Mt. Evans.

To the left of the snowfields are The Aprons, two obvious slabs with many route possibilities on them. Left of The Aprons is another buttress called Pika Rock (and probably 20 other names). I have listed only one climb on each of The Aprons, though I know of many people, myself included, who have climbed on these slabs over the years. Almost all of the routes are in the 5.7-5.8 range with some runouts. Because of the "climb anywhere" nature of these slabs it wasn't possible to list all of the many variations. The climbs are in the neighborhood of 700' long and, in addition the weather, the main hazard is the tourist generated rockfall from the summit.

Lower down the road is Lincoln Lake Slab, also with one reported route: Jabba the Hut. There is room for many other routes on these slabs.

Jeff Lowe and Dan Hare were responsible for the route Road Warrior. Ken Trout with partners that included Jerry Rock, Noel Childs, Kirk Miller, Pete Pradoni, and Eric Winkelman accounted for all others except for Rusty Dagger which was established by Miller and Rock. Angelo de la Cruz and Bradford put up Summer Snow on the First Apron.

Mt. Evans Area Rocks and Routes:

A. West Slabs
1. Kurt Smith Route 5.13a/b
2. Project
3. Toxic Chalk Syndrome 5.10d   Pro: To 4", extra ½" to 1".
4. Time to Climb 5.10b   Pro: To 5".
5. Bolt Like Mad (BLM) 5.12a/b
6. The Shaft 5.12a
7. Kurt Smith Route 5.12c

B. Monument Rock
8. Childs-Miller Rock Route 5.11b R   Pro: To 3".
9. Project
10. Gottenborg-Schovajsa Route 5.9 R   Pro: To 3".

C. The Black Wall
11. Coffee Achievers 5.10d   Pro: To 5", extra ½" to 5".
12. Project?
13. Parallel Universe 5.10b A4 R   Pro: Doubles through 4", rurps to 2" pins, bat hooks and copperheads.
14. Project?
15. Rusty Dagger 5.9 A3   Pro: Doubles through 3.5", pins through 2".
16. Undertow 5.10b A4+   Pro: Doubles through 4", pins through ½".
17. Road Warrior 5.10d   Pro: To 6", extra 3.5" to 6".
18. Good Evans 5.11a   Pro: To 4", extra ¼" to 2.5".
19. Rappel Route 5.11a   Pro: To 4", extra 1" to 4".
20. Cary Granite 5.11c   Pro: To 4", extra 1" to 2.5"
21. Alpine Ice   Moderate, not shown.

D. The Aprons: First Apron
22. Summer Snow 5.7+ R   Face and cracks to 600-foot dihedral on right side of Apron. Pro: To 4".

Second Apron
23. Slab Route 5.7+ R   Pro: To 4".

Third Apron
24. Cheap Date 5.9   Pro: To 5".

E. Lincoln Lakes Slab
25. Jabba the Hut 5.10c/d   Not shown. Follows a long thin crack on the left end, on and obvious orange face. Faces east. Pro: To 3".

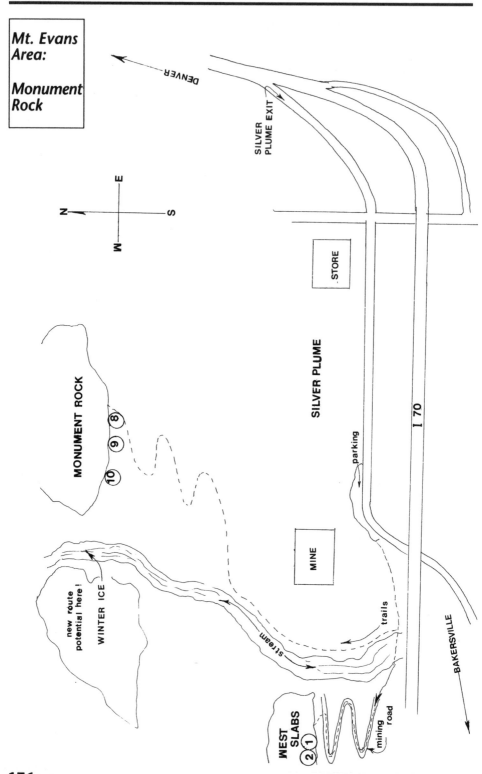

Mt. Evans
Area:

Monument
Rock

A. West Slabs

1. Kurt Smith Route 5.13a/b
2. Project
3. Toxic Chalk Syndrome 5.10d.
4. Time to Climb 5.10b

5. Bolt Like Mad (BLM) 5.12a/b
6. The Shaft 5.12a
7. Kurt Smith Route 5.12c

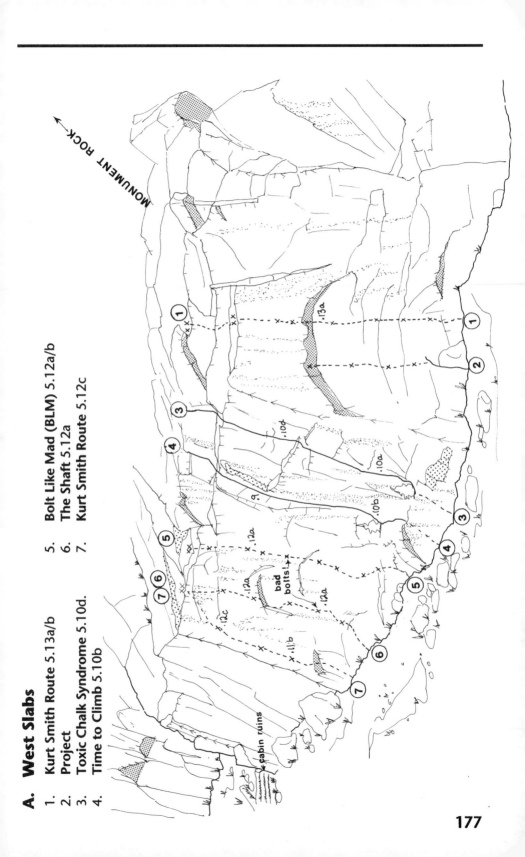

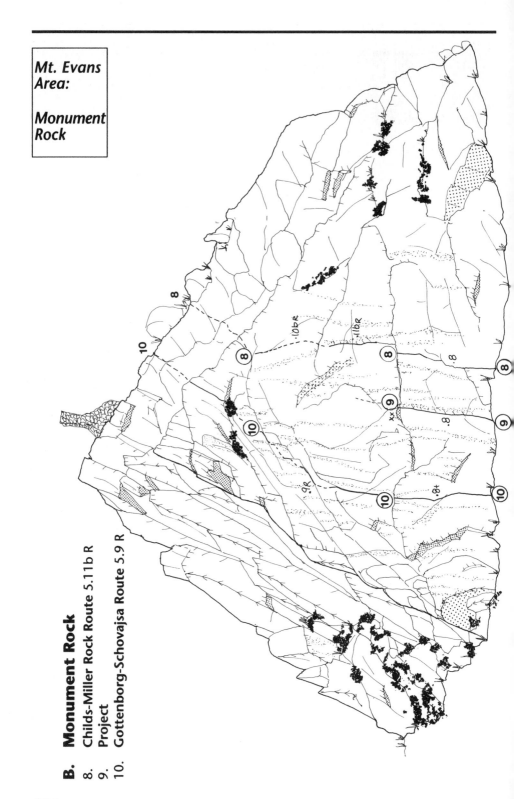

B.   Monument Rock
8.   Childs-Miller Rock Route 5.11b R
9.   Project
10.   Gottenborg-Schovajsa Route 5.9 R

Brian Brown leading **Queen of Hearts,** North Turkey Creek.

C. The Black Wall

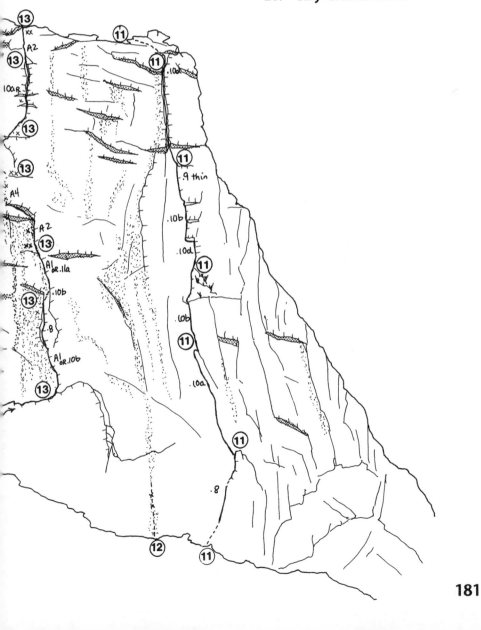

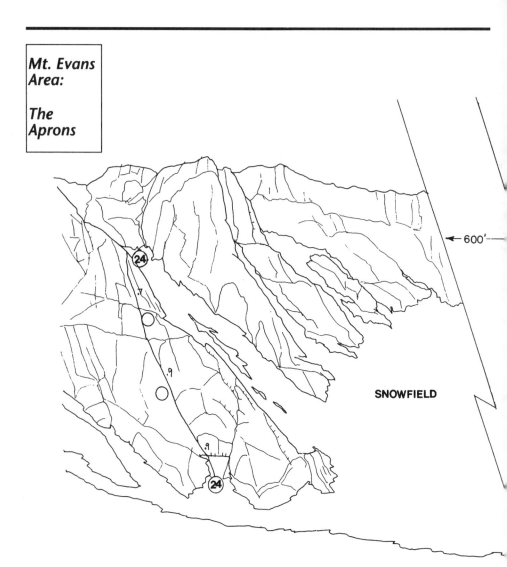

Mt. Evans Area:

The Aprons

600'

SNOWFIELD

D. The Aprons

First Apron

22. Summer Snow 5.7+ R

Second Apron

23. Slab Route 5.7+ R

Third Apron

24. Cheap Date 5.9

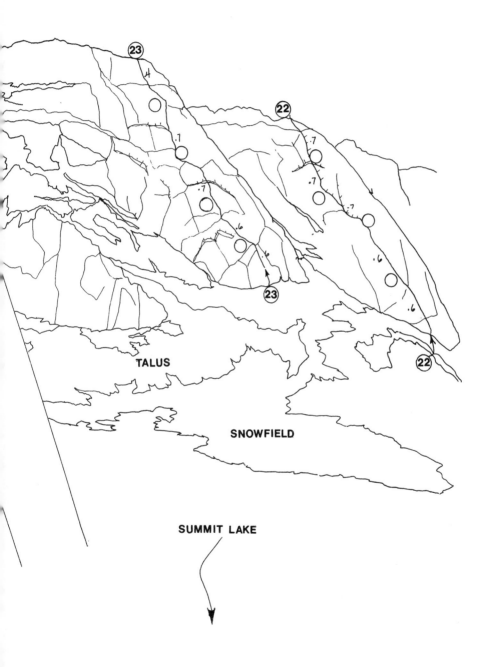

TALUS

SNOWFIELD

SUMMIT LAKE

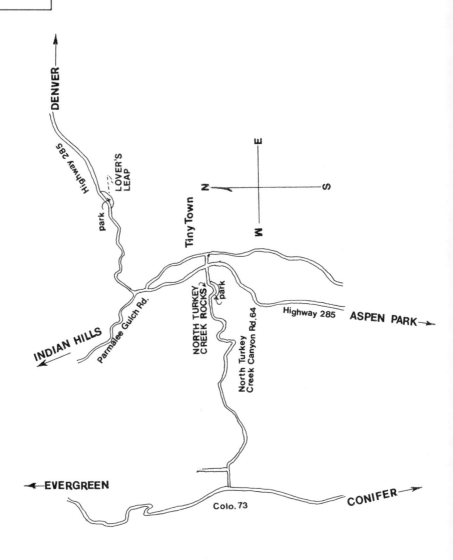

Highway 285

This area features a wide variety of climbs, mostly on gniess, and some of the longest climbs close to Denver. Lover's Leap is a 450-foot high cliff located about 3 miles up Highway 285 from Soda Lakes Road on the left side of the canyon. It's faces offer an array of mostly lower-end climbs of a very alpine nature. These same climbs, with the right conditions, provide hard, protectable winter mixed routes. Three miles past Lover's Leap is North Turkey Creek Canyon Road. Take this to the right for .7 mile to the next area, a sprawling mass of boulder problems and climbs from 15' to 160' high, with a variety of climbing difficulty levels. This area is extremely popular with beginning to intermediate climbers.

Many of the climbs in these areas are old; put up in the 1920s and '30s by the Colorado Mountain Club (CMC) and the US Army. Most of the older climbs on Lover's Leap can be attributed to these two groups. North Turkey Creek Canyon has been a popular bouldering spot for a number of years. Many of the standard boulder problems were put up by Chuckie Grossman, Dan Trygstad, Dave and Chris Bell, Ken Trout, Olaff Mitchell and others.

Most of the rock at North Turkey Creek is very close to the road and private residences. Please be very considerate of where you park and of picking up trash. This area has already seen one closure for about a year.

In addition to the rock climbs on Lover's Leap and the bouldering/short climbs to be found at North Turkey Creek and the nearby Morrison bouldering area, there is a short 80' ice climb located up Bear Creek Canyon Road. It is on the south side of the road and located about halfway between Idledale and Kittredge.

Emergency numbers

911 or Jefferson County Sheriff's Department (303)271-5304.

Camping and recreation

There is really no camping or other recreational opportunities this low in the canyon, with the exception of some hiking in Mt. Falcon State Park.

A. Lover's Leap

1. **Original Route** 5.6   Pro: To 4".
2. **Ye Olde Hysterical Route** 5.10b   Pro: To 4".
2a. **5.10c/d variation**   Pro: To 4".
2b. **Yohr variation** 5.9   Pro: To 4".
3. **Hubble-Drier Route** 5.9 R   Pro: To 3.5".
4. **Where Tunas Flop** 5.10b   Pro: To 3".
5. **Lover's Leap** 5.7+   This is an excellent mixed route. Pro: To 5".
6. **No Holds Barred** 5.9   Pro: To 3".
7. **Something for Nothing** 5.10a R   Pro: To 3", extra small.
8. **Procrastination** 5.7 R   Pro: To 3.5".
9. **Winter Route** (Rating is dependent on weather conditions.)
9a. **Donelan variation** 5.7
10. **Winter Route II** (Rating is dependent on weather conditions.)

B. Licorice Reunion Buttress

11. **Scare Tactics** 5.10a   Pro: To 3".
12. **Shadow Dancer** 5.10c   Pro: To 3.5".

C. Wimpy's Burger Stand

13. **Love Me Do** 5.6   Pro: To 4".
14. **Where's the Beef?** 5.10b R   Pro: To 2.5".
15. **The Cutting Board** 5.8+   Pro: To 4".
16. **Mind Games** 5.9   Pro: To 3".
17. **Leon's Way** 5.9+ R

D. North Turkey Creek

18. **5.8 Crack**   Pro: To 2.5".
19. **Chimney Climb** 5.5   Pro: To 3".
20. **Green Slab Indirect** 5.9+   Pro: To 3".
21. **Green Slab** 5.7   Pro: To 3.5".
22. **Sucker** 5.8+   Pro: To 3".
23. **Bell Route variation** 5.8+   Pro: To 4".
24. **Bell Route** 5.9   Pro: To 3".
25. **Wuthering Corner** 5.8   Pro: To 4".
26. **5.8 Crack** TR
27. **5.9 Crack** TR
28. **5.12 Crack** 5.11c/d TR
29. **Queen of Spades** 5.9-   Pro: To 3".
30. **Queen of Hearts** 5.6 or 5.9   Pro: To 2.5".
31. **Into a Corner** 5.6+   Pro: To 2.5".
32. **Roof Route** 5.7+   Pro: To 3".
33. **Unnamed** 5.9   Pro: To 2.5".
34. **King of the Jungle** 5.10b TR
35. **Marginal Error** 5.9+   Pro: To 3".
36. **Warhead** 5.6   Pro: To 4".
37. **Young Lizards** 5.9+   Pro: To 2.5".
38. **Valley Rescue** 5.8   Pro: To 3".
39. **Glory Hunters** 5.9+/5.10a TR
40. **5.7 Corner**   Pro: To 3".

Steve Van Meter, Winter 1984 ascent of **4th of July Crack**, Lover's Leap. Photo: Peter Hubbel

DESCEND EAST FACE

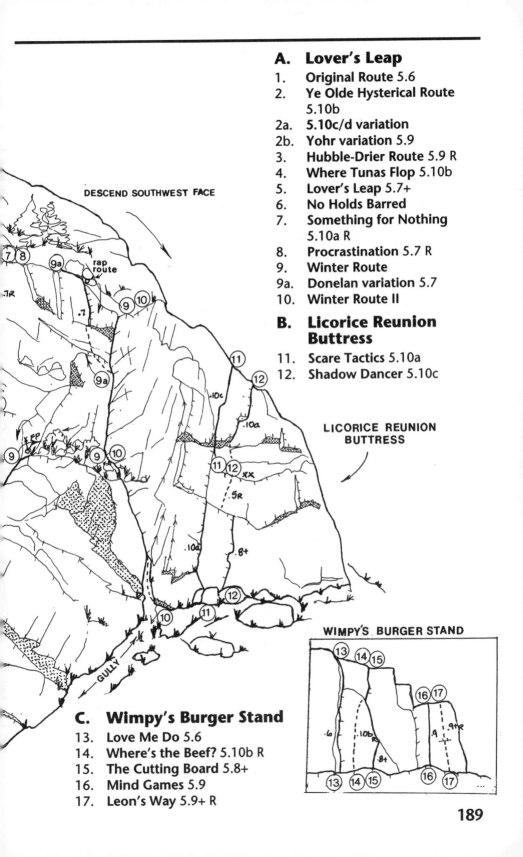

A. Lover's Leap
1. Original Route 5.6
2. Ye Olde Hysterical Route 5.10b
2a. 5.10c/d variation
2b. Yohr variation 5.9
3. Hubble-Drier Route 5.9 R
4. Where Tunas Flop 5.10b
5. Lover's Leap 5.7+
6. No Holds Barred
7. Something for Nothing 5.10a R
8. Procrastination 5.7 R
9. Winter Route
9a. Donelan variation 5.7
10. Winter Route II

B. Licorice Reunion Buttress
11. Scare Tactics 5.10a
12. Shadow Dancer 5.10c

C. Wimpy's Burger Stand
13. Love Me Do 5.6
14. Where's the Beef? 5.10b R
15. The Cutting Board 5.8+
16. Mind Games 5.9
17. Leon's Way 5.9+ R

189

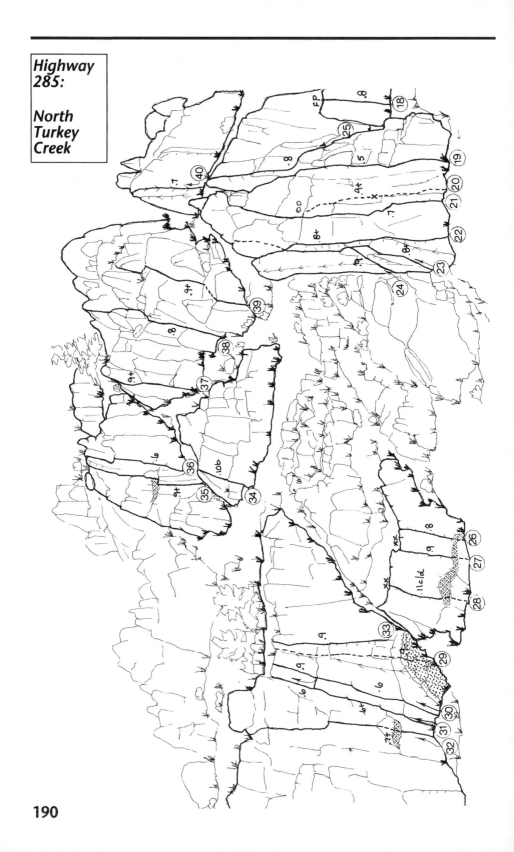

D. North Turkey Creek

18. 5.8 Crack
19. Chimney Climb 5.5
20. Green Slab Indirect 5.9+
21. Green Slab 5.7
22. Sucker 5.8+
23. Bell Route variation 5.8+
24. Bell Route 5.9
25. Wuthering Corner 5.8
26. 5.8 Crack TR
27. 5.9 Crack TR
28. 5.12 Crack 5.11c/d TR
29. Queen of Spades 5.9-
30. Queen of Hearts 5.6 or 5.9
31. Into a Corner 5.6+
32. Roof Route 5.7+
33. Unnamed 5.9
34. King of the Jungle 5.10b TR
35. Marginal Error 5.9+
36. Warhead 5.6
37. Young Lizards 5.9+
38. Valley Rescue 5.8
39. Glory Hunters 5.9+/5.10a TR
40. 5.7 Corner

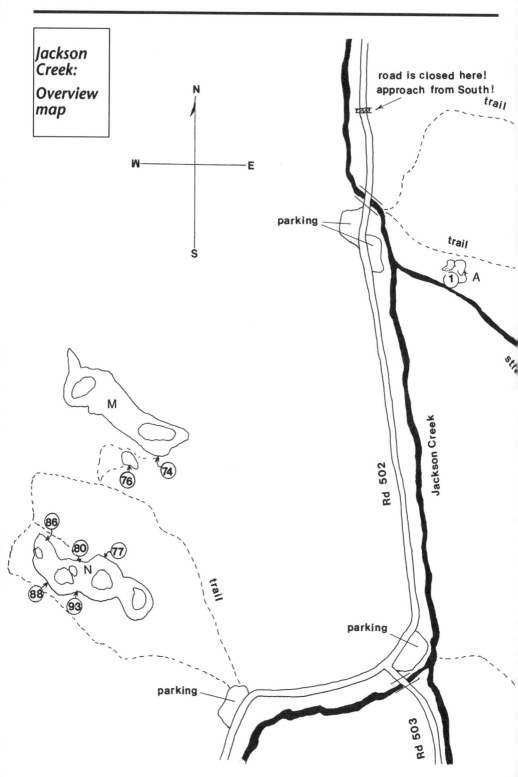

Jackson
Creek:

Overview
map

N

W——————E

S

road is closed here!
approach from South!

trail

parking

trail

1 A

M

74

76

86

80 77

N

88

93

trail

Jackson Creek

Rd 502

parking

parking

Rd 503

str

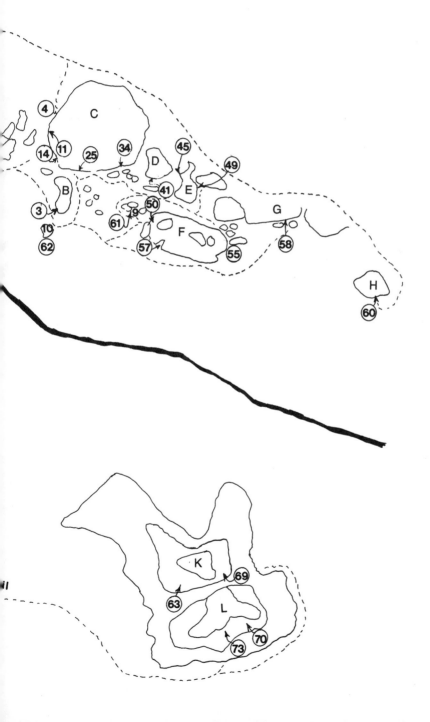

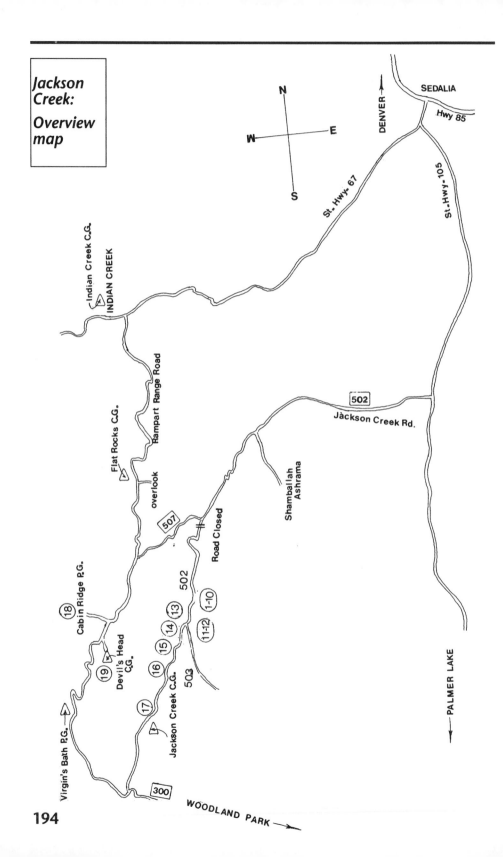

Jackson
Creek:
Overview
map

N
W — E
S

SEDALIA

DENVER →

Hwy 85

St. Hwy. 67

St. Hwy. 105

Indian Creek C.G.

INDIAN CREEK

Rampart Range Road

502

Jackson Creek Rd.

Flat Rocks C.G.

overlook

507

Road Closed

Shamballah Ashrama

502

Cabin Ridge P.G.

18

1-10

13

14

15

11-12

Devil's Head C.G.

19

16

503

PALMER LAKE

Virgin's Bath P.G.

17

Jackson Creek C.G.

300

WOODLAND PARK →

Jackson Creek

The Jackson Creek Area has long been popular with dirt bikers and four-wheelers but has been considered somewhat of a secret among climbers. Even though it was briefly covered in *South Platte Rock Climbs and Garden of the Gods* (Chockstone Press, 1988) many of the routes were not listed due to lack of information.

Cecil Ouellette and Dick Woodford made what is possibly the first recorded ascent here of the Taj Mahal in 1957. The Colorado Mountain Club (CMC) has been using the back (west) side of Devil's Head as a practice area for a number of years, reaching the top by way of the hiking trail and fire tower stairs. There are a number of fine top rope climbs, both crack and face to be found in these corridors. Bill Forrest has been climbing here for about 20 years, but, as is his nature, hasn't recorded or reported any of his routes. He probably has done most of the major crack lines although the current names do not reflect his ascents.

Since the South Platte guide came out, a group of climbers consisting of Steve and Sharon Holonitch, Gene Ellis, Gary Walker, and Alan Mosiman have been extensively developing the area and are responsible for 90% of the current routes. The rock in Jackson Creek is typical South Platte granite, at least in the northern (Taj Mahal) end of the valley. The rock on the Devil's Head Massif is not quite as sound nor are the crack systems as continuous, but the climbing is still enjoy-able. Many of the climbs are bolt protected slab and face climbs, sometimes requiring a selection of standard gear. There are some fine Yosemite style cracks on the south face of the Taj Mahal in a beautiful amphitheater, as well as a two-pitch face route. The Jackson Creek Dome Area has a fine selection of bolted slab routes ranging in difficulty from 5.5 to mid-range 5.11 as well as quite a few crack climbs. Cabin Ridge Rock is located just west of the Jackson Creek Valley off Rampart Range Road. The Devil's Head Campground Rock is located just west of the parking area for the campground. The climbing on both rocks is again on South Platte granite, with the climbing on Cabin Ridge Rock offering cleaner climbing due to its south facing nature. These rocks offer some nice climbing with a lot of diversity and minimal approach.

Directions

To get to Jackson Creek, take Highway 85 to Sedalia and go west on Highway 67. Highway 105 is on your left after you cross the railroad tracks and you have two options here: either continue west until you reach Rampart Range Road and then turn south; or take Highway 105 to Jackson Creek Road, turning west onto Jackson Creek Road and turning south into the valley. At the time of this writing, Jackson Creek Road was closed due to a washout from this end, so instead of turning south here, continue to Rampart Range Road. Turn south to reach the southern entrance and turn north into the valley.

To reach Cabin Ridge Rock, follow Rampart Range Road south past the 8-mile marker. The Cabin Ridge turnoff is marked and is on your left. Park at the parking area, walk west on the trail, dropping off of the ridge before you reach the rock formation and walk around to the south face.

To reach the Devil's Head Campground Rock, follow Rampart Range Road to the Devil's Head parking area. The rock sits above the parking area to the west. There are camping spots all along the valley and a couple of National Forest Service campgrounds. This is a very popular spot for dirt bikers and so is a little noisy at times. There are some popular hiking trails; though I wouldn't recommend it for mountain biking simply because of the faster traffic. At times this area becomes trashed out. Please clean up any trash you find, whether or not it's yours. Maybe people will get the message. Please respect other climbers' projects and routes. Leave the bolt hangers in place so that other people may enjoy the routes.

Jackson Creek Rocks and Routes

A. Levitation Slab
1. **Dancing with the Crystal Queen** 5.8   Pro: Bolts.
B. Lower Dome
2. **Creeper** 5.9   Pro: To 4".
The Chief
3. **Stealth Trojan** 5.11c
C. Jackson Creek Dome (West Face Routes)
4. **Fuzzy Little Crack** 5.8   Pro: To 1".
5. **Cold Fusion** 5.10b TR
6. **Time Traveler** 5.8 TR
7. **Wild Weasel** 5.8 TR
8. **Paint Your Wagon** 5.8 R   Pro: To 6".
9. **Missouri Breaks** 5.8 R   Pro: To 3".
10. **Living on Borrowed Time** 5.9 TR
11. **Beta Blocker** 5.10c R   Pro: To 3".
12. **Buns in the Sun** 5.5/5.6   Pro: To 3".

13. **Nervous Disorder** 5.11c
14. **Hot Rize** 5.10a   Pro: To 1.5".
15. **Cold Frize** 5.8   Pro: To 3".

The following climbs start on a bench behind a rock formation in front of the main wall:

16. **Alien Elite** 5.10a   Pro: To 2.5".
17. **Mythical Kings and Iguanas** 5.9   Pro: To 1".
18. **One Track Pony** 5.8+   Pro: To 2.5".
19. **D. Winger** 5.7+
20. **Shortcut** 5.2 X
21. **Moronic Convergence** 5.5 X
22. **La La Land** 5.5 X

South Face Routes:

23. **Face the Face** 5.11a
24. **Flaming Monkey** 5.7   Pro: To 3".
25. **Energy Vortex** 5.9   Pro: To 3".
25a. **Alternate start** 5.9
26. **Living in Sin** 5.7 X   Pro: To 6".
27. **Mr. Chips** 5.9- R   Pro: #2 Friend.
28. **Consenting Adults** 5.10a
29. **Ramp Route** 5.6 R   Pro: To 3".
30. **In a Wrinkle** 5.8+   Pro: To 3".
31. **Snail Trail** 5.8+   Pro: To 3".
32. **Creaturistic** 5.11b   Climbs face in chimney.
32a. **Chimney variation**   Climbs chimney.
33. **Hard Attack** 5.9+ TR
34. **Wild Thing (aka Creature Comfort)** 5.9+
35. **Lego Land** 5.9
36. **Hang Ten** 5.7 R
37. **Time Out** 5.8
38. **Crispy Critters** 5.10a/b
39. **Tease** 5.8
40. **Nipple Flipper** 5.10a/b   Pro: To #1 or #1.5 Friend.

D. New Age Slab

41. **Psychic Intuition** 5.7+ R
42. **Astral Projection** 5.7 R
43. **Out of Body Experience** 5.8
44. **Out of Mind Experience** 5.9

E. Winger Wall

45. **Pringle's Prow** 5.10a   Pro: #2 RP, #2 Friend.
46. **Pringle's Crack** 5.8   Pro: To 3".
47. **My Evil Twin** 5.7
48. **I Need a Nurse** 5.8   Pro: To 3".
49. **Raven** 5.9   Not shown, climbs north wall of chimney.
     Pro: To 3".

F. Mega Dome

50. **Granite Rain** 5.9+   Pro: To 3".
51. **Don't Bother** 5.8+ R   Pro: To 5", extra 3" to 5".
52. **Bongo Flake** 5.10a   Pro: To 3".
53. **Unnamed** 5.8
54. **El Bosco** 5.10b
55. **Left Hand of Darkness** 5.10a   Pro: #1 TCU.
56. **Project**
57. **Dances with Beavers** (Project)

G. The Amphitheater

58. **Crystal Cruise** 5.11a
59. **Shadows on the Wall** 5.8   Pro: To 3".

H. Mini Dome

60. **Rat Lips** 5.8+ Not shown. South face, far right. Pro: Bolts.

I. The Grotto

61. **Fetal Flutters** 5.9+/5.10a   Pro: To 3".

J. Southwest Slab

62. **Robo** 5.5 TR (Not shown.)

K. Split Rock: Upper Face routes

63. **Accidental Tourist** 5.9+
64. **Bone Dome** 5.9+
65. **Come What May** 5.9+
66. **Project** 5.9+ TR
67. **Project** 5.8 TR
68. **Project** 5.8+ TR
69. **The Peter Dee** 5.9

L. Lower Face routes

70. **Que Pasa** 5.6   Pro: To 2.5".
71. **The Stroll** 5.8
72. **Clown** 5.8   Pro: Miscellaneous to 2".
73. **Howler** 5.9-   Pro: Miscellaneous to 2".

M. Flat Head Dome

74. **Project**
75. **Flat Foot** 5.11a   Pro: To 4".
76. **PI Patrol** 5.10d   Pro: To 3".

N. Taj Mahal: North Face routes

77. **Finger of Destruction** 5.11a
78. **Mind Games** 5.9   Pro: To 5", extra 3.5" to 5".
79. **Standing in a Slide Zone** 5.7   Pro: None.
80. **Pili Pili** 5.9   Pro: To 3".
81. **Dotted Line** 5.7 X   Pro: None.
82. **Chimneychanga** 5.8+   Pro: To 4".

83. **Traverse Below the Roof** 5.7 R   Pro: To 3".
84. **Inside Taj Mahal** 5.7   Pro: To 4".
85. **Genetic Impressions** 5.5 A2   Pro: To 4".
86. **Ouellette-Woodford Route (aka Northwest Face Friction Route 1957)** 5.8   Pro: To 3".
87. **1957 Route Variation**

South Face routes

88. **Unknown face climb** 5.10d/5.11a Pro: Miscellaneous to ¾".
89. **Top part of Ouellette-Woodford Route** 5.7
90. **Unknown crack climb** 5.10c Pro: To 3.5", extra 2" to 3".
91. **Air to the Thrown variation** 5.10b
92. **Air to the Thrown** 5.10d A1   Pro: To 4.5".
93. **Bad to the Bone** 5.11d   Pro: To 4".
94. **The King and Eyes** 5.9+   Pro: To 5", extra 3" to 4.5".

O. Raspberry Dome

95. **Calypso** 5.9-   Pro: To 5", extra 3" to 5".
96. **Go Figure** 5.10b   Pro: To 4.5".
97. **Unknown** 5.9+   Pro: To 6", extra 4" to 6".
98. **Rejuvenation** 5.10d   Pro: To 3".

P. Spire Rock

99. **Nutbuster** 5.10a   Pro: To 6".

Q. Devil's Head

100. **Unknown** 5.9   Pro: To 3.5".
101. **Unknown** 5.8   Pro: To 5".
102. **Dariush of Balanat** 5.9+   Pro: To 4".
103. **Satan's Satire** 5.10a   Pro: To 5", extra 4" to 5".
104. **Dance with the Devil** 5.10b   Pro: To 5", extra 4" to 5".
105. **Unknown** 5.10+ A2?
106. **Forrest-Van Meter Route** 5.7+/5.8-   Pro: To 5".
107. **Baal** 5.9+   Pro: To 4", extra 3"-4".
108. **Mark of the Devil** 5.9   Pro: To 3", extra 2" to 3".
109. **Bacarat** 5.10c   Pro: To 6", extra 5" and 6".

R. Cabin Ridge Rock

110. **Smokestack** 5.8.   Pro: To 3".
111. **Cabin Fever** 5.9   Pro: To 2".
112. **Unknown**
113. **Project**
114. **2nd Thoughts** 5.9-   Pro: To 6", extra 4" to 6".
115. **Original Route** 5.9+   Pro: To 4".

S. Devil's Head Campground Area

116. **Constipation** 5.8+   Pro: To 5".
117. **Colder than Hell** 5.9 R   Pro: To 4".
118. **Happy Camper** 5.7   Pro: To 6".

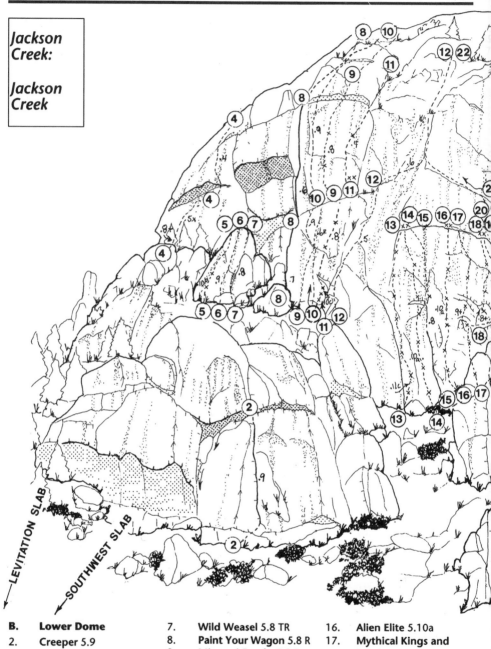

Jackson Creek:

Jackson Creek

LEVITATION SLAB

SOUTHWEST SLAB

B.	**Lower Dome**	7.	Wild Weasel 5.8 TR	16.	Alien Elite 5.10a
2.	Creeper 5.9	8.	Paint Your Wagon 5.8 R	17.	Mythical Kings and
	The Chief	9.	Missouri Breaks 5.8 R		Iguanas 5.9
3.	Stealth Trojan 5.11c	10.	Living on Borrowed	18.	One Track Pony 5.8+
			Time 5.9 TR	19.	D. Winger 5.7+
C.	**Jackson Creek Dome**	11.	Beta Blocker 5.10c R	20.	Shortcut 5.2 X
	(West Face Routes)	12.	Buns in the Sun 5.5/5.6	21.	Moronic Convergence
4.	Fuzzy Little Crack 5.8	13.	Nervous Disorder 5.11c		5.5 X
5.	Cold Fusion 5.10b TR	14.	Hot Rize 5.10a	22.	La La Land 5.5 X
6.	Time Traveler 5.8 TR	15.	Cold Frize 5.8		

200

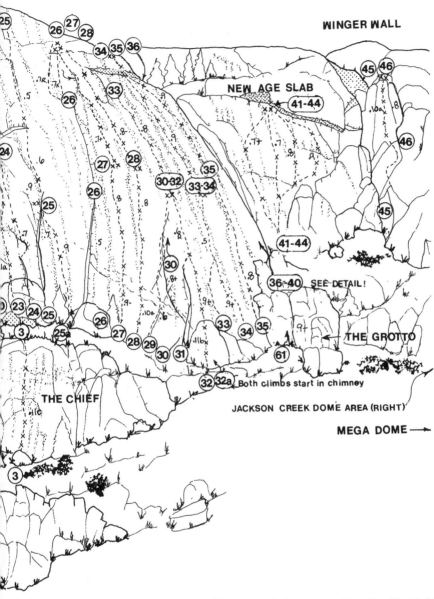

WINGER WALL

NEW AGE SLAB

THE GROTTO

SEE DETAIL!

Both climbs start in chimney

THE CHIEF

JACKSON CREEK DOME AREA (RIGHT)

MEGA DOME ───▶

23.	Face the Face 5.11a	32a.	Chimney variation	41.	Psychic Intuition 5.7+ R	
24.	Flaming Monkey 5.7	33.	Hard Attack 5.9+ TR	42.	Astral Projection 5.7 R	
25.	Energy Vortex 5.9	34.	Wild Thing (aka	43.	Out of Body	
25a.	Alternate start 5.9		Creature Comfort) 5.9		Experience 5.8	
26.	Living in Sin 5.7 X	35.	Lego Land 5.9	44.	Out of Mind	
27.	Mr. Chips 5.9- R	36.	Hang Ten 5.7 R		Experience 5.9	
28.	Consenting Adults 5.10a	37.	Time Out 5.8			
29.	Ramp Route 5.6 R	38.	Crispy Critters 5.10a/b	**E.**	**Winger Wall**	
30.	In a Wrinkle 5.8+	39.	Tease 5.8	45.	Pringle's Prow 5.10a	
31.	Snail Trail 5.8+	40.	Nipple Flipper 5.10a/b	46.	Pringle's Crack 5.8	
32.	Creaturistic 5.11b					
		D.	**New Age Slab**			

201

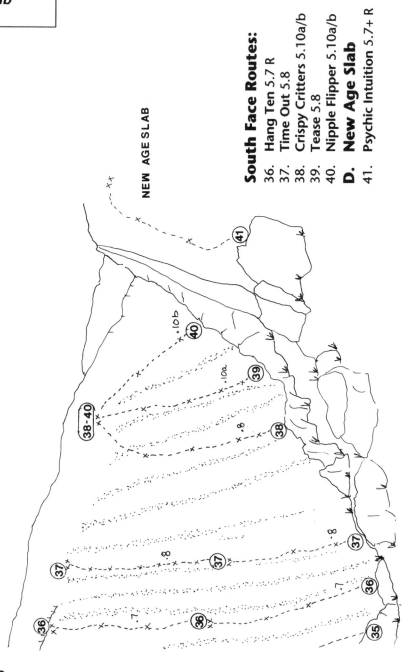

NEW AGE SLAB

South Face Routes:

36. Hang Ten 5.7 R
37. Time Out 5.8
38. Crispy Critters 5.10a/b
39. Tease 5.8
40. Nipple Flipper 5.10a/b
D. New Age Slab
41. Psychic Intuition 5.7+ R

E. Winger Wall

45. Pringle's Prow 5.10a
46. Pringle's Crack 5.8
47. My Evil Twin 5.7
48. I Need a Nurse 5.8
49. Raven 5.9

F. Mega Dome

50. Granite Rain 5.9+
51. Don't Bother 5.8+ R
52. Bongo Flake 5.10a

53. Unnamed 5.8
55. Left Hand of Darkness 5.10a
56. Project

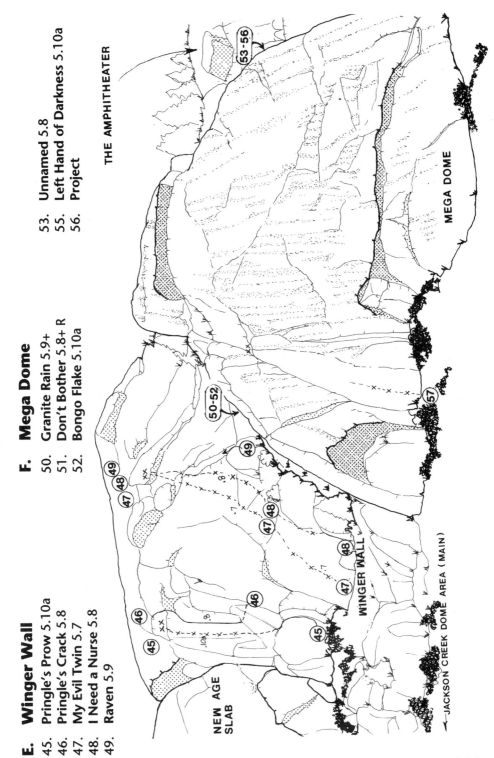

THE AMPHITHEATER

MEGA DOME

NEW AGE SLAB

WINGER WALL

— JACKSON CREEK DOME AREA (MAIN)

203

Jackson Creek:

Mega Dome

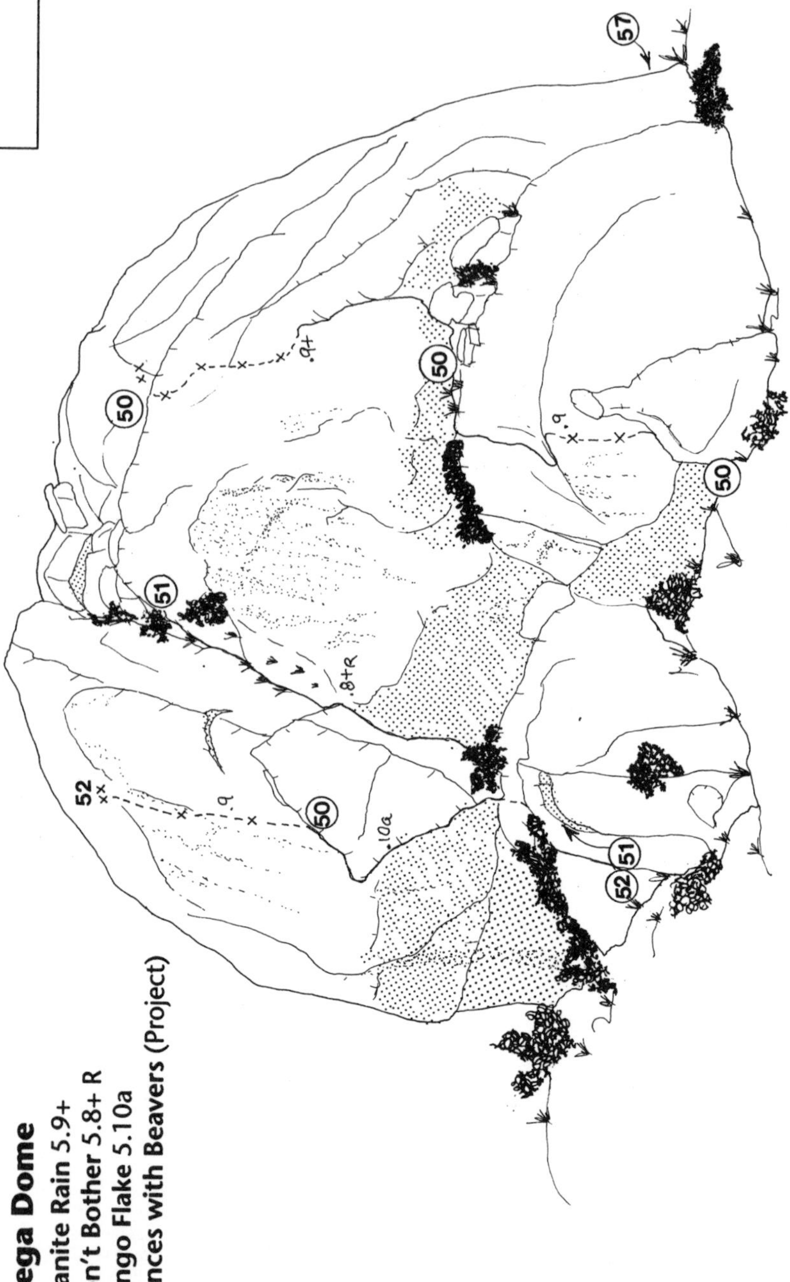

F. Mega Dome

50. Granite Rain 5.9+
51. Don't Bother 5.8+ R
52. Bongo Flake 5.10a
57. Dances with Beavers (Project)

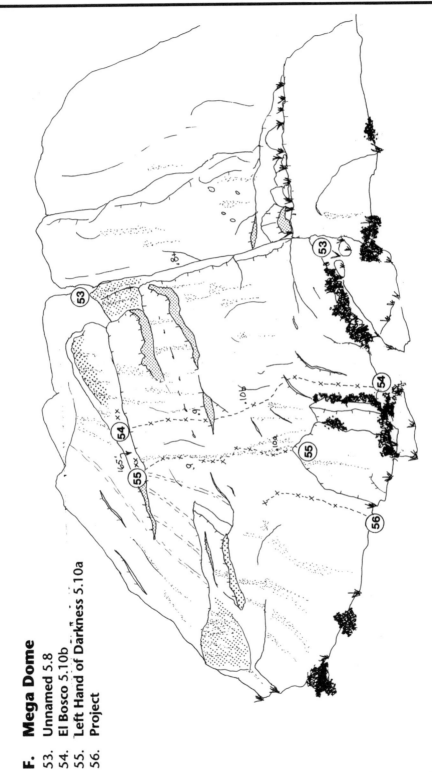

F. Mega Dome

53. **Unnamed 5.8**
54. **El Bosco 5.10b**
55. **Left Hand of Darkness 5.10a**
56. **Project**

G. The Amphitheater

58. Crystal Cruise 5.11a
59. Shadows on the Wall 5.8

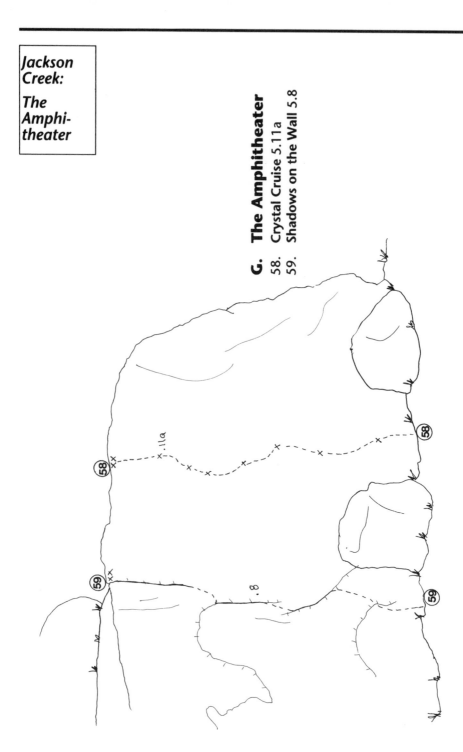

K. Split Rock: Upper Face routes

63. Accidental Tourist 5.9+
64. Bone Dome 5.9+
65. Come What May 5.9+
66. Project 5.9+ TR
67. Project 5.8 TR
68. Project 5.8+ TR
69. The Peter Dee 5.9

L. Lower Face routes

70. Que Pasa 5.6
71. The Stroll 5.8
72. Clown 5.8
73. Howler 5.9-

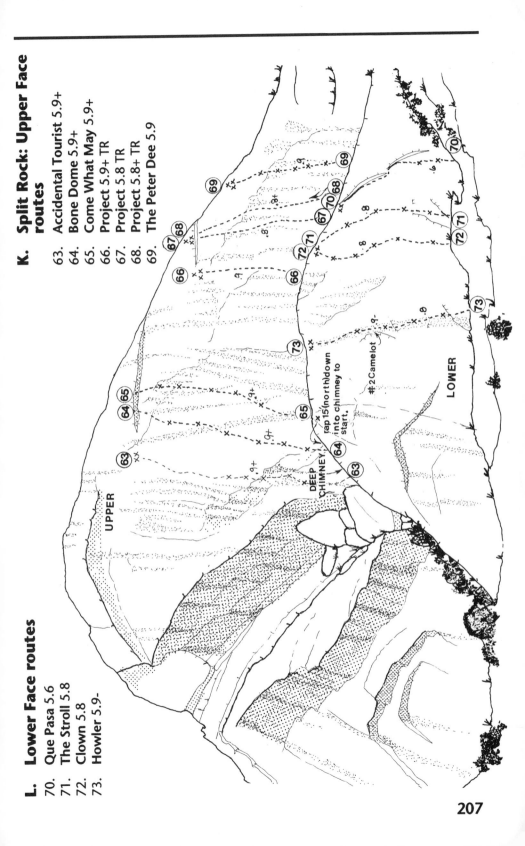

UPPER

LOWER

DEEP CHIMNEY

rap 15 (north) down into chimney to start.

#2 Camelot

207

Jackson Creek:

Flat Head Dome

M. Flat Head Dome

74. Project
75. Flat Foot 5.11a
76. Pl Patrol 5.10d

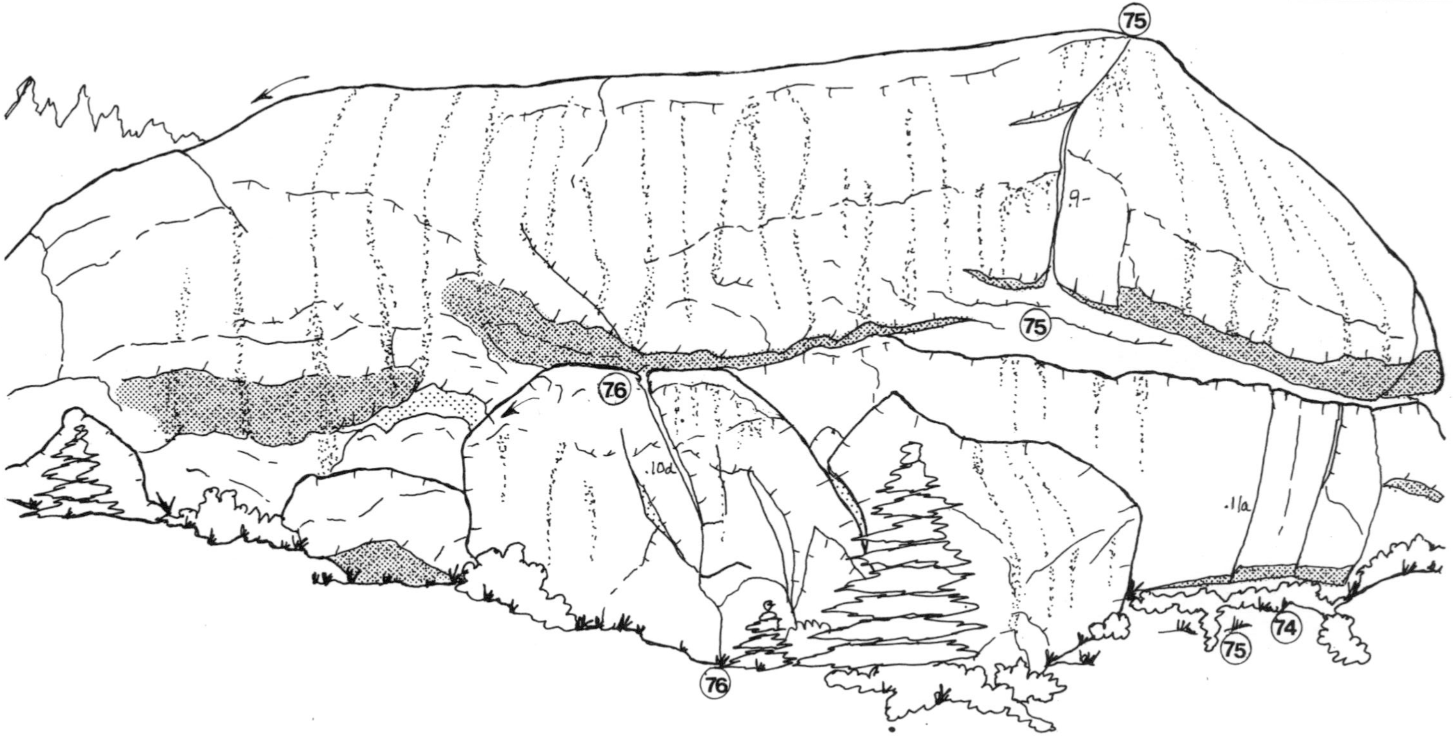

N. Taj Mahal: North Face routes

77. Finger of Destruction
    5.11a
78. Mind Games 5.9
79. Standing in a Slide Zone
    5.7
80. Pili Pili 5.9
81. Dotted Line 5.7 X
82. Chimneychanga 5.8+
83. Traverse Below the Roof
    5.7 R
84. Inside Taj Mahal 5.7
85. Genetic Impressions 5.5
    A2

86. Ouellette-Woodford Route
    (aka Northwest Face
    Friction Route 1957) 5.8
87. 1957 Route Variation

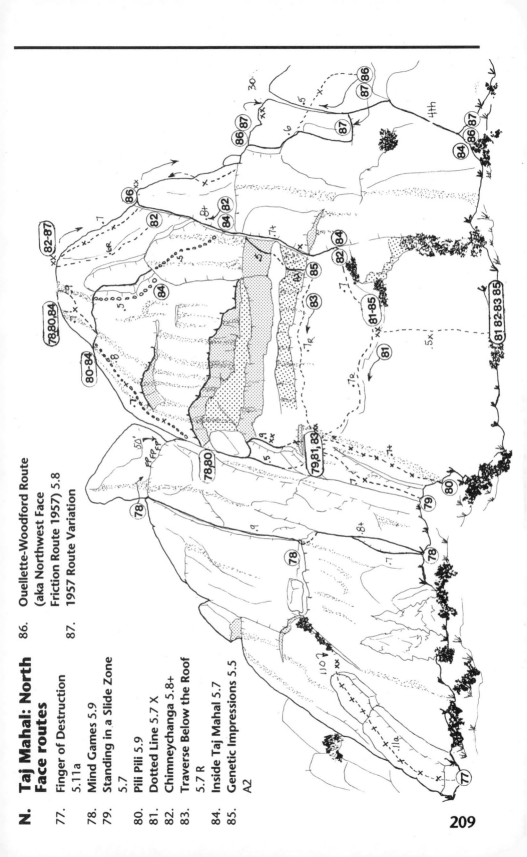

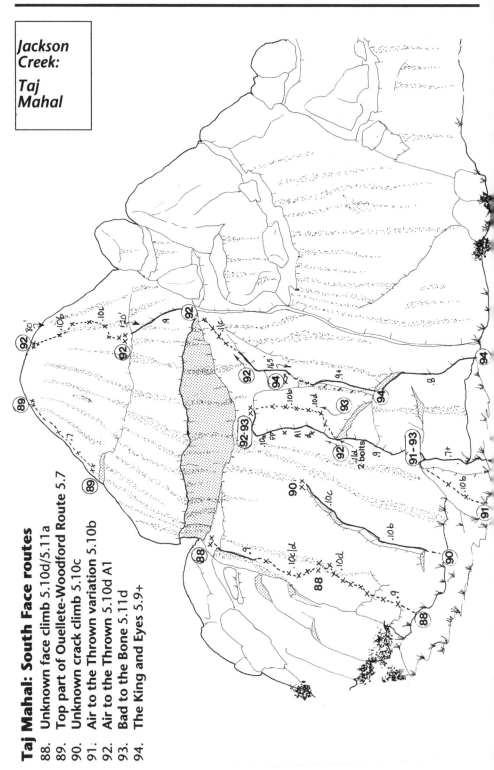

Taj Mahal: South Face routes

88. Unknown face climb 5.10d/5.11a
89. Top part of Ouellete-Woodford Route 5.7
90. Unknown crack climb 5.10c
91. Air to the Thrown variation 5.10b
92. Air to the Thrown 5.10d A1
93. Bad to the Bone 5.11d
94. The King and Eyes 5.9+

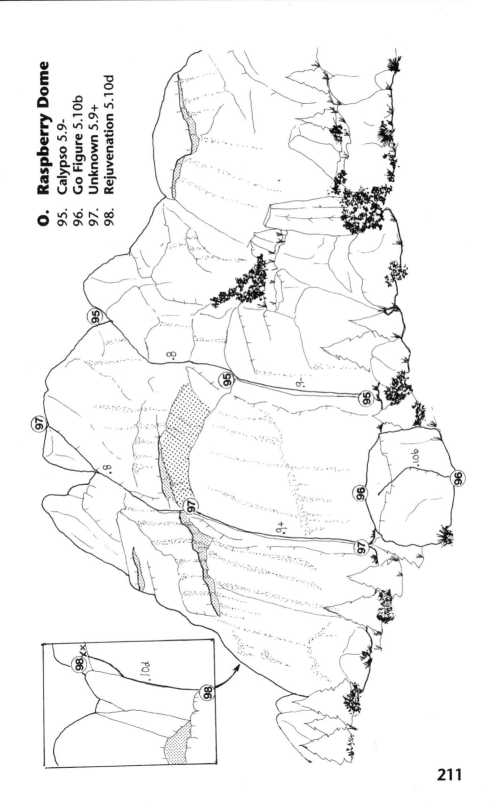

O. Raspberry Dome
95. Calypso 5.9-
96. Go Figure 5.10b
97. Unknown 5.9+
98. Rejuvenation 5.10d

211

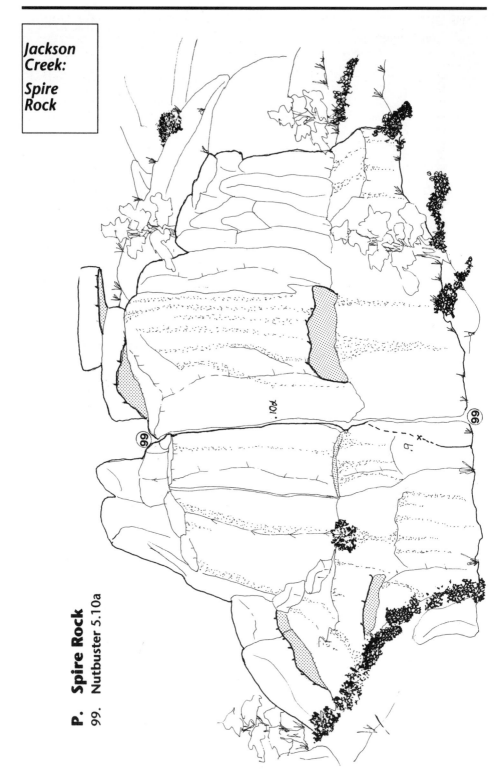

Jackson Creek:

Spire Rock

P. Spire Rock
99. Nutbuster 5.10a

212

Peter Hubbel, **Left Hand of Darkness** 5.10a, Jackson Creek Dome. Photo by Chris Roark.

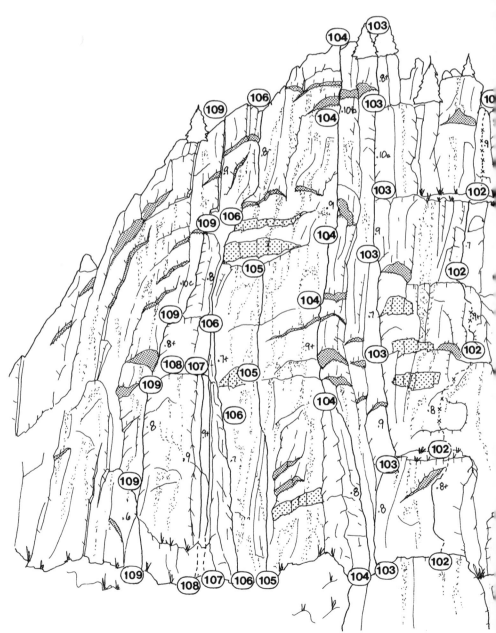

214

Q. Devil's Head

100. **Unknown** 5.9
101. **Unknown** 5.8
102. **Dariush of Balanat** 5.9+
103. **Satan's Satire** 5.10a
104. **Dance with the Devil** 5.10b
105. **Unknown** 5.10+ A2?
106. **Forrest-Van Meter Route** 5.7+/5.8-
107. **Baal** 5.9+
108. **Mark of the Devil** 5.9
109. **Bacarat** 5.10c

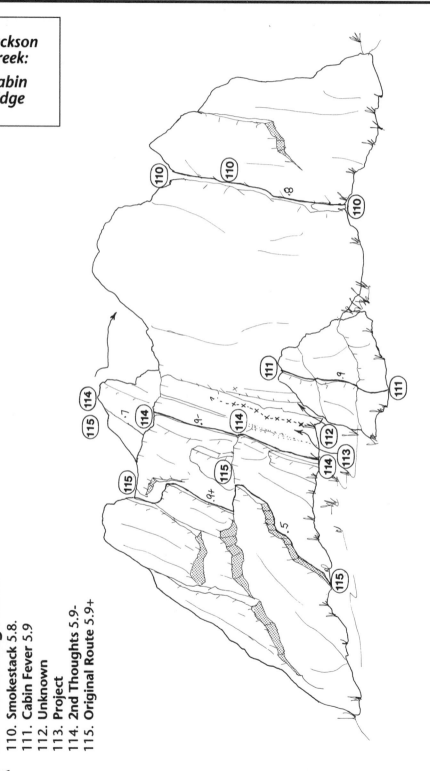

R. Cabin Ridge Rock
110. Smokestack 5.8.
111. Cabin Fever 5.9
112. Unknown
113. Project
114. 2nd Thoughts 5.9-
115. Original Route 5.9+

S. Devil's Head Campground Area

116. Constipation 5.8+
117. Colder than Hell 5.9 R
118. Happy Camper 5.7

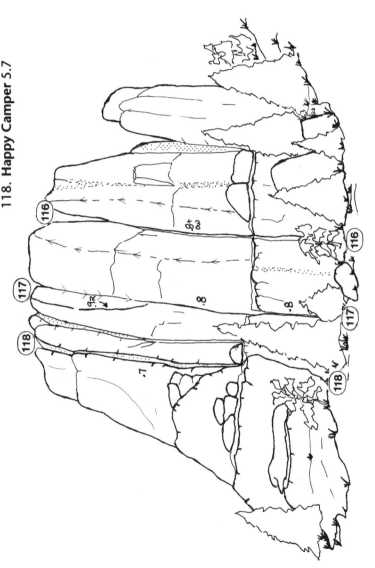

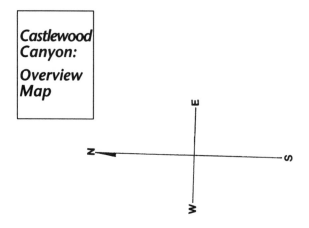

Castlewood Canyon:

Overview Map

E

N

S

W

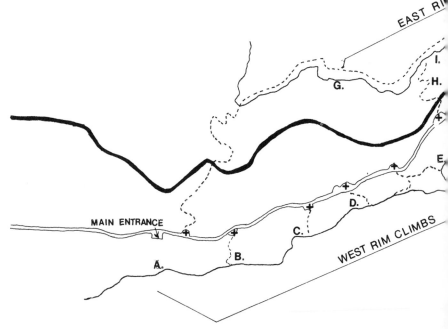

EAST RI

I.

H.

G.

E.

D.

MAIN ENTRANCE

C.

B.

A.

WEST RIM CLIMBS

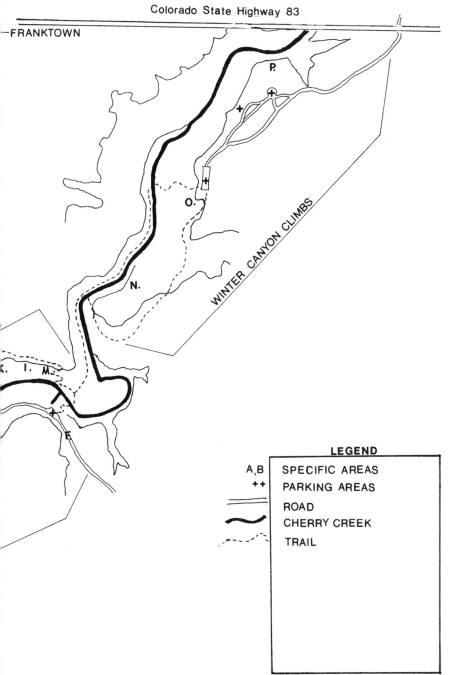

Colorado State Highway 83

—FRANKTOWN

P.

+

+

O.

WINTER CANYON CLIMBS

N.

K. I. M.

A.

F.

LEGEND

A,B | SPECIFIC AREAS
++ | PARKING AREAS
‗‗ | ROAD
〜 | CHERRY CREEK
⸌⸍ | TRAIL

Castlewood Canyon State Park

Castlewood Canyon State Park is the eastern most area covered in this guide. Located east of Castlerock and west of Franktown, Castlewood Canyon not only has a wealth of rock climbs of all difficulty levels, but also has some great ice climbs in the winter, making it Colorado's easternmost ice climbing area.

Many of the early climbs were done by the Colorado Mountain Club (CMC), which was introduced to the area by Dr. Fred Crowle. The original documentation of the climbs and area was the work of Larry Griffin. Alan Mosiman, Bill Coffin, Charlie Winger and friends started climbing here in the early 1970s and were responsible for most of the routes on Grocery Store Wall. Alan also published the first guidebook to the area in 1987.

Since then, Castlewood Canyon has seen an increase in the number of climbers and climbs. Most of the climbs can be attributed to: Steve and Sharon Holonitch, Jerry Harder, Judy Jacoby, Tim Hanson, Chris Drysdale, Tod Anderson, Dave Fortner, Uber Mike, Eric Leonard, Richard Wright and Alan Mosiman. Chris Drysdale put out the most recent guide in 1990 and Tim Hanson has a collection of nicely detailed, but non-published, topos that are up-to-date.

Directions

To get there from Colorado Springs, follow Highway 83 north to the southern Winter Canyon Entrance. From Denver, take I-25 south to the Castlerock/Franktown exit. Go left at the light which puts you on Wilcox, the main drag through Castlerock.Follow this for .4 mile to the light at the junction of 86 and Wilcox. Go left here towards Franktown for 5.9 miles to the Castlewood Canyon Road. Take this right for 2.2 miles to the park entrance. Please make sure to pay the $3.00 entrance fee – you will ticketed if you don't. Note: The Road is not maintained during winter – towing fees exceed $100.00.

Considerations

The rock of Castlewood Canyon is unique enough to merit its own name, Castlerock Conglomerate. The rock provides climbs that feature cracks, roofs, thin faces, pockets, corners and pebble pulling and offers about the same diversity as Clear Creek Canyon. The vertical faces are in the 30' to 50' range and host climbs that cover the span of climbing difficulty, from 5.3 to 5.13. Many of the climbs listed are unprotectable and exist as top-rope only climbs. These climbs are either obvious from the ground, follow blank faces with no bolts, or have no protection suggestions on the topos. When in doubt, just top rope it. Most of the newer, sport climbs are to be found on the eastern rim. These are primarily bolt protected climbs of a harder nature.

The rock lends itself to small camming gear placements. Even if you plan to do just bolted sport climbs, some small cams will be a welcome addition to your rack. Due to the coarse, rope-destroying nature of the rock (not to mention finger shredding), pad your ropes when you top rope a climb. It is also wise to bring some extra long slings or another rope to back up some of the single anchors that exist at the top of some of the older routes.

Some things to be aware of, especially during the summer months, are: prairie rattlers sunning themselves on the rocks, bees and wasps in certain areas, and mosquitoes. Bring some bug juice! Poison ivy may also be found at the base of some of the climbs.

There is now a bolting ban, the same that Eldorado Canyon has. Please respect this ban, use the toilet facilities, pick up any trash and help a little with trail maintenance where it's needed.

Castlewood Canyon: West Rim Climbs
A. Five and Dime Wall
1. BC Winger 5.8+   Pro: To 3".
2. Maneater 5.9-
3. Die Rottenwand 5.11b
4. Sheer Lat Attack 5.9+   Pro: To 12".
5. Ramper Room 5.6+   Pro: To 4".
6. Skin Flint 5.10c/d   Pro: To 2".
7. Why Ask Why? 5.11a/b
8. Barn Door 101 5.10a/b   Pro: To 3".
9. The Slide 5.5+
10. Camper van Beethoven B1/B2

B. Grocery Store Wall
11. Castor Oil Downclimb Class 4
12. Gorilla Milk Right Edge 5.7+
13. Gorilla Milk Direct 5.9-
14. Strawberry Jam 5.5   Pro: To 4".
15. Pit in the Sky 5.10c/d
16. Franktown Brewery 5.4
17. Pecan Pit 5.8-
18. Rainbow Bread 5.9+
19. Purdy's Prune 5.6

20. **Nut Practice** 5.4
21. **Mossy Mantle** Class 4
22. **Burnt Pizza** 5.6
23. **Short Ribs** 5.5
24. **Yukon Jack** 5.7
25. **Banana Flip** 5.6
26. **Banana Peel** 5.8
27. **Banana Split Chimney** 5.3
28. **From Russia with Love** 5.10a
29. **Banana Shake** 5.9
30. **Guacamole Face** 5.11a/b
31. **Teething Biscuit** 5.10a
31a. **Unknown** 5.10b?
32. **Bad Juju** 5.10b
33. **Snickers** 5.8+/5.9
34. **Palm Tickler** 5.7   Pro: To 3".
35. **Popcorn Fart** 5.10a
36. **Popcorn** 5.8
37. **Lollipop** 5.8+
38. **Lollipop Direct** 5.9
39. **Duck Soup** 5.8   Pro: To 3".
40. **Piece o' Cake** 5.6   Pro: To 3".
40a. **Bouldering Traverse** 5.9-
41. **BLT (Alternate start)** 5.8
42. **BLT** 5.9
43. **Chicken Choker** 5.9
44. **Starvation** 5.5   Pro: To 4".
45. **Up the Brown** 5.10c/d
46. **French Toast** 5.6
47. **Blood Pudding** 5.9+
48. **Caramel Corner Layback** 5.5   Pro: To 4".
49. **Caramel Corner** 5.5   Pro: To 4".
50. **Frosted Flakes** 5.10b
50a. **Sundance** 5.10b/c
51. **Raindance** 5.9
52. **Raindance Crack** 5.10b
53. **Bozo No No** 5.11a
54. **Unnamed** 5.11c/d
55. **Gatoraide** 5.11c/d or 5.13a
56. **Licorice Stick** 5.7+   Pro: To 4".
57. **You Name It** 5.12c/d
58. **Pretzel Logic** 5.11b
59. **Vanilla Fudge** 5.9
60. **Rat's Nest Right** 5.7
61. **Rat's Nest Left** 5.8
62. **Tortilla Flats** 5.9
63. **What's Homogenized?** 5.11b/c

64. **Peppermint Patty** 5.10c/d
65. **Zucchini** 5.4
66. **Peaches and Scream** 5.5
67. **Rocky Mountain Barking Saber-Tooth Tiger** 5.8
68. **Fudge Face** 5.10b/c
69. **Fudge Farce** 5.11b   Climbs face of dihedral.
70. **Hot Fudge Direct** 5.9   Pro: To 4".
71. **Donut Hole** 5.12a or 5.11b
72. **Hot Fudge** 5.8+   Pro: To 4".
73. **Petrified Turd** 5.8   Pro: To 3".
74. **Shake and Bake** 5.11b
75. **Cactus Flower Upper** 5.10b
76. **Cactus Flower Lower** 5.9
77. **Hamburger** 5.10b
78. **Hamburger Helper** 5.10b
79. **Hot Tuna (aka Tuna Helper)** 5.9+/5.10a
80. **Short Cake** Class 4
81. **Crystal Lyte** 5.10b
82. **Crystal Lyte** (Alternate start) 5.6
83. **Bone Eater** 5.2

C. Neanderthal Wall

84. **Up the Red** 5.10c/d
85. **Wall of Webs** 5.10b
86. **Cro-Mag Crack** 5.10d
87. **The Squeeze** 5.11c   Pro: To 6".
88. **Chicken Wing Crack** 5.10c   Pro: To 6".
89. **Unnamed** 5.12d/5.13a
90. **The Fingers Have It** 5.7+   Pro: To 3".
91. **Pack the Walls** 5.5   Pro: To 4".
92. **Where's the Jam?** 5.11c
93. **Are You Experienced?** 5.5+   Pro: To 5".
94. **Adajam** 5.5+   Pro: To 6".
95. **Corner Crack** 5.10a
96. **The Sneeze** 5.10b
97. **Rufus** 5.8
98. **Landlubber** 5.10d
99. **Cheater Five** 5.11b
100. **The Grind** 5.11c
101. **The Way Out** 5.7+   Pro: To 3".
102. **The Way In** 5.8   Pro: To 4".
103. **The Umph** 5.7+   Pro: To 4".
104. **Primal Jam** 5.11c   Pro: To 3".
105. **The Mosh** 5.9   Pro: To 3".
106. **The Mosh Variation** 5.8+   Pro: To 4".
107. **The Rock Rat** 5.11a
108. **Bad Case of Hives** 5.10a
109. **Left Corner** 5.10a

D. The Cave Wall

110. Hourglass Flake 5.11b   Pro: To 2".
· 111. Time Passages 5.10c/d   Pro: To 2".
112. The Good, The Bad and The Dirty 5.10d   Pro: To 4".
113. Snowden's Intro 5.8+   Pro: To 4".

E. Porky's Wall

114. Porky's Revenge 5.7+   Pro: To 10".
115. Pinch Crack 5.10c/d
116. Hand Pain 5.8-   Pro: To 3".

F. Alien Tuna Area

117. Alien Tuna 5.10a   Project, not shown. Located west of sign. Steep red face with roof, no anchors.

Center Area Climbs
H. North Sentry

1N. B2 Traverse
2N. Fingers 5.11a/c   Pro: To 1.5".

South Sentry

1S. Cracker Pox 5.6   Pro: To 3".
2S. Why Bother 5.9-

The Buoux Block

1B. Lazy Daze 5.4
2B. New Crack on the Block 5.6
3B. Bridge of Sighs 5.9
4B. Confederate 5.13a
5B. Unknown 5.12c
6B. Bop Till You Drop 5.11c/d

East Rim Walls
G. Dungeon Area

1. Unnamed 5.9/5.10   Stem or face.
2. Unnamed 5.10a/b
3. Unnamed 5.11a
4. Unnamed 5.10a
5. Unnamed 5.9+   Shares same anchors with #4.

I. Falls Wall

6. Gonzo 5.11d
7. Swinging Sirloin 5.11c
8. Lichen Rain 5.7   Pro: To 4".
9. Out of Arms Reach 5.10b
10. Tendon Terror 5.12b/c
11. Arborist Arms 5.11b/c
12. Building Bottrell 5.11b
13. Bitch 5.10a/b   Pro: To 6".
14. Steam Rock Fever 5.8-   Pro: To 3".
15. The Fat Raisin Sings 5.11b
16. Not Long for This World 5.10c   Pro: To 2".

17. **Internal Affairs** 5.11b
18. **It's Flaky** 5.7   Pro: To 2".
19. **Chimney Sweep** 5.5   Pro: To 4".
20. **Ledge Out** 5.5   Pro: To 4".
21. **Elliot and the Flying Tsetse** 5.10b/c
22. **Flaming Fingers Traverse** B2
23. **Unnamed** 5.11a
24. **Blue Event Horizon** 5.12b/c
25. **Blackout** 5.12d   Pro: To 3".
26. **Lactic Tactics** 5.10d   Pro: To 3".
27. **Downclimb Area**

J. Project X Wall
28. **Rest in Pieces** 5.9+
29. **Nuclear Blue** 5.11a or 5.11c
30. **Project X** 5.12a/b
31. **Radiation Control Area** 5.12b/c
32. **Stemasaurus** 5.12b/c
33. **Unnamed** 5.10a

K. Hedgeclipper Area
34. **Beta Slave** 5.10b/c
35. **Patrick Hedgeclipper** 5.11b
36. **Entry Level** 5.8+
37. **Heavy Duty Judy** 5.10c
38. **Radiation Fear** 5.11a
39. **First Dibs** 5.10d
40. **Dope on a Rope** 5.10a   Pro: To 3".
41. **Bolted by Committee** 5.12a
42. **Pebble Beach** 5.11d
43. **Unnamed** 5.10a/b
44. **Downclimb Area**

L. Hanson's Wall
45. **Unnamed** 5.10d/5.11a
46. **Unnamed** 5.11a/b
47. **Unnamed** 5.11a
48. **Unnamed** 5.11a/b
49. **Project** 5.12a

M. Vulture Wall
50. **Vulture Culture** 5.7+   Pro: To 3".
51. **Vulture Club** 5.8   Pro: To 3".
52. **The Reaper** 5.11b
53. **Pay Homage** 5.12b
54. **Unnamed** 5.11b
55. **A Step in Time** 5.8+   Pro: To 1.5".
56. **Lightning Strikes** 5.10b   Pro: To 1.5".
57. **Unnamed** 5.10c/d
58. **Downclimb Area**

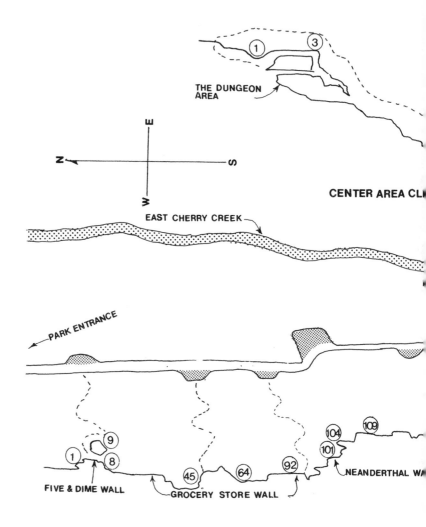

THE DUNGEON
AREA

CENTER AREA CL

EAST CHERRY CREEK

PARK ENTRANCE

FIVE & DIME WALL

GROCERY STORE WALL

NEANDERTHAL W

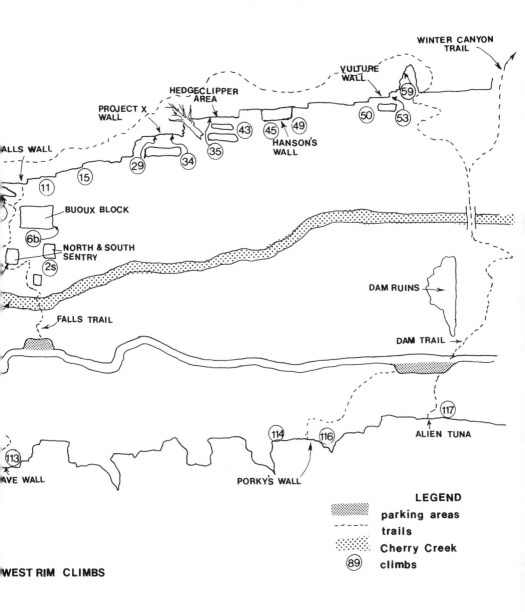

LEGEND

parking areas

trails

Cherry Creek

⑧⑨ climbs

WEST RIM CLIMBS

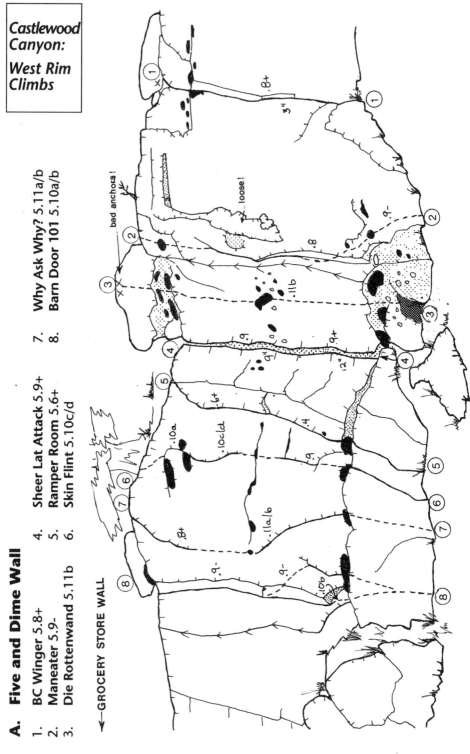

Castlewood Canyon:

West Rim Climbs

A. Five and Dime Wall

1.	BC Winger 5.8+	4.	Sheer Lat Attack 5.9+
2.	Maneater 5.9-	5.	Ramper Room 5.6+
3.	Die Rottenwand 5.11b	6.	Skin Flint 5.10c/d
		7.	Why Ask Why? 5.11a/b
		8.	Barn Door 101 5.10a/b

← GROCERY STORE WALL

228

A. Five and Dime Wall

8. Barn Door 101 5.10a/b
9. The Slide 5.5+
10. Camper van Beethoven B1/B2

B. Grocery Store Wall

11. Castor Oil Downclimb Class 4
12. Gorilla Milk Right Edge 5.7+
13. Gorilla Milk Direct 5.9-

14. Strawberry Jam 5.5
15. Pit in the Sky 5.10c/d
16. Franktown Brewery 5.4
17. Pecan Pit 5.8-
18. Rainbow Bread 5.9+

19. Purdy's Prune 5.6
20. Nut Practice 5.4
21. Mossy Mantle Class 4
22. Burnt Pizza 5.6

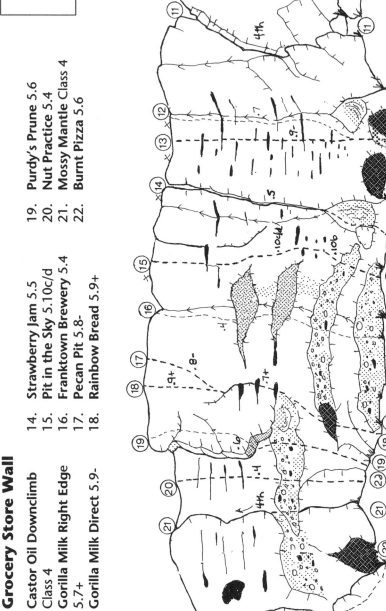

FIVE AND DIME WALL →

230

B. Grocery Store Wall

22. Burnt Pizza 5.6
23. Short Ribs 5.5
24. Yukon Jack 5.7
25. Banana Flip 5.6
26. Banana Peel 5.8

27. Banana Split Chimney 5.3
28. From Russia with Love 5.10a
29. Banana Shake 5.9
30. Guacamole Face 5.11a/b
31. Teething Biscuit 5.10a

31a. Unknown 5.10b?
32. Bad Juju 5.10b
33. Snickers 5.8+/5.9
34. Palm Tickler 5.7

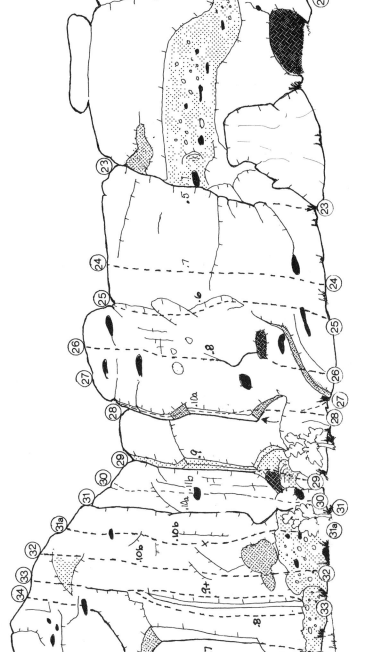

231

B.   Grocery Store Wall

34.   Palm Tickler 5.7
35.   Popcorn Fart 5.10a
36.   Popcorn 5.8
37.   Lollipop 5.8+
38.   Lollipop Direct 5.9
39.   Duck Soup 5.8

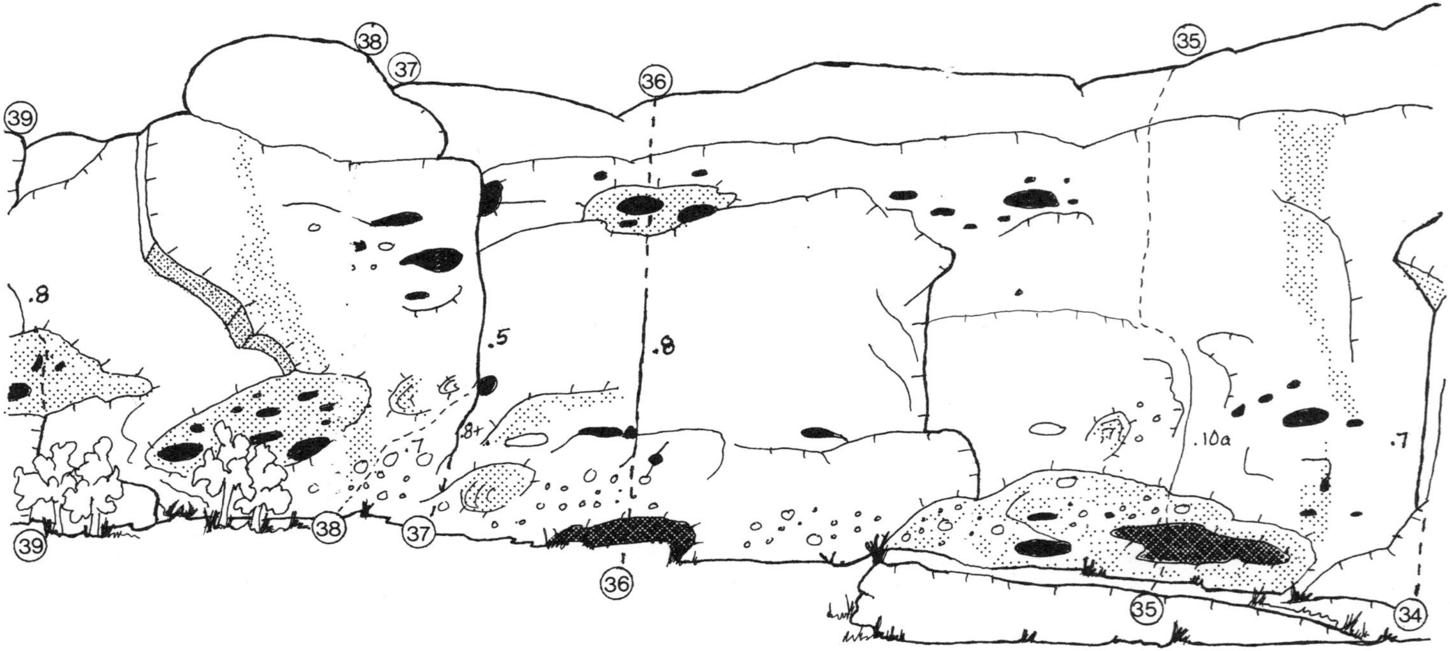

B. Grocery Store Wall

39. Duck Soup 5.8
40. Piece o' Cake 5.6
40a. Bouldering Traverse 5.9-
41. BLT (Alternate start) 5.8

42. BLT 5.9
43. Chicken Choker 5.9
44. Starvation 5.5

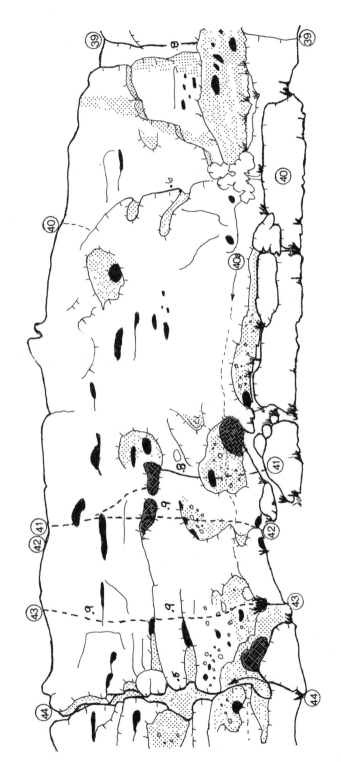

233

Castlewood
Canyon:

*West Rim
Climbs*

B. Grocery Store Wall

44. Starvation 5.5
45. Up the Brown 5.10c/d
46. French Toast 5.6
47. Blood Pudding 5.9+
48. Caramel Corner Layback 5.5

49. Caramel Corner 5.5
50. Frosted Flakes 5.10b
50a. Sundance 5.10b/c
51. Raindance 5.9

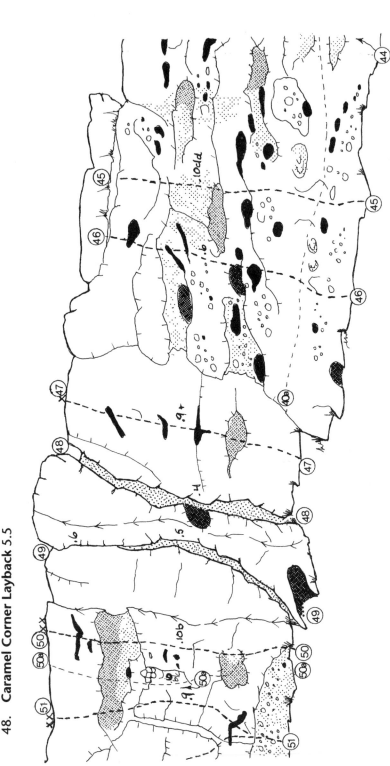

B. Grocery Store Wall

51. Raindance 5.9
52. Raindance Crack 5.10b
53. Bozo No No 5.11a
54. Unnamed 5.11c/d

55. Gatoraide 5.11c/d or 5.13a
56. Licorice Stick 5.7+
57. You Name It 5.12c/d
58. Pretzel Logic 5.11b

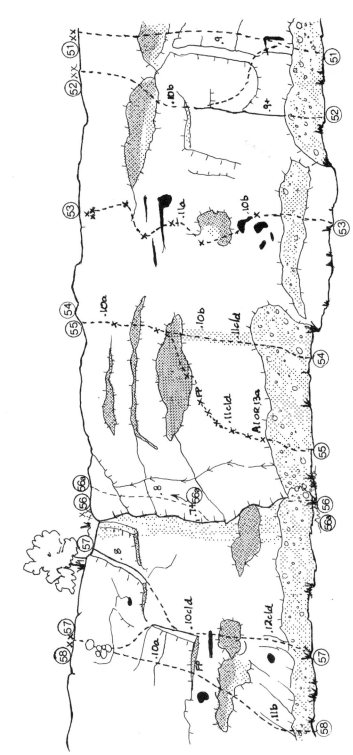

235

B.   Grocery Store Wall

58. Pretzel Logic 5.11b
59. Vanilla Fudge 5.9
60. Rat's Nest Right 5.7
61. Rat's Nest Left 5.8
62. Tortilla Flats 5.9
63. What's Homogenized?
     5.11b/c
64. Peppermint Patty 5.10c/d

65. Zucchini 5.4
66. Peaches and Scream 5.5
67. Rocky Mountain Barking
     Saber-Tooth Tiger 5.8
68. Fudge Face 5.10b/c
69. Fudge Farce 5.11b
70. Hot Fudge Direct 5.9
71. Donut Hole 5.12a, 5.11b

72. Hot Fudge 5.8+
73. Petrified Turd 5.8
74. Shake and Bake 5.11b
75. Cactus Flower Upper
     5.10b
76. Cactus Flower Lower 5.9
77. Hamburger 5.10b

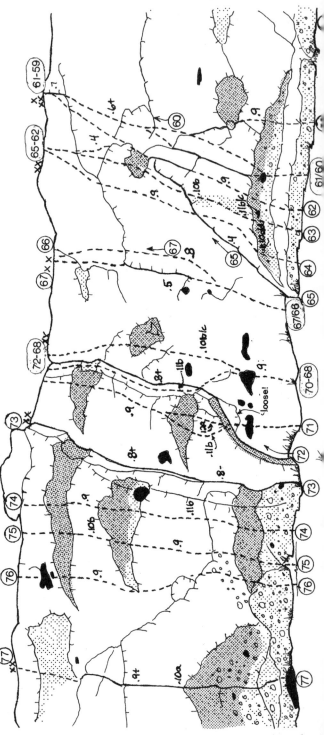

B. Grocery Store Wall

77. Hamburger 5.10b
78. Hamburger Helper 5.10b
79. Hot Tuna (aka Tuna Helper) 5.9+/5.10a
80. Short Cake Class 4
81. Crystal Lyte 5.10b
82. Crystal Lyte (Alternate start) 5.6
83. Bone Eater 5.2

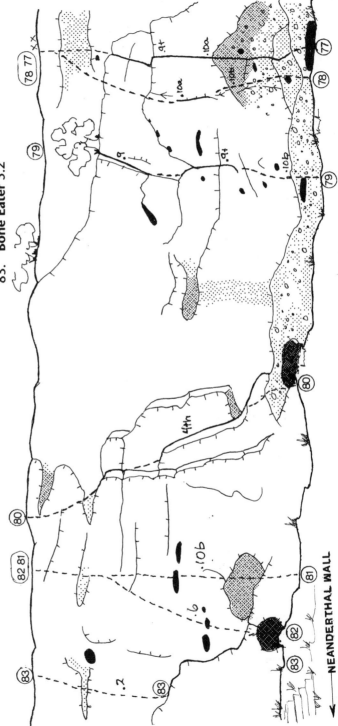

237

B. Grocery Store Wall

83. Bone Eater 5.2

C. Neanderthal Wall

84. Up the Red 5.10c/d
85. Wall of Webs 5.10b
86. Cro-Mag Crack 5.10d
87. The Squeeze 5.11c

88. Chicken Wing Crack 5.10c
89. Unnamed 5.12d/5.13a
90. The Fingers Have It 5.7+

Castlewood
Canyon:

*West Rim
Climbs*

GROCERY STORE WALL →

C. Neanderthal Wall

89. Unnamed 5.12d/5.13a
90. The Fingers Have It 5.7+
91. Pack the Walls 5.5
92. Where's the Jam? 5.11c
93. Are You Experienced? 5.5+

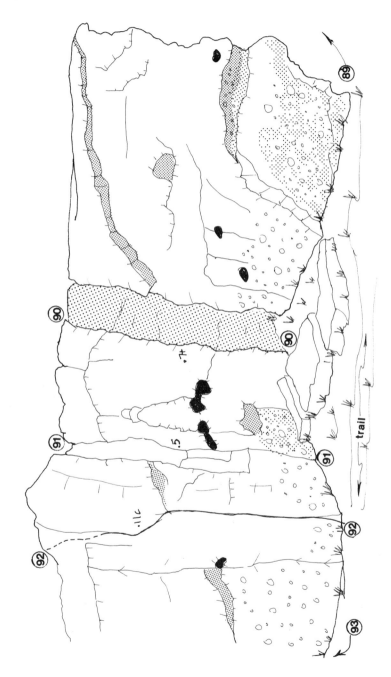

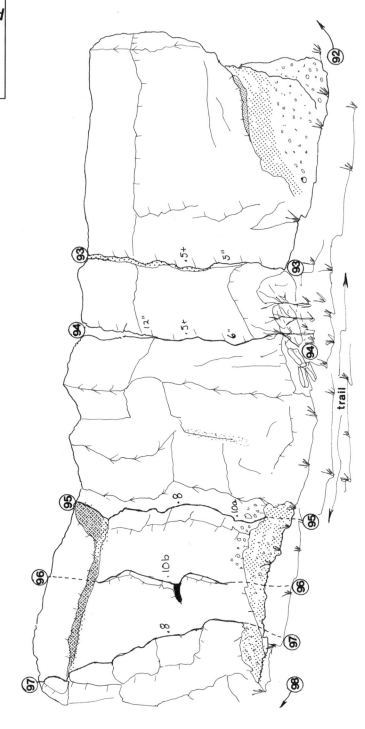

Castlewood
Canyon:

West Rim
Climbs

C. Neanderthal Wall

92. Where's the Jam? 5.11c
93. Are You Experienced? 5.5+
94. Adajam 5.5+

95. Corner Crack 5.10a
96. The Sneeze 5.10b
97. Rufus 5.8

C. Neanderthal Wall

97. **Rufus** 5.8
98. **Landlubber** 5.10d
99. **Cheater Five** 5.11b
100. **The Grind** 5.11c
101. **The Way Out** 5.7+

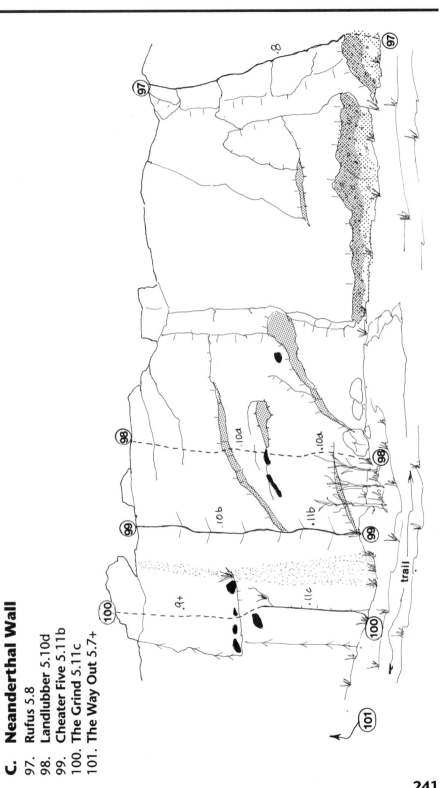

Castlewood Canyon:

West Rim Climbs

C. Neanderthal Wall

100. The Grind 5.11c
101. The Way Out 5.7+
102. The Way In 5.8
103. The Umph 5.7+

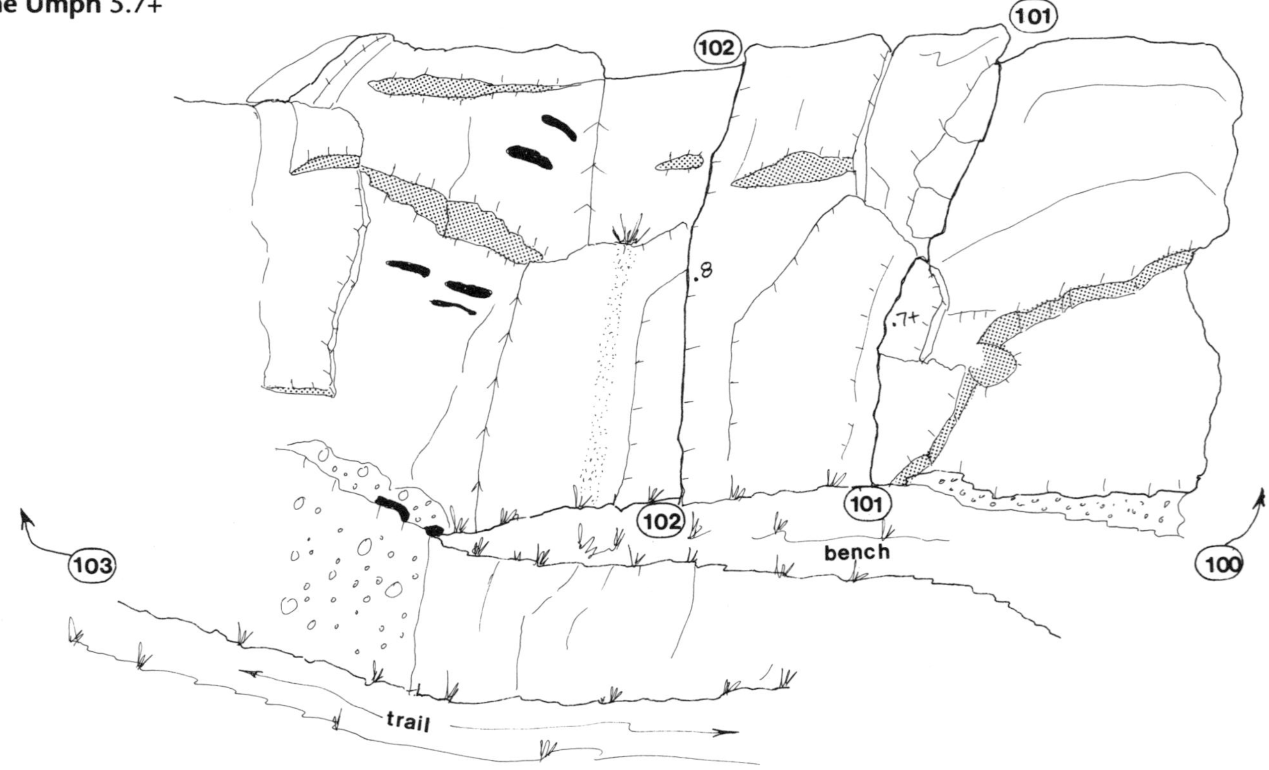

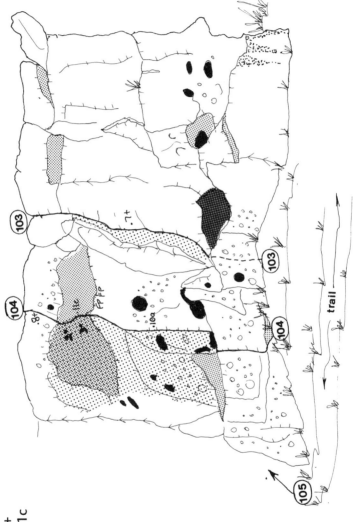

C. Neanderthal Wall
103. The Umph 5.7+
104. Primal Jam 5.11c
105. The Mosh 5.9

C. Neanderthal Wall
104. Primal Jam 5.11c
105. The Mosh 5.9
106. The Mosh Variation 5.8+
107. The Rock Rat 5.11a

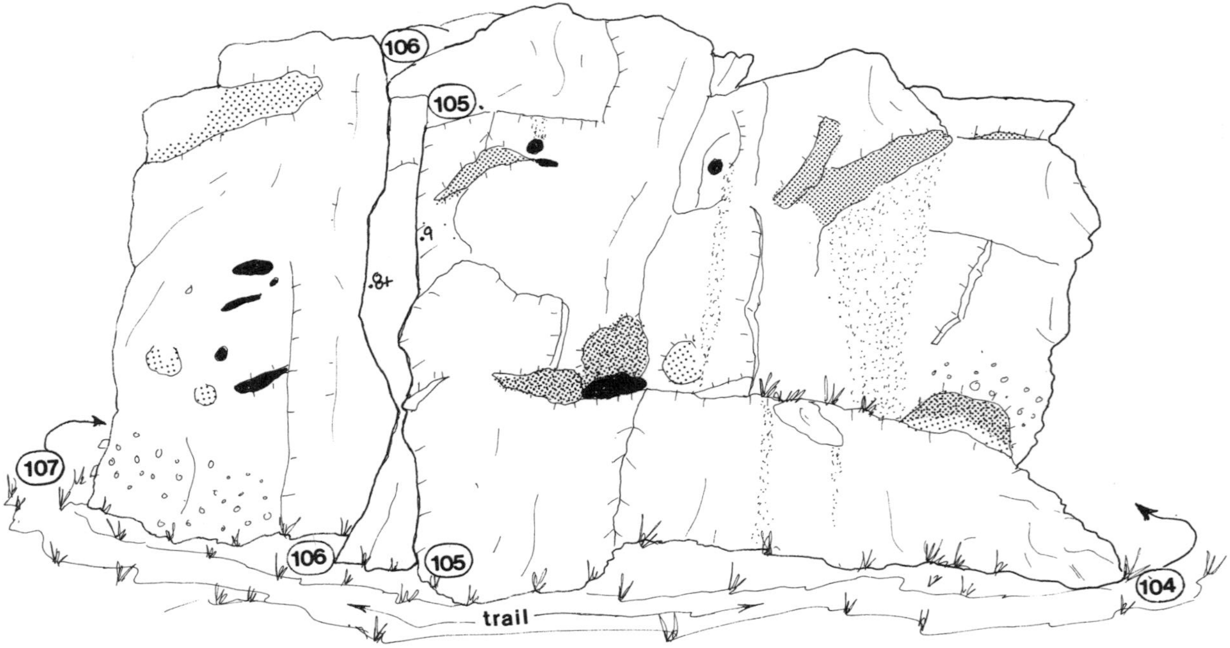

244

C. Neanderthal Wall

106. The Mosh Variation 5.8+
107. The Rock Rat 5.11a
108. Bad Case of Hives 5.10a
109. Left Corner 5.10a

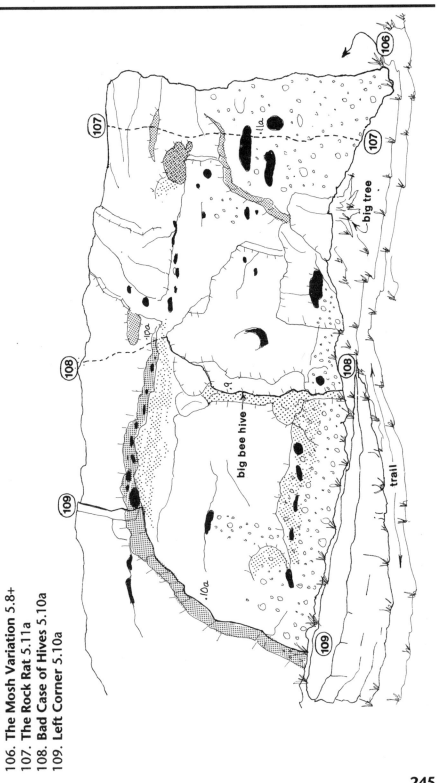

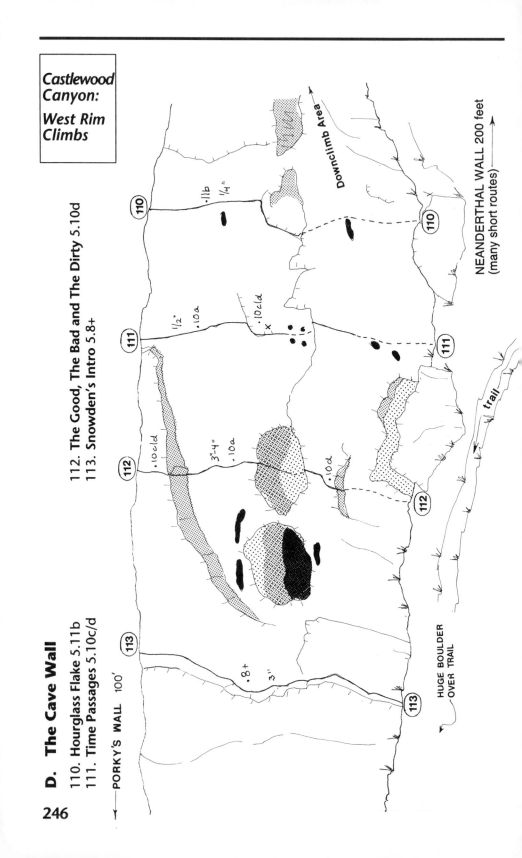

Castlewood
Canyon:

*West Rim
Climbs*

D. The Cave Wall

110. Hourglass Flake 5.11b
111. Time Passages 5.10c/d

112. **The Good, The Bad and The Dirty 5.10d**
113. Snowden's Intro 5.8+

← PORKY'S WALL 100'

NEANDERTHAL WALL 200 feet →
(many short routes)

HUGE BOULDER
OVER TRAIL

Downclimb Area

trail

.11b
¼"

½"
.10a
.10c/d
×

.10c/d
3"–4"
.10a
.10d

.8+
3"

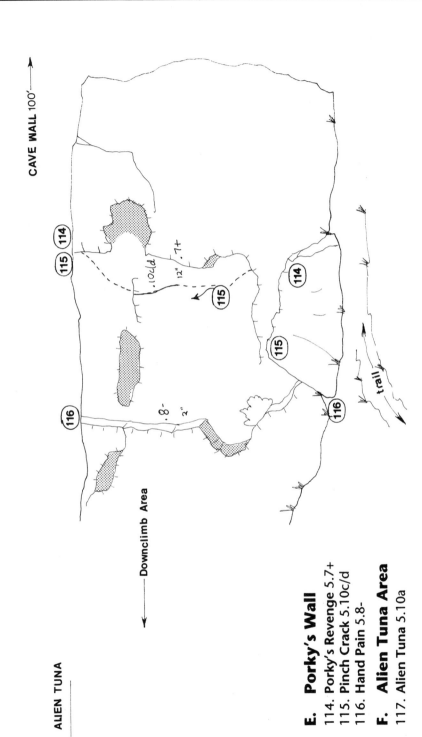

E. Porky's Wall

114. Porky's Revenge 5.7+
115. Pinch Crack 5.10c/d
116. Hand Pain 5.8-

F. Alien Tuna Area

117. Alien Tuna 5.10a

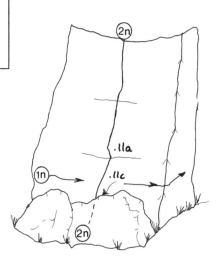

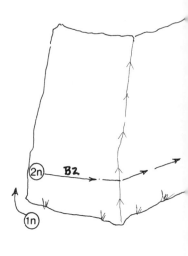

H. North Sentry

1N. B2 Traverse
2N. Fingers 5.11a/c

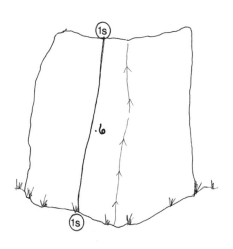

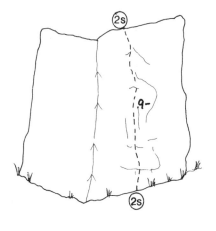

South Sentry

1S. Cracker Pox 5.6
2S. Why Bother 5.9-

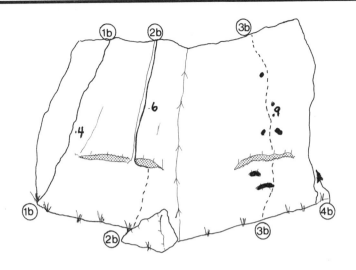

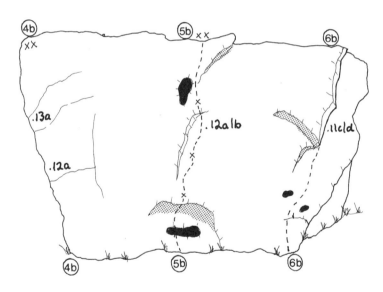

The Buoux Block

1B. **Lazy Daze** 5.4
2B. **New Crack on the Block** 5.6
3B. **Bridge of Sighs** 5.9
4B. **Confederate** 5.13a
5B. **Unknown** 5.12c
6B. **Bop 'till You Drop** 5.11c/d

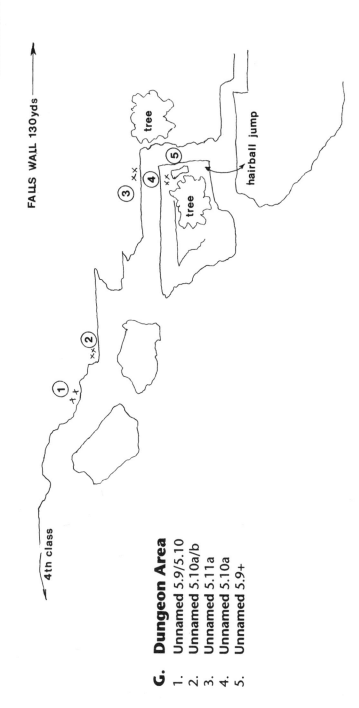

Castlewood Canyon: East Rim Climbs

FALLS WALL 130yds →

4th class

tree

tree

hairball jump

G. Dungeon Area

1. Unnamed 5.9/5.10
2. Unnamed 5.10a/b
3. Unnamed 5.11a
4. Unnamed 5.10a
5. Unnamed 5.9+

250

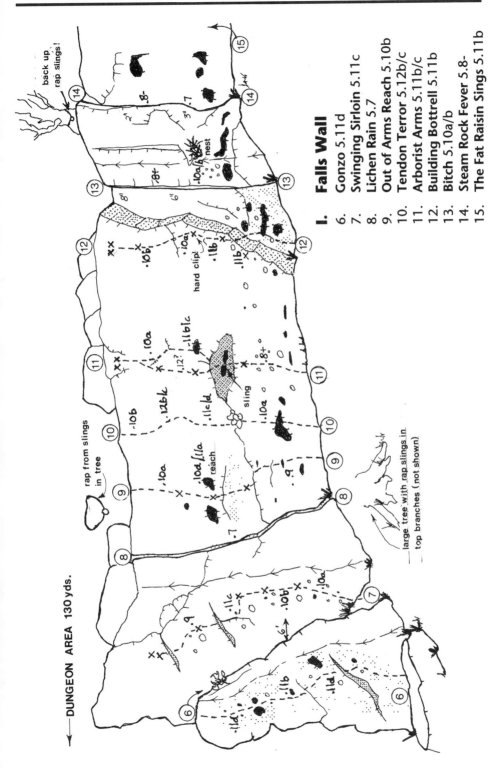

I. Falls Wall

6. Gonzo 5.11d
7. Swinging Sirloin 5.11c
8. Lichen Rain 5.7
9. Out of Arms Reach 5.10b
10. Tendon Terror 5.12b/c
11. Arborist Arms 5.11b/c
12. Building Bottrell 5.11b
13. Bitch 5.10a/b
14. Steam Rock Fever 5.8-
15. The Fat Raisin Sings 5.11b

DUNGEON AREA 130 yds.

back up rap slings!

nest

rap from slings in tree

large tree with rap slings in top branches (not shown)

hard clip!

sling

reach

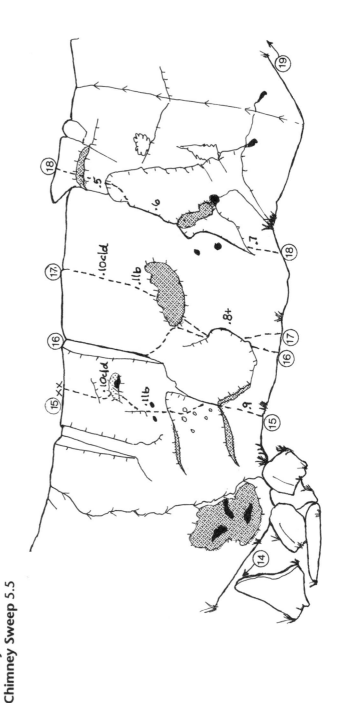

I.   Falls Wall

14.   Steam Rock Fever 5.8-
15.   The Fat Raisin Sings 5.11b
16.   Not Long for This World 5.10c
17.   Internal Affairs 5.11b
18.   It's Flaky 5.7
19.   Chimney Sweep 5.5

252

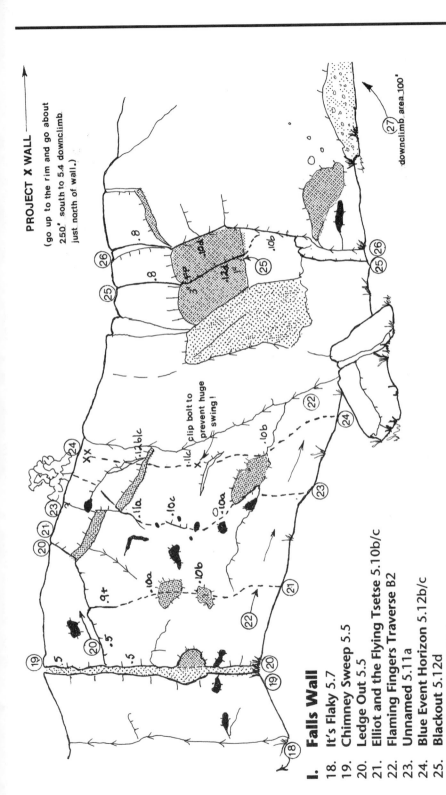

PROJECT X WALL →

(go up to the rim and go about 250' south to 5.4 downclimb just north of wall.)

I. Falls Wall

18. It's Flaky 5.7
19. Chimney Sweep 5.5
20. Ledge Out 5.5
21. Elliot and the Flying Tsetse 5.10b/c
22. Flaming Fingers Traverse B2
23. Unnamed 5.11a
24. Blue Event Horizon 5.12b/c
25. Blackout 5.12d
26. Lactic Tactics 5.10d
27. Downclimb Area

253

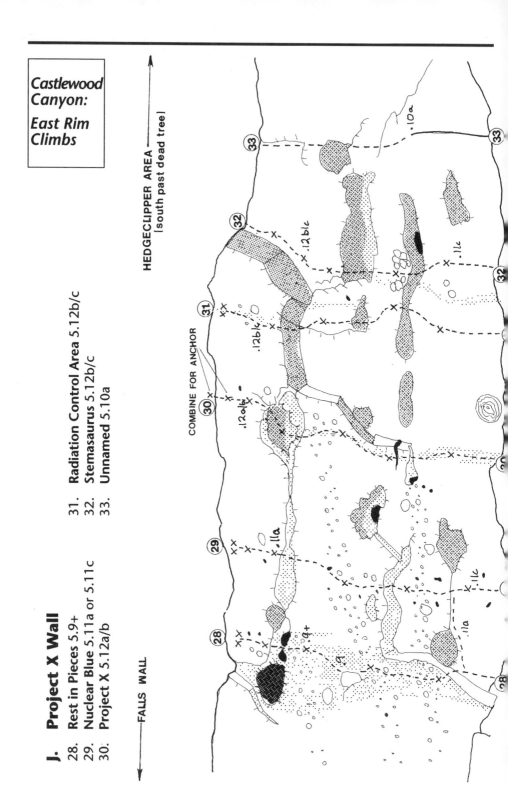

J. Project X Wall

28. Rest in Pieces 5.9+
29. Nuclear Blue 5.11a or 5.11c
30. Project X 5.12a/b

31. Radiation Control Area 5.12b/c
32. Stemasaurus 5.12b/c
33. Unnamed 5.10a

Castlewood Canyon:

East Rim Climbs

HEDGECLIPPER AREA
[south past dead tree]

COMBINE FOR ANCHOR

FALLS WALL

K. Hedgeclipper Area

34. Beta Slave 5.10b/c
35. Patrick Hedgeclipper 5.11b
36. Entry Level 5.8+
37. Heavy Duty Judy 5.10c
38. Radiation Fear 5.11a
39. First Dibs 5.10d

40. Dope on a Rope 5.10a
41. Bolted by Committee 5.12a

—— PROJECT X WALL

255

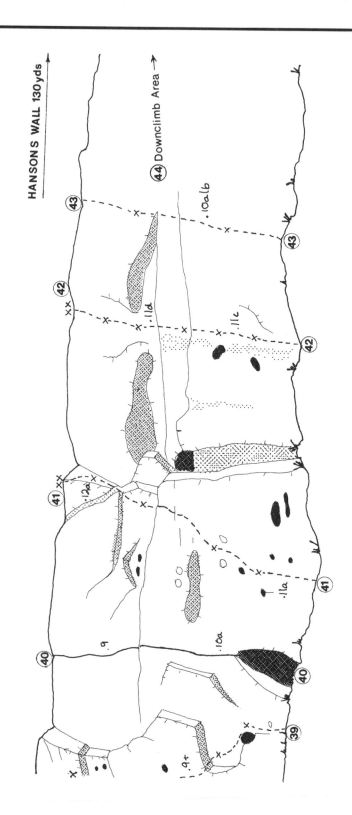

K. Hedgeclipper Area

39. First Dibs 5.10d
40. Dope on a Rope 5.10a
41. Bolted by Committee 5.12a

42. Pebble Beach 5.11d
43. Unnamed 5.10a/b
44. Downclimb Area

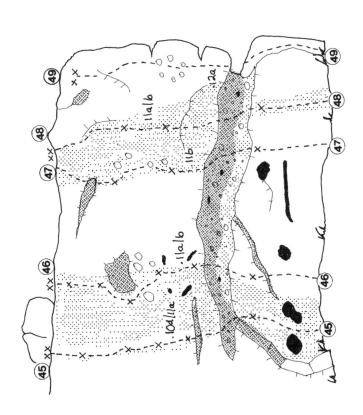

L. Hanson's Wall

45. Unnamed 5.10d/5.11a
46. Unnamed 5.11a/b
47. Unnamed 5.11a
48. Unnamed 5.11a/b
49. Project 5.12a

VUITURE WALL →

← HEDGECLIPPER AREA 130 yds

Castlewood Canyon:

East Rim Climbs

Hang long sling off anchors before leading!

.11b

.10b

.12b

.12a

.11b

nest

loose

.7

.7

.7+

← HANSON'S WALL

M. Vulture Wall

50. Vulture Culture 5.7+
51. Vulture Club 5.8
52. The Reaper 5.11b
53. Pay Homage 5.12b
54. Unnamed 5.11b
55. A Step in Time 5.8+

M. Vulture Wall

54. Unnamed 5.11b
55. A Step in Time 5.8+
56. Lightning Strikes 5.10b
57. Unnamed 5.10c/d

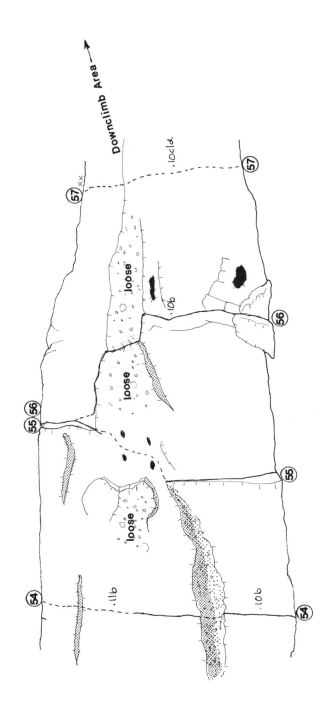

Ice Climbs:
N. The Ice Garden

1. **The Incisor**   35', WI3+   Exposed to sun.
2. **Tears for Fears**   45', WI3+   Exposed to sun.
3. **I'm Not Worthy**   35', WI2, 5.2   Dihedral to short chimney.
4. **Smear Tactics**   35', Class 3
5. **?**
6. **Vertebral Column**   35', WI2+, 5.2   Pillar to short chimney.
7. **Practice Gully**   35', Class 3

O. The Nerve Center

8. **Cranial Nerve**   45', WI4   Classic steep dihedral.
9. **Peripheral Stimulation**   55', WI4+
10. **Synergetic Interruption**   50', WI5, 5.5   Rocking chimney to thin pillar to hand traverse.

P. The Cascade

11. **West Cascade**
12. **Central Cascade**
13. **East Cascade**   Class 3 to WI2   Central is hardest, room for many variations.
14. **?**   WI2+   Two short steps, two more pitches just west of #14.
15. **?**   One good short pillar, gets lots of sun.

Other ice climbs, not shown on overview map, but also in Castlewood Canyon:

The Turgid Penetrator   55', WI5   This climb is found just north of the overlook at The Falls parking lot area. There are also some 40' 45° slabs south of the overlook with 10'-15' of vertical at the bottom.

There is another ice climb located just north of the Dungeon Area, but it gets lots of sun and needs good conditions.

The climb **Licorice Stick** on Grocery Store Wall makes for an excellent mixed climb, but needs great conditions to be in shape.

There are also many short and intermittent seeps in the Winter Canyon Area, especially in The Ice Garden area than are shown. Also many of the areas on the north rim would be good mixed climbs under the right conditions.

It is possible in winter and spring to spend the morning in 50 degree weather climbing ice and then to go to the other side of the canyon in the sun and rock climb the rest of the day. Keep in mind that the road isn't maintained and that a towing fee would cost around $100.

Little is known about the bolted routes in this area of the canyon. The author would appreciate information on these climbs. Please send any information to Front Range Crags, care of Chockstone Press, PO Box 3505, Evergreen, Colorado 80439.

N. The Ice Garden

1. **The Incisor**   35', WI3+
2. **Tears for Fears**   45', WI3+
3. **I'm Not Worthy**   35', WI2, 5.2
4. **Smear Tactics**   35', Class 3
5. **?**
6. **Vertebral Column**   35', WI2+, 5.2
7. **Practice Gully**   35', Class 3

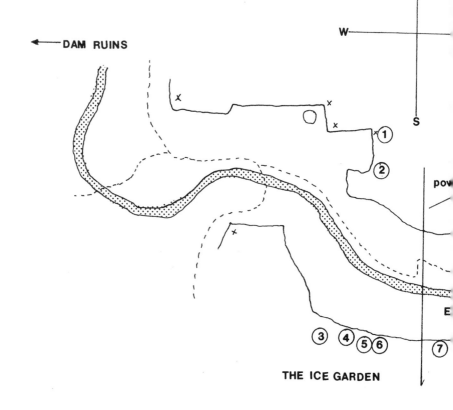

THE ICE GARDEN

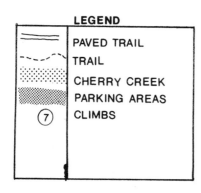

LEGEND

PAVED TRAIL

TRAIL

CHERRY CREEK

PARKING AREAS

⑦ CLIMBS

O. The Nerve Center

8. **Cranial Nerve**   45', WI4
9. **Peripheral Stimulation**   55', WI4+
10. **Synergetic Interruption**   50', WI5, 5.5

P. The Cascade

11. **West Cascade**
12. **Central Cascade**
13. **East Cascade**   Class 3 to WI2
14. **?**   WI2+
15. **?**

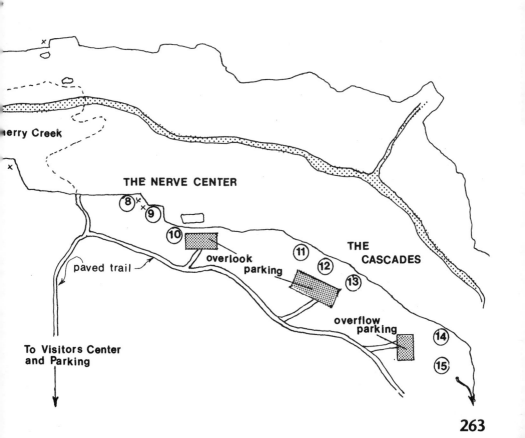

Guide Services:

The Boulder Rock
2952 Baseline Road
Boulder, CO 80303
(303)447-2804

CATS
2400 30th Street
Boulder, CO 80301
(303)939-9699

Colorado Mountain School
351 Moraine Ave.
Estes Park, CO 80517
(303)586-5758

Bob Culp Climbing School
1335 Broadway
Boulder, CO 80302
(303)442-8355

Desert Ice Mountain Guide
1606 Banyan #1
Ft. Collins, CO 80526
(303)493-2849

Eldorado Mountain Guides
PO Box 1644
Nederland, CO 80466
(303)589-5629

Free West Rock Guides
PO Box 732
Boulder, CO 80306
(303)939-0019

International Alpine School
PO Box 3037
Eldorado Springs, CO 80025
(303)494-4904

Steve Young
PO Box 4801
Estes Park, CO 80517
(303)586-0571

Lichen Mountain Works
116 Deer Pass Road
Manitou Springs, CO 80829
(719)685-1625

Equipment/Dealers:

Adventure Outfitters
514 S. College Ave.
Ft Collins, CO 80524
(303)224-2460

Basecamp Mountain Sports
821 Pearl Street
Boulder, CO 80302
(303)443-6770

The Boulder Mountaineer
1335 Broadway
Boulder, CO 80302
(303)447-2804

The Boulder Mountaineer
330 Highway 170
Eldorado Springs, CO
(303)499-1185

Grand West Outfitters
3250 N. Academy Blvd.
Colorado Springs, CO 80917
(719)596-3031

Grand West Outfitters
801 Broadway
Denver, CO 80203
(303)825-0300

Mountain Chalet
226 North Tejon
Colorado Springs, CO 80903
(719)633-0732

The Mountain Miser
209 West Hampden
Englewood, CO 80110
(303)761-7070

The Mountain Shop
632 South Mason
Ft. Collins, CO 80524
(303)493-5720

Mountain Sports
821 Pearl Street
Boulder, CO 80302
(303)443-6770

Neptune Mountaineering
627 South Broadway
Boulder, CO 80303
(303)499-8866

The North Face
629K South Broadway
Boulder, Co 80303
(303)499-1731

The North Face
2490 S. Colorado Blvd.
Denver, CO 80222
(303)758-6366

REI
4100 E. Mexico, Bldg. C
Denver, CO
(303)756-3100

REI
8991B Harlan
Westminster, CO
(303)429-1800

Wilderness Sports
358 East Elkhorn
Estes Park, CO 80517
(303)586-6548

Resoling Services:

Komito Boots
235 West Riverside
Estes Park, CO 80517
(303)586-5391
(800)422-2668

Moring Custom Boots
2583 Highway 74
PO Box 718
Evergreen, CO 80439
(303)674-2806

Rock and Resole
2500 N. 47th St., #11
Boulder, CO 80301
(303)274-0414

Stepping Stones
2910 N. Wood Ave.
Colorado Springs, CO 80907
(719)634-3575

Climbing Gyms:

The Boulder Rock
2952 Baseline Rd.
Boulder, CO 80303
(303)447-2804

CATS
2400 30th Street
Boulder, CO 80301
(303)939-9699

Healthworks
415 East Monroe
Ft. Collins, CO 80525
(303)226-8786

Paradise Rock Gym
6260 N. Washington, #5
Denver, CO 80216
(303)286-8168

The Point Athletic Club
53533 Van Gordon St.
Lakewood, CO 80228
(303)988-1300

Thrillseekers
1912 S. Broadway
Denver, CO 80210
(303)733-8810

Westminister Climbing Wall
Westminister Rec Center
10455 Sheridan Blvd.
Westminister, CO
(303)460-9690

Suggested Readings:

Most titles are available through local climbing stores or from Chessler Books, PO Box 2436, Evergreen, CO 80439, (800)654-8502 or (303)670-0093.

Cheney, Steve. *For Turkeys Only* (Bob Couchman, 19650 Blue Clover Lane, Monument, CO 80132.) Covers the Turkey Rock area and Sheep's Nose in the South Platte.

Horan, Bob. *Front Range Bouldering* (Chockstone Press, Evergreen, CO.) Covers most of the Front Range bouldering from Horsetooth Reservoir to Morrison.

Hubbel, Peter and Rolofson, Mark. *South Platte Rock Climbing and Garden of the Gods* (Chockstone Press, Evergreen, CO.) Covers most of the South Platte region from Highway 285 to Garden of the Gods.

Rossiter, Richard. *Boulder Climbs North* (Chockstone Press, Evergreen, CO.) Covers climbing in the Boulder area from Skunk Canyon north, including Boulder Canyon.

— *Climber's Guide to Rocky Mountain National Park* (Chockstone Press, Evergreen, CO 80439.) Covers Lumpy Ridge and all of the climbing in the High Country.

Rolofson, Mark. *1993 Boulder Sport Climbs* (Mark Rolofson, PO Box 732, Boulder, CO 80306, 303-939-0019.) Covers selected sport climbs in Clear Creek Canyon, The West Bank, North Table Mountain, Mickey Mouse Wall, North and South St. Vrain.

Luebben, Craig. *A Rockclimber's Guide to Greyrock* (Craig Luebben, 2100 West Drake, Ft. Collins, CO 80524, 303-493-2849.) Covers the Greyrock area in the Poudre Canyon.

Gene Ellis climbing top pitch of **Mr. Misty** 5.10a, Mt. Thoridin. Photo by Peter Hubbel.

270

Access: It's everybody's concern

the ACCESS FUND

THE ACCESS FUND, a national, non-profit climbers' organization, is working to keep you climbing. The Access Fund helps preserve access and protect the environment by providing funds for land acquisitions and climber support facilities, financing scientific studies, publishing educational materials promoting low-impact climbing, and providing start-up money, legal counsel and other resources to local climbers' coalitions.

Climbers can help preserve access by being responsible users of climbing areas. Here are some practical ways to support climbing:

- **COMMIT YOURSELF TO "LEAVING NO TRACE."** Pick up litter around campgrounds and the crags. Let your actions inspire others.

- **DISPOSE OF HUMAN WASTE PROPERLY.** Use toilets whenever possible. If none are available, choose a spot at least 50 meters from any water source. Dig a hole 6 inches (15 cm) deep, and bury your waste in it. *Always pack out toilet paper* in a "Zip-Lock"-type bag.

- **UTILIZE EXISTING TRAILS.** Avoid cutting switchbacks and trampling vegetation.

- **USE DISCRETION WHEN PLACING BOLTS AND OTHER "FIXED" PROTECTION.** Camouflage all anchors with rock-colored paint. Use chains for rappel stations, or leave rock-colored webbing.

- **RESPECT RESTRICTIONS THAT PROTECT NATURAL RESOURCES AND CULTURAL ARTIFACTS .** Appropriate restrictions can include prohibition of climbing around Indian rock art, pioneer inscriptions, and on certain formations during raptor nesting season. Power drills are illegal in wilderness areas. *Never chisel or sculpt holds in rock on public lands, unless it is expressly allowed* – no other practice so seriously threatens our sport.

- **PARK IN DESIGNATED AREAS,** not in undeveloped, vegetated areas. Carpool to the crags!

- **MAINTAIN A LOW PROFILE.** Other people have the same right to undisturbed enjoyment of natural areas as do you.

- **RESPECT PRIVATE PROPERTY.** Don't trespass in order to climb.

- **JOIN OR FORM A GROUP TO DEAL WITH ACCESS ISSUES IN YOUR AREA.** Consider clean-ups, trail building or maintenance, or other "goodwill" projects.

- **JOIN THE ACCESS FUND.** To become a member, *simply make a donation (tax-deductable) of any amount.* Only by working together can we preserve the diverse American climbing experience.

The Access Fund. Preserving America's diverse climbing resources.
The Access Fund • P.O. Box 17010 • Boulder, CO 80308